Also by Jane Watson Hopping
**The Pioneer Lady's
Country Kitchen**
*A Seasonal Treasury of
Time-Honored American Recipes*

THE PIONEER LADY'S
COUNTRY CHRISTMAS

My Grandfather and Grandmother Meekins with baby Archie

THE PIONEER LADY'S COUNTRY CHRISTMAS

JANE WATSON HOPPING

Author of THE PIONEER LADY'S COUNTRY KITCHEN

*Old-fashioned Recipes and
Memories of Christmas Past*

WINGS BOOKS
New York

Copyright © 1996 by Jane Watson Hopping

Grateful acknowledgment is made to the following for permission to reprint previously published material:

BRETHREN PRESS: "The Touch of the Master's Hand" from *The Touch of the Master's Hand* by Myra Brooks Welch. Copyright © 1957 by House of the Church of the Brethren. Used by permission of Brethren Press, a division of the Church of the Brethren.

CONTEMPORARY BOOKS, INC.: "An Old-fashioned Welcome," First-Name Friends," and "Home (A Heap o' Livin')" from *Collected Verses of Edgar A. Guest.* Copyright 1934 by Contemporary Books, Inc. Reprinted by permission of Contemporary Books, Inc.

RUPERT CREW LIMITED: "Christmas Blessing by Patience Strong. Reprinted by permission of Rupert Crew Limited.

MACMILLAN PUBLISHING COMPANY and THE SOCIETY OF AUTHORS: Excerpt from "Sea Fever" from *Poems* by John Masefield (New York: Macmillan, 1953). Canadian rights administered by Macmillan Publishing Company; open-market rights administered by the Society of Authors as the literary representative of the Estate of John Masefield. Reprinted by permission of Macmillan Publishing Company and the Society of Authors as the literary representative of the Estate of John Masefield.

The Charles E. Tuttle Co., Inc.: Excerpt reprinted from the poem "Seeing the Girls Home in Vermont," from *Rhymes of Vermont Rural Life,* by Daniel L. Cady, second series, 1922, by permission of the Charles E. Tuttle Co., Inc., Rutland, Vt.

MARY B. WALL: "Afterglow" by Mary B. Wall. Reprinted by permission of Mary B. Wall.

This 1998 edition is published by Wings Books®, a division of Random House Value Publishing, Inc., New York, by arrangement with Jane Watson Hopping.

Wings Books® and colophon are trademarks of Random House Value Publishing, Inc.

Random House
New York • Toronto • London • Sydney • Auckland
http://www.randomhouse.com/

Printed and bound in the United States of America

Library of Congress Cataloging-in-Publication Data
Hopping, Jane Watson.
    The pioneer lady's country Christmas: a gift of old-fashioned recipes and memories of Christmas past / Jane Watson Hopping.
        p.   cm.
    Includes index.
    Originally published: New York: Villard, 1989.
    ISBN: 0-517-18349-8
    1. Christmas cookery. 2. Christmas—United States. I. Title.
[TX739.2.C45H66 1998]
641.5'68—dc21   97-47138
                                                        CIP

Photo on p. 270 © 1988 by Regina DeLuise

Designed by Joseph B. DelValle

Manufactured in the United States of America

9 8 7 6 5 4 3 2 1

FOR RAYMOND, RANDY, COLLEEN, AND MARK

And I saw the happy mother, and a group surrounding her
  That knelt with costly presents of frankincense and myrrh;
And I thrilled with awe and wonder, as a murmur on the air
  Came drifting o'er the hearing in a melody of prayer;—

Then the vision, slowly failing, with the words of the refrain,
  Fell swooning in the moonlight through the frosty window-pane;
And I heard the clock proclaiming, like an eager sentinel
  Who brings the world good tidings,—"It is Christmas—all is well!"

—From "Das Krist Kindel"
by James Whitcomb Riley

ACKNOWLEDGMENTS

While writing this old-fashioned Christmas book has been a great deal of pleasure for me, I've never lost sight of the fact that the contributions of others have enriched it and certainly in a large way made it possible.

So, many thanks Sheila (my sister) for the hard work you do on the lovely pieces of decorative art for my books. Your flash phone calls with messages of encouragement are a joy! I've so often thought that the outpouring of love you share speaks of greatness of heart and depth of character.

Raymond (dear husband of thirty-nine years): Thanks for doing so many routine chores without a grumble. And while I tease you about it, thanks for being my most enthusiastic fan.

My gratitude to good friends Lee Ryland Arlandson and Marlys Franklin who dug through trunks and boxes to share the photographs of old-time family members; thanks most particularly for the delightful pictures of the children.

Again thanks to Meg and to everyone at the Jane Rotrosen Agency for turning my pumpkin into a coach.

And my ongoing thanks to Alison Acker (my editor) and to the other folks at Villard.

A toast to Edgar A. Guest whose poetry has added holiday cheer to the book and, of course, to my favorite Hoosier poet, James Whitcomb Riley. A few words of praise for the lovely old-time art of Will Vawter and Howard Chandler Christy. And many thanks to the poets whose delightful Christmas poetry first came to my attention when published by Ideal Publishing Co., and who have so generously allowed us to enjoy their work again here.

My thanks also go to Regina DeLuise, for the photograph she took of a Christmas angel we know.

Now, it gives me pleasure to voice appreciation for all the folks at home in Auburn, Loomis, Roseville, and Citrus Heights and in the Medford area, and for those good people everywhere who buy and enjoy my books.

CONTENTS

CHRISTMAS MEMORIES

Remember the joys of Christmas,
How they linger deep in our past,
Memories of sleigh-bells and angels,
Visions that hauntingly last!

Raggedy Anns in their cradles,
Trains and trucks made of wood,
Stories and songs about Santa,
Trying so hard to be good.

How sweet the babe in the manger,
(T'was Billie McCord's brother Joe)
The choir sang "Holy Night" softly,
Small Magi gestured, graceful and slow.

Our thoughts so easily grow tender,
As the mantle of time we part,
Leaving naught but a crib and an infant,
And bright memories alive in our heart.

—J.W.H.

INTRODUCTION: SEASON OF THE HEART

In early childhood our mother explained to us that richness in life depended on a blend of past, present, and future, that our sources of strength came from that which has gone before, and our dreams were flights into the future, a time yet to come. She taught us to look gently over our shoulder, and she taught us that the qualities most needed in a successful present were personified in the Christmas story.

Through the cold and stormy days that I have spent writing this book, I find myself remembering the wisdom with which Mother guided us and the love that flowed over us. For me her spirit will always be entwined with the Christmas traditions. I can see her, an apron over her cotton dress, a kitchen spoon in her hand, standing at the door as we hurried in from school, tightly gripping paper Santa Clauses with cotton whiskers and colored paper chains streaming out behind us. "Merry Christmas! Merry Christmas!" we would call out to everyone we knew and sometimes to those we didn't know, and if the strangers smiled at us, we would wish them a "Happy New Year," too.

Once the seasonal juices began to flow, we could not hold Grandpa —who lived with us—down. By mid-December he was as eager as a boy to put up the Christmas tree, and each year he began early to talk about leaving it up until mid-January. He was Mother's father and our favorite Grandpa, so we humored him and took pleasure in his eagerness. We would all straggle out into the nearby hills to find "our" tree, Daddy and Grandpa carrying the saws and axes. Amid much laughter, teasing and boisterous singing of "Jingle Bells" and other lively old carols, we searched for a thick-branched fir tree, and also brought home boughs of mistletoe full of tiny rose-cream berries, which we cut out of the tops of giant oaks, and arms full of wild, red berries.

Tired and hungry we would bear our treasures home about dusk. Grandpa would always make a deal with Mother: He would nail the x-shaped "foot" on the bottom of the tree and get it ready to be "set up" that evening in our tiny living room if she would "get a bite of supper together."

When the tree was ready and supper eaten, we would all string endless chains of popcorn and cranberries while Mother began baking cookies and gingerbread men to hang on the tree along with polished aromatic Arkansas Black apples, which were a dark, deep rich red.

By bedtime, the tree was up, its base covered with a tablecloth and soft snowy-white quilt batting and its boughs hung with fragrant home-made ornaments and store-bought candy canes.

Knowing our tree would be up early in the season and that Grandpa, a playful sort of man, would be full of holiday cheer, relatives and neighbors would soon begin to drop in, bringing gifts, plates of cookies like Aunt Clary's Chocolate Fruit Drops, Aunt Mary's Oatmeal Macaroons, and Old English Ginger Nuts, and greetings. Sharing went on at a feverish pitch. Mother and the aunties baked, using great ingenuity, digging deep into flour bins and tin cans of raisins; filling baskets, plates, and colorful tins with festive goodies with names like Sheila's Cherry Bliss for the visitors.

Those were the days when the Christmas season stirred in our hearts the joyous belief that Christ had come to enlighten the world. Thoughts of God, the baby Jesus, and Mary and Joseph were on everyone's mind. We children began to practice songs for church or school pageants. Our parents, aunts, and uncles misted up or joyfully praised our efforts as we sang for them our newly learned songs: "Away in a Manger" and "Silent Night! Holy Night!"

Out of those memories of Christmas at home in the country has come this book, which is first and foremost an old-fashioned cookbook, like those of the past that recognize the bond between "good eating" and "good living." Second, it is a nostalgic glance at how we were, not so long ago, when most of us depended on subsistence farming for our livelihood. And it is very much about Christmas and about the loved ones of our past, about their almost unbelievable stoicism in the face of hardship, the love and strength that sustained them, and the power that their close relationships and staunch values brought them.

The recipes are those of down-home, self-taught country cooks and the list of ingredients is of simple, readily available staples plus a few extra items, goodies like raisins, nuts, and a little honey or molasses. The recipes, both traditional and family favorites like Gretchen's Honey *Lebkuchen,* A Christmas Delight, and A Delicious Light Fruitcake are easy to make and when baked will fill even the smallest house or apartment with the fragrance and flavor of an old-fashioned Christmas in the country.

Spiced with bits of old-time poetry, photographs of my family and those of friends, decorative art, stories and recipes, the book intentionally tries to revive the past, for only a moment to pull back the veil of time. It is about Wise Men and immigrants, snow birds and carolers, old women made softly beautiful by long and gentle lives, angels who winged their way through the night, Christmas bells and school pageants. And mid such bits of nostalgia are joyful sleigh rides revisited, jolly old elves, and recipes like Aunt El's Old-fashioned Walnut and Sweet Potato Pie, Maud's Excellent Lemon Mincemeat Pie (which contains no meat and which she served with everyone's favorite ham dinner), Aunt Irene's Angel Torte, Old-fashioned Sugarplums, and Grandma Hopping's Turkish Delight.

This book speaks not only to the joyful times—the feasting and celebrating, gift giving, chiming of Christmas bells, the generous outpouring of good will, and childlike excitement—but to the tender, nostalgic lonesome times as well, the looking back, the remembering of places and people that linger gently on the mind.

As I have written this book, I have wondered if perhaps we, you and I, could share the warmth of Christmas, the heart-changing emotions and attitudes that fuel mankind's dreams of a heart more tender and hands more willing and kind. And perhaps during this holy time, we could softly ponder upon who we are, and what kind of Christmas legacy we want to leave to our children.

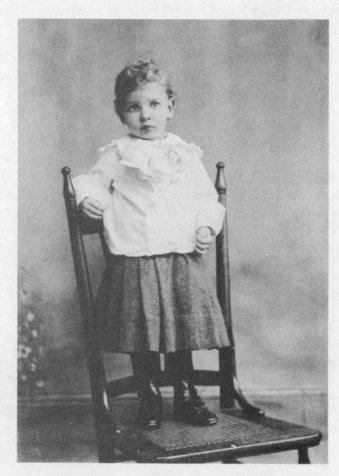

A glimpse of Christmas past

THEM OLD CHEERY WORDS

Pap he allus ust to say,
  "Chris'mus comes but onc't a year!"
Liked to hear him thataway,
  In his old split-bottomed cheer
By the fireplace here at night—
Wood all in,—and room all bright,
Warm and snug, and folks all here:
"Chris'mus comes but onc't a year!"

Me and 'Lize, and Warr'n and Jess
  And Eldory home fer two
Weeks' vacation; and, I guess,
  Old folks tickled through and through,
Same as we was,—"Home onc't more
Fer another Chris'mus—shore!"
Pap 'ud say, and tilt his cheer,—
"Chris'mus comes but onc't a year!"

—James Whitcomb Riley

The
Pioneer Lady's
Country Christmas

THERE'S A SONG
IN THE AIR

When Indian summer fades and the year drifts to a close, winter sweeps down from the north, putting a nip in the air and a blanket of snow over the earth. On cue, starting just after Thanksgiving, all across the nation —from churches, schools, and street corners—comes the sound of music, of bells, and the joyful lifting of voices. Little children softly sing "Silent Night, Holy Night,/All is calm, all is bright," and carolers ring out the ancient songs of jubilation:

> Joy to the earth! the Savior reigns;
> Let men their songs employ;
> While fields and floods, rocks, hills and plains,
> Repeat the sounding joy.
> Repeat the sounding joy.

And, like a rich counterpoint, an old-time spiritual rides the night wind, hauntingly reminding us of times gone by:

> When I was a sinner, I sought both night and day,
> I asked the Lord to help me and He showed me the way.
> Go, tell it on the mountain,
> Over the hills an' everywhere,
> Go, tell it on the mountain,

That Jesus Christ is born.
    Go over the hills and everywhere,
    Go tell it on the mountains, Go!

In every city and hamlet, old men trying out for a Christmas play have to be coaxed into learning to scoff like Ebenezer Scrooge, while small boys practice the immortal words of Tiny Tim.

On street corners the Salvation Army stands, ringing bells, carrying out the historic mission of mercy and love which was begun in 1865 by "General" William Booth, a Methodist minister who took the gospel into the streets, and gave food, shelter, and clothing to those who needed it most, thereby bringing the message of Christ to many.

O little town of Bethlehem,
How still we see thee lie!
Above thy deep and dreamless sleep
The silent stars go by;
Yet in thy dark streets shineth
The everlasting Light;
The hopes and fears of all the years
Are met in thee tonight.

HOLIDAY PLANS AFOOT

It seems like only yesterday that ours was a nation of rural villages, each boasting little more than a grocery store, church, school, barbershop—all strung out along Main Street. Nestled as they were in farm country, supported by and supporting a gaggle of everyday folks—most of whom knew each other—such little towns became in a broad sense a family concern. They were tightly knit, particularly so in life-threatening emergencies and at Christmas, at which time differences were put aside.

Each year by the first of December the buzzing local conversation left off talking about cows, farrowing, and the price of grain, and folks began to speculate on whether or not it would snow for Christmas. Men began to confer as to whether Arch McCord's widow needed extra wood, meat, or milk over the holidays. Fatherless children were counted, and a local farm machinery dealer or a cattle buyer (who would skin you in a cattle deal) would up and take responsibility for seeing that these children "had Christmas."

The women naturally would take care of such things as Christmas baskets—you could count on the women of the churches and the school for such things. They would bake endless fruitcakes, pies, and cookies to go along with homemade preserves and jellies that had been put away during the summer with just such purpose in mind.

Everyone believed that mid-January was soon enough to get back to the never-ending cycle of the seasons, the plowing and planting, caring for newborn lambs, and upgrading the machinery for the new year. For now, planning the holiday season would be enough.

CHRISTMAS BLESSING

God bless our little home today and all our family,
the ones that gather round the hearth,
and those across the sea.

And some of us have gone away, and drifted far apart,
but Christmas ties the cords of friendship
close around the heart.

May all our fancied grievances be banished from the mind,
and may we greet each other
with a wish that's good and kind.

May nothing false creep in to spoil the perfect harmony,
and may we speak sweet words of love
and peace and harmony.

—Patience Strong

MOTHER'S HANDMADE CHRISTMAS BASKETS

The remaining turkey from our Thanksgiving feast was barely baked into richly flavored pies and the other leftovers (pickles, cranberry sauce, vegetables, and bits of cakes and pies) set out to finish off before Mother drew up plans for Christmas baskets that we would give to old folks and friends who might need a little something extra.

By early December she had ready several hand-worked baskets made of fine grape or blackberry vines or from willow whips and had made new calico napkins with which to line them. The baking schedule was organized, and recipes and supplies were gathered. All was ready for the baking.

Finally, about the third week in December, mother would begin by baking at least four dozen glittering sugar-sprinkled star cookies, then add Christmas-tree cookies decked out with green frosting and gold ornaments, reindeer cookies, colorful stained-glass cookies, bars containing rich fillings, and coconut almond cookies, all of which would be tucked into the baskets. Then, when the baskets were brimming, we children would be bundled up and sent all around our neighborhood to deliver them.

OUR FAVORITE
CHRISTMAS SUGAR COOKIES

This dough makes a delicious plain sugar cookie and lots of delightful variations.

1 cup butter or margarine, plus a
    scant 1 tablespoon for greasing
    cookie sheet
2 cups granulated sugar or 2 cups,
    packed, light brown sugar
3 eggs, beaten to a froth
⅓ cup milk
1 tablespoon vanilla extract

5 cups all-purpose flour, plus about
    ½ cup flour for rolling out
    dough
1 tablespoon baking powder
1 scant teaspoon salt
Plain or colored granulated sugar, for
    sprinkling on cookies

Very lightly grease a 15x12x1-inch cookie sheet with the scant 1 table-spoon butter; set aside. In a large bowl, cream the 1 cup butter. Gradually add the sugar, beating until fluffy. In a separate bowl, combine the eggs, milk, and vanilla. Sift together the 5 cups flour, baking powder, and salt. To the butter-sugar mixture, alternately add the egg mixture and flour mixture. Cover the bowl and refrigerate until firm to the touch, about 30 minutes.

Meanwhile, preheat oven to 375°F. When dough is chilled, turn onto a lightly floured surface. Shape into a ball and divide into 4 equal portions; return all but 1 portion to the refrigerator. Roll out dough on the floured surface about ¼ inch thick and cut out with Christmas cookie cutters into stars, reindeers, Santas and the like. Sprinkle with plain or colored, granulated sugar and place about 2 inches apart on the prepared cookie sheet. Repeat with the remaining 3 portions of dough. (Note: Since over-rolled dough toughens, reserve all scraps from each cutting until dough has been used, then roll them together for a final cutting.)

Bake until done and lightly browned around the edges, 12 to 15 minutes. Immediately remove from pan and cool on a wire rack or on a piece of kraft paper (an opened brown grocery bag will do). When cool, store in an airtight container until ready to serve.

Makes about 4 dozen cookies.

Stained-Glass Cookies
Spread a thin layer of tart jelly (use as many different colors of jelly as possible) on top of the cut-out Christmas sugar cookies before baking.

Fruit-Filled Cookies

Prepare the Christmas sugar cookie dough and chill. Meanwhile, make a fruit filling as follows: In a small saucepan, combine ⅓ cup light brown sugar, ⅓ cup boiling water, 1 cup raisins, a dash of salt, and 2 teaspoons butter. Cook until thick; cool.

Or, for another delicious filling, combine ½ cup chopped dates (or figs, dried apples, peaches, or pears), ½ cup boiling water, juice from half a lemon, ½ cup granulated with light fruits or packed light brown sugar with dark fruits, (depending on the fruit used), 1 tablespoon cornstarch, and a dash of salt. Cook until thick; cool.

Once the filling is cool, roll the chilled dough ⅛ inch thick and cut into 1½ to 2-inch rounds; place a teaspoon of filling on each cookie and cover with a second cookie; press edges together with the tines of a fork and prick the top to allow the steam to escape. Bake as directed for the basic Christmas sugar cookies.   *Makes about 2 dozen.*

Coconut Almond Cookies

Add ½ cup grated coconut and ½ cup slivered almonds to the Christmas sugar cookie dough, folding them in just before refrigerating dough. When chilled, turn dough onto a lightly floured surface and shape into a ball. Pinch off pieces about the size of a walnut and roll into a ball in the palms of your hands; place 2 inches apart on a lightly greased cookie sheet and very lightly press down with your fingertips to flatten. Bake as directed for the basic Christmas sugar cookies.   *Makes about 4 dozen.*

AUNT EL'S PASTEL CHRISTMAS COOKIES

These colorful cookies, in delicate contrast to the richly spiced and fruited sweets of the holidays, were everyone's favorite. Aunt El made them in five flavors and colors. Grandpa riddled the plates, eating only the vanilla and lemon cookies which he called "dunkin' cookies," and my little sister Sheila loved the Ribbon Cookies (recipe follows), which were made of the five colors of dough pressed together before baking, taking them apart to eat each color, one at a time.

1 cup butter or margarine, plus 1 tablespoon for greasing cookie sheet
2 cups sugar
3 egg whites, lightly beaten
6 cups all-purpose flour, plus ½ cup for rolling out dough

1 teaspoon salt
1 tablespoon baking powder
Yellow, green, pink, and orange food coloring
Vanilla extract
Lemon extract
Almond extract

Cinnamon oil
Orange flavoring

Nuts or candied fruit for decorating
tops, optional

Grease a large cookie sheet with the 1 tablespoon butter; set aside. In a large bowl, cream the 1 cup butter until light. Gradually add the sugar, beating until fluffy; fold in the egg whites. Sift together the 6 cups flour, baking powder, and salt, stirring to blend; add to butter mixture, mixing well. Turn dough onto a lightly floured surface and shape into a ball. Divide into 5 equal portions.

With the food coloring,, color 1 of the portions light yellow, 1 light green, 1 light pink, and 1 light orange. Next, add flavoring as follows: flavor the uncolored portion with *1 teaspoon* vanilla; flavor the yellow portion with ½ to ⅔ *teaspoon* lemon extract; the green portion with ¼ to ½ *teaspoon* almond extract; the pink portion with *2 drops* of cinnamon oil; and the light-orange portion with *1 teaspoon* orange flavoring. Refrigerate until firm to the touch.

Preheat oven to 325°F. Remove 1 portion of dough at a time from the refrigerator; roll out about ⅛ inch thick on a lightly floured surface and cut out with cookie cutters into fancy shapes, including stars and snowflakes. If desired, decorate with nuts or candied fruit. Place on the prepared cookie sheet, 1 to 2 inches apart, and bake until cookies are lightly browned on the bottoms (when done, the tops should still be light and pastel-colored), about 12 minutes. Remove from pans and cool on an opened brown grocery bag.

Makes about 5 dozen cookies, depending on cutters used.

Ribbon Cookies
For colorful ribbons: Once the pastel Christmas cookie dough has been colored and flavored, roll it out about ⅓ inch thick. Alternately stack the different-colored layers to a thickness of about 2 inches, brushing between the layers with a little *egg white* beaten to a froth; press layers lightly together, then cut into 2-inch strips. Wrap loosely in waxed paper and refrigerate until thoroughly chilled, then slice crosswise about ¼ inch wide and bake as directed for the pastel cookies.

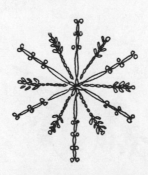

OLD-FASHIONED APPLESAUCE COOKIES

These cookies and their slight variations were so popular with old folks that younger women and girls baked them by the dozens, tucked them generously into Christmas baskets, and served them at all sorts of functions.

½ cup butter or margarine, plus 1 tablespoon for greasing cookie sheet

2 cups sifted all-purpose flour, plus 2 tablespoons flour for coating walnuts and raisins

1 teaspoon ground cinnamon

½ teaspoon freshly ground nutmeg

½ teaspoon salt

¼ teaspoon ground cloves

1 cup chopped walnuts

1 cup dark raisins, finely minced

1 cup, packed, brown sugar (light preferred)

1 cup usweetened, unspiced applesauce

1 egg, well beaten

1 teaspoon baking soda

Preheat oven to 375°F. Grease a large cookie sheet with the 1 tablespoon butter; set aside. Into a medium-size bowl, sift together the 2 cups flour, cinnamon, nutmeg, salt, and cloves; set aside. In a separate bowl, dust the walnuts and raisins with the 2 tablespoons flour; set aside.

Cream the ½ cup butter in a large bowl; gradually add the sugar and continue beating until fluffy. In a small bowl, combine the applesauce and egg until well blended; stir in the baking soda. Add the applesauce mixture to the butter-sugar mixture, beating lightly until thoroughly mixed. Next, add the flour mixture, stirring to make a soft dough. Fold in the walnuts-raisin mixture until well incorporated. Drop by rounded teaspoonfuls onto the prepared cookie sheet, 2 or 3 inches apart.

Bake until the cookies have a cake-like texture and are lightly browned and firm to the touch, about 15 to 20 minutes. Remove from oven, let cool on the cookie sheet for about 5 minutes, then transfer to a wire rack to finish cooling. Store cooled cookies in an airtight container until ready to serve. Use within 3 or four days, or freeze for later use. *Makes about 4 dozen cookies.*

CRISP PECAN COOKIES

This old-fashioned recipe was written by hand in Aunt Veda's cookbook. She marked it "Christmas Cookies," but all the family knew that it turned up in all seasons, and sometimes, despite its name, it became a walnut, butternut, or hazelnut cookie.

1 cup butter or margarine, plus 1 tablespoon for greasing cookie sheet
1 pound (2⅓ packed cups) brown sugar (light brown preferred)
2 eggs, well beaten

2½ cups sifted all-purpose flour, plus 2 tablespoons flour for dusting pecans
½ teaspoon baking soda
¼ teaspoon salt
1 to 2 cups chopped pecans

Preheat oven to 350°F. Lightly grease a large cookie sheet with the 1 tablespoon butter; set aside. In a large bowl, cream the 1 cup butter; gradually add the sugar and beat until light. Add the eggs, stirring until well blended. Sift the 2½ cups flour with the baking soda and salt and add to the butter-sugar mixture, stirring until a soft dough is formed. In a small bowl, dust the pecans with the 2 tablespoons flour, then add to the cookie dough, stirring until well incorporated. Drop by teaspoonfuls onto the prepared cookie sheet, about 2 inches apart. Bake until lightly browned, 12 to 15 minutes. Remove from oven and immediately transfer cookies to a wire rack to cool (or cool them on an opened brown grocery bag). When completely cooled, store in an airtight container until ready to serve. *Makes about 5 dozen cookies.*

🌿 SHEILA'S NIMBLE FINGERS

For generations the women in our family have been very skilled with the crochet hook. Grandpa's sisters made endless doilies, table cloths, and edgings in intricate designs. The old aunties sold their lovely work, which was always in demand, to the town women and generously gave it away at Christmas.

In our generation the skill is in my sister Sheila's nimble fingers, and her work—beautifully done—graces our tables and touches up our dresses.

🌿 A CHRISTMAS ROSE INSERT

Old-time women loved to insert a bit of hand-crocheted lace into the front of their homemade dresses. Such lace, made of strong cotton thread, would often be removed from a dress when the dress became faded and worn; then the lace would be washed, gently ironed, and laid away in a trunk to be used again and again in new dresses.

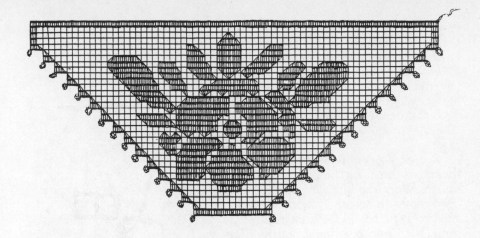

Sheila's instructions for making this old-fashioned rose pattern are not difficult to follow. She suggests you study the instructions carefully before starting the project. And she encourages you to check the visual guide frequently.

MATERIALS

350 yards size 50 crochet thread (if you cannot find 50 crochet thread, ask for size 50 tatting thread)
Size 12 crochet hook

To work the foundation chain, crochet 211 *chain stitches.*

Row 1: A *treble crochet stitch* is made by placing the thread around the hook twice, then putting the hook in the 4th chain from the hook. With thread over the hook pull stitch through 2 loops at a time; repeat, pulling through 2 loops at a time until one loop is left. Stitch is completed. Work a treble crochet stitch in the 4th chain stitch from the hook; then treble crochet in the following 207 chain stitches. Crochet 3 chain stitches and turn.

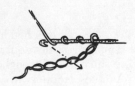

Row 2: Treble crochet in the next three stitches, forming a *filet square;* then crochet 2 chain stitches. Next, skip 2 treble crochet stitches from the previous row, and treble crochet to form an *open mesh square.* Work 67 more open mesh squares. Treble crochet in the last 4 stitches. Chain 3 stitches and turn.

Row 3: Work a treble crochet stitch in the next three stitches, making a filet square. Work the following 34 squares in open mesh. In square 35 work a *right filet* and in 36 a *left filet.* Work squares 37 through 68 into open mesh squares. Treble crochet in 69 to form a filet square. Chain 3 stitches and turn.

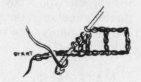

Row 4: Next, crochet 1 filet square. Work the following 33 squares in open mesh. Crochet 1 right filet square, 2 filet squares, and 1 left filet square. Work squares 38 through 68 in open mesh. Treble crochet 69 into a filet square. Next work 9 chain stitches and then make a *slip stitch* in the 6th chain stitch from the hook and turn.

Row 5: Treble crochet in the next 3 stitches, making a filet square. Work the following squares, 2 through 26, in open mesh. Treble crochet in the next 2 squares, making 2 filet squares. Then work 1 left filet square. Crochet squares 30 through 37 in filet squares. Work squares 38 through 40 in open mesh squares. Next, work 1 right filet square. Crochet squares 42 through 67 in open mesh. Crochet square 68 into a right filet, followed by 1 filet square. Chain 9 and make a slip stitch in the 6th stitch from the hook and turn.

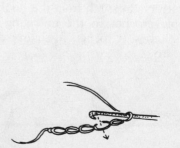

Row 6: Start this row with 1 filet square followed by 1 right filet square. To finish the project follow the visual guide. When the insert is finished the crocheted piece is reversed so that the wide edge becomes the top or neck edge and the narrow edge the bottom of the insert.

VEDA'S ALMOND LACE COOKIES

As these cookies came out of the oven, Veda with flying hands rolled them around the handle of a wooden spoon to shape them before they hardened, then laid them on a piece of waxed paper and dusted them lightly with powdered sugar, giving them an elegant appearance. When they were hard and cool, she served them on a delicate antique pink glass plate.

You can serve these cookies at a tree-trimming party, a family Christmas get-together, or a school or church function to a chorus of "how light," "delicious," and "yums."

⅔ cup almonds, ground to a fine
    powder
½ cup granulated sugar
½ cup butter or margarine
1 tablespoon all-purpose flour
2 tablespoons milk
About ½ cup powdered sugar,
  optional

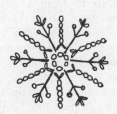

Preheat the oven to 350°F. In a large skillet with a heavy bottom (cast-iron preferred), combine the almonds, granulated sugar, butter, flour, and milk. Cook over low heat until the butter melts and ingredients are well blended, stirring constantly. Keep the mixture warm over very low heat as you drop it by well-rounded teaspoonfuls, about 2 inches apart, onto a large greased cookie sheet. Bake until golden brown, about 5 minutes. Remove from oven and immediately transfer cookies to a piece of waxed paper to cool (they will cool and harden rather quickly), or, while still pliable, roll over a spoon handle to shape into tubes. Dust with powdered sugar, if you wish.   *Makes about 2 dozen cookies.*

SHEILA'S CROCHETED LACE FOR COLLARS AND CUFFS

At one sitting, women of the past could crochet enough of this string lace to trim the collars and cuffs of their best dresses, the ones they wore to church. Patterns like these, crocheted not along a chain-stitch base but worked lengthwise like a string, were made for new Christmas dresses and were considered so simple that even little girls could make them.

SNOW FLOWER LACE

MATERIALS

Size 20 or 30 crochet thread
Size 11 crochet hook

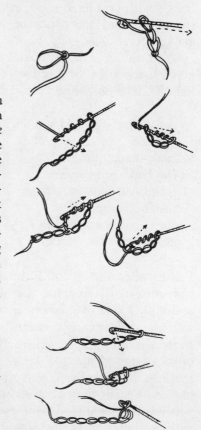

To make the flowers, crochet 8 *chain stitches* and join to form a circle; then chain 5 stitches more. Work 3 *double treble stitches* into the circle. (*Note:* A double treble stitch is made by wrapping the thread around the hook 3 times, then inserting the hook into the circle and pulling the looped stitch back up the hook through 2 loops; repeat until one loop is left.) Retain the last loop of each stitch (4 loops in all) and form a cluster by pulling thread through all of them at once. Chain 5 more stitches, then *slip stitch* (pull thread through 2 loops) into the circle, which makes one petal. Work 2 more petals using the instructions above.

For the fifth petal, chain 5 and make 4 double treble stitches, retaining the last loop of each of the 5 stitches; then form a cluster by pulling thread through all of them at once. For additional flowers repeat from the beginning. Frequently check the visual guide.

🌿 WOODLAND FERNS

MATERIALS

Size 20 to 30 crochet thread
Size 11 crochet hook

Measure the length of lace needed for your project; add one inch for every yard (37 chain stitches). To make the foundation chain, crochet enough chain stitches to make a base (when measuring the chain, don't stretch the thread).

Row 1: Double crochet in the first *chain stitch*; skip the second chain stitch. To double crochet, loop thread over the hook. Insert hook into chain length; pull through loop. Then pull thread through 2 loops; finally pull the thread through the last 2 loops. Repeat to the end of the chain. Then work 3 chain stitches and turn.

Row 2. Work a shell in the third space from the end as follows: *treble crochet 3* times. Chain 2 stitches, then treble crochet in the same space, which completes the shell. Skip two spaces and make a shell in the next space, using instructions above. Treble crochet in the last space, work 3 chain stitches, and turn.

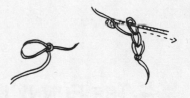

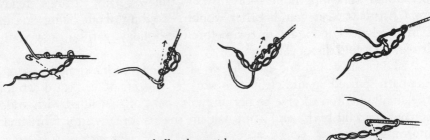

Row 3: To make a *shell edge with a picot*, treble crochet 3 times in chain 2 space. Chain 5 stitches and *slip stitch* in the 5th stitch from the hook to form a loop. Treble crochet 3 times and repeat pattern to the end of the lace.

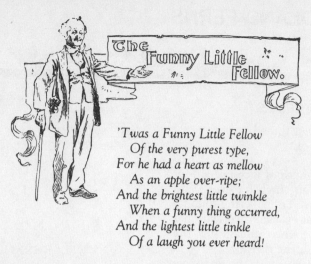

'Twas a Funny Little Fellow
Of the very purest type,
For he had a heart as mellow
As an apple over-ripe;
And the brightest little twinkle
When a funny thing occurred,
And the lightest little tinkle
Of a laugh you ever heard!

—James Whitcomb Riley

THE FUNNY LITTLE FELLOW

When Mama was a little girl she lived in a big house on a prairie farm. Theirs was a hardworking life, but one filled with fluffy chicks in spring, hay lofts in summer, and in winter, sledding, skating, newborn lambs, and Christmas.

In those days almost everyone had a hired man or two living on the farm, helping with chores and eating at the kitchen table with the family. Mother fondly recalls a little fellow named Cap, who in December would work long hours—on his own time—getting "things" ready for Christmas. Our grandmother would tease him about being one of Santa's elves. Then a day or two before the holiday, without a by-your-leave, he would disappear.

The family would find extra firewood stacked for Grandma's cooking, the barn spruced up and clean as a whistle, buckets of feed set down for the small children to give to pet animals, balls of suet filled with grain set out for wild birds, and a fire laid in the parlor-stove for Christmas morning.

Then, on New Year's Day, Cap would return, a smile on his face and gifts for us all and not a word about where he had been. There would be *Schnecken* and *Pfeffernüsse*, *Scheiterhaufen*, and an unwritten recipe for some other dish—memorized and carefully stored—a special gift for Grandmother.

SCHNECKEN (CARAMEL BUNS)

Sometimes called caramel buns, *Schnecken* are delightful served fresh from the oven with piping hot coffee, but our friend Hanna loved them when they were about half-cooled, served with a tall glass of icy-cold milk.

1 package dry or granulated yeast
¼ cup lukewarm water (105°F to 115°F)
1 cup plus 2 tablespoons granulated sugar
¾ cup butter or margarine, melted
½ cup lukewarm milk
1½ teaspoons salt
2 eggs, well beaten
1 cup dairy sour cream

6½ cups all-purpose flour
¾ cup raisins
1½ cups chopped pecans plus 24 reserved pecan halves
1 teaspoon finely grated lemon peel
1 cup, packed, light brown sugar
1 teaspoon ground cinnamon
4 tablespoons butter or margarine, melted
2 tablespoons cold water

In a large bowl, combine the yeast, warm water, and 2 tablespoons of the granulated sugar. Let sit 5 to 10 minutes before adding other ingredients. When the yeast has developed a bubbly head, add ½ cup more sugar, and the ¾ cup butter, milk and salt; stir until sugar and salt dissolve. Combine the eggs and sour cream in a small bowl, blending well; add to the yeast mixture; then add 4½ cups of the flour, beating by hand about 5 minutes to form a soft dough and develop the gluten (if desired, use an electric mixer). Cover bowl with a clean kitchen towel and refrigerate overnight.

The next day, let the dough rise in a warm place until doubled in bulk, about 45 minutes. Turn onto a floured surface and knead in the *remaining 2 cups* flour. Divide dough in half and roll each half into a rectangle about ¼ inch thick; on each rectangle spread half of the raisins, chopped pecans, and lemon peel. Combine the *remaining ½ cup* granulated sugar with the cinnamon and sprinkle half of mixture on top of each rectangle; roll up rectangles lengthwise like jelly rolls.

Mix together the brown sugar, the 4 tablespoons butter, and the cold water; spoon 1 tablespoon of the mixture into each of 24 muffin cups and place a pecan half in each cup. Slice the *Schnecken* crosswise into 1½-inch pieces and place in well greased muffin cups. Let rise in a warm place until doubled in bulk, about 30 to 45 minutes. Bake in a preheated 400°F oven until golden brown and firm to the touch, about 25 minutes; then reduce oven setting to 350°F and continue baking 10 minutes longer. *Makes 2 dozen Schnecken.*

PFEFFERNÜSSE (PEPPERNUT COOKIES)

While the name of these delicious old-fashioned cookies rolls awkwardly off an American tongue, they are well worth the time to make. Many years after Cap was gone, we learned that these cookies were called peppernuts in English and that old-time German cooks ripened the dough for two to three days before baking them; they stored the baked cookies in an airtight container with a piece of apple to mellow for one to two weeks before eating.

4 cups sifted all-purpose flour
1 tablespoon ground cinnamon
1 teaspoon freshly grated nutmeg
1 teaspoon ground cloves
1 teaspoon baking soda
½ teaspoon salt
¼ teaspoon black pepper
1 tablespoon cardamom seed
1 teaspoon anise seed
2 tablespoons butter or margarine, softened

2½ cups powdered sugar
5 large eggs, separated and at room temperature
Finely grated rind from 1 lemon
1 cup candied citron, finely chopped
½ cup candied orange peel, finely chopped

In a large bowl, sift together the flour, cinnamon, nutmeg, cloves, baking soda, salt, and pepper. Add the cardamom and anise seed. In a separate large bowl, cream the butter; gradually add the sugar, beating until light and fluffy. Add the egg yolks, blending well; then add the flour-spice mixture, lemon rind, and candied fruits, stirring until well blended. Beat the egg whites until stiff but not dry and fold into the batter. Cover with plastic wrap or aluminum foil; refrigerate for about 1 hour.

Once the batter has chilled, shape into small balls; arrange on a clean kitchen towel placed in a cool dry place. Let stand overnight (or up to two weeks if desired). Bake in a preheated 350°F oven until light brown, 15 to 20 minutes. Remove from oven and place on kraft paper to cool. Store in an airtight container.   *Makes about 9 dozen cookies.*

SCHEITERHAUFEN

Serve this pudding either hot or cold and win compliments from all the family.

1 tablespoon butter or margarine, for greasing pan
1 one-pound loaf white bread,

(remove crust if you wish) thinly sliced (French bread preferred)
5 medium-size apples, peeled and

thinly sliced
¼ cup golden raisins
Juice from 1 lemon (about 2
  tablespoons)
3 tablespoons honey
1 teaspoon ground cinnamon

½ teaspoon freshly grated nutmeg
2 eggs, well beaten
3 cups milk
1 teaspoon vanilla extract
About ¼ cup powdered sugar, more
  if you wish

Preheat oven to 375°F. Butter an 11x7½x1½-inch Pyrex loaf pan. Line the bottom and sides of the pan with the bread, using as much as is needed. In a medium-size bowl, thoroughly combine the apple slices, raisins, lemon juice, honey, cinnamon, and nutmeg; spoon mixture over the bread in the pan. Rinse the bowl and in it blend together the eggs, milk, vanilla, and powdered sugar to taste. Pour the egg mixture over the apple mixture; let sit for about 10 minutes. Bake uncovered until pudding is firm and golden brown, 45 to 50 minutes. Remove from oven and place pan on a wire rack to cool. Serve while still warm or serve at room temperature. *Makes 8 to 10 servings.*

GRETCHEN'S HONEY LEBKUCHEN WITH A SIMPLE POWDERED SUGAR GLAZE

When Mother was a girl, these spicy frosted gingerbread cookies filled with hazelnuts, candied citron, and candied orange peels were a favorite gift from German farm women to their neighbors at Christmastime.

5 cups sifted all-purpose flour
1 teaspoon baking powder
1 teaspoon ground cinnamon
½ teaspoon freshly grated nutmeg
½ teaspoon ground ginger
½ teaspoon ground cloves
5 eggs
1¾ cups light honey, at room
  temperature (clover honey
  preferred)
1 tablespoon lemon juice
Finely grated rind from 1 lemon
  (about 2 teaspoons)

⅔ cup finely chopped hazelnuts
  (preferred) or slivered
  almonds, plus 36 halves or
  slices for decorating tops of
  cookies
½ cup chopped candied citron
½ cup chopped candied orange peel
A Simple Powdered Sugar Frosting
  (recipe follows)
About ½ cup quartered or halved
  candied cherries, for decorating tops
  of cookies

Measure out 4 *cups* of the flour and sift with the baking powder, cinnamon, nutmeg, ginger, and cloves (the *remaining 1 cup* flour will be needed for finishing dough or rolling it out); set aside. In a large bowl, beat the eggs with the honey until a thick and rich yellow; add the lemon juice and lemon rind. Gradually add the flour-spice mixture to the egg-honey mixture, stirring well. Add just enough of the remaining sifted flour to make a fairly stiff dough that is not sticky. Blend in the ⅔ cup hazelnuts, candied citron, and candied orange peel. Wrap the dough in plastic wrap or aluminum foil; refrigerate overnight.

The next day and when ready to bake, preheat oven to 400°F. Divide the dough into thirds; roll out one piece at a time ¼ inch thick. Cut dough into 2-inch round cookies or into 1x2-inch bar cookies and place about 2 inches apart on a lightly greased cookie sheet. Bake until cookies are lightly browned and tops spring back when lightly pressed, 8 to 10 minutes. Remove from oven and transfer to a wire rack to cool. When thoroughly cooled, frost with the simple powdered sugar frosting, then immediately decorate with halved or sliced hazelnuts and the candied cherries. Once frosting is dry, serve immediately or store in an airtight container until ready to serve.   *Makes about 3 dozen cookies.*

A Simple Powdered Sugar Glaze

1 cup powdered sugar
4 to 5 tablespoons heavy cream or
   milk

Combine the sugar and enough cream to make mixture a good spreading consistency, stirring until smooth. Spread a small amount on each cooled cookie or dip top of cookie in the glaze. Use immediately.
          Makes enough to glaze about 3 dozen Lebkuchen.

JANE WATSON HOPPING

Effie as a girl

🌿 SONGFESTS

In farm country, boys and girls alike helped get the crops planted and harvested, cows milked and pigs fed. Most of the time there was so much work to do from spring until late fall that people hardly left home. Then in November, when the butchering was done, the apples were all picked and tucked away, the great squashes laid by in a warm spot indoors for winter, the elevators filled with grain, and hay stacked "clean to the rafters" in the barns, social life resumed.

All young men fourteen years of age and older, scrubbed at skin that was tanned dark by more than half a year of outside work, washed hair that had grown too long or wild for courting, patted on a little bay rum, and rode into town to dances, church socials, and songfests. In those days it helped to know how to dance and to have a good singing voice since both dancing and singing were very popular at social events.

Sometimes young men would get together and sing to impress all the girls. Spirits were high so the songs tended to be a bit rowdy. Then, as the holidays approached and fellows had singled out special girls, the songs became less boisterous, and more romantic and tender.

Young men, all fired up by now would look moon-eyed and sing "By the light of the silvery moon,/I want to croon to my honey I'll sing love's tune." And others were so addled by the delightful companionship of girls that they could hardly walk straight:

SEEING THE GIRLS HOME IN VERMONT

Of course, when Winter took his seat,
And clubs and things begun to meet,
And singing school was running strong,
And magic lanterns come along—
'Twas nothing strange that girls and boys
Should kinder share each other's joys;
But, when you scarcely hadn't seen
A girl sense grass was getting green,
It took some nerve, I'll tell you that,
To walk right up to Minnie Pratt,
Or Flora Flagg, or Susie Guile,
Or any girl that dressed in style,
And ask if you could see her home,
A-jest as if you owned a brome.

My Gracious! If she smiled and said,
"With pleasure, Mr. Buttonhead,"
You felt a load fall off your back
As heavy as a pedlar's pack,
And grabbed her arm with such a pinch
She side-stepped 'bout a half an inch;
Recovering from this slight alarm,
You eased a trifle on her arm,
And walked along so brave and true
You didn't care who spotted you;
And when she said, "Good evening, Ben,"
You vowed you'd not be scart again,
But it's a fact—you ain't to blame—
You'll be worked up about the same.

—Daniel Cady

JANE WATSON HOPPING

Then a few weeks before Christmas, attendance at churches rose and religious music predominated as everyone began to practice the ancient carols.

AUNT IDA LOUISE'S CHOCOLATY WACKY CAKE WITH DUSTED POWDERED-SUGAR LACE

I don't remember when Aunty learned to make this "stir-up-in-a-pan" cake, but I do remember watching her lay a lacy paper doily over the top and dust it with powdered sugar. As a child I loved to listen to her tales about old-time songfests and could barely resist the urge to touch the lacy sugar pattern left on the cake top when she had removed the doily.

1½ cups all-purpose flour
1 cup sugar
¼ cup unsweetened cocoa powder
1 teaspoon baking soda
½ teaspoon salt
1 tablespoon cider vinegar

1 teaspoon vanilla extract
⅓ cup vegetable oil
1 cup cold water
Powdered sugar, for decorating top of cake, optional

Preheat oven to 350°F. Into an ungreased 9-inch round cake pan, sift together the flour, sugar, cocoa, baking soda, and salt. Shake the pan until ingredients are level, then with the back of a large spoon make three wells in the mixture. Into the first well pour the vinegar, in the second well pour the vanilla, and into the remaining well the oil. Pour the cold water over the entire top. Then use a large fork to stir the ingredients together, lifting and stirring the dry ingredients off the bottom and out of the corners of the pan until they are well incorporated and the batter is almost smooth, with only a few small lumps. (*Note:* this mixing should take about 1½ to 2 minutes.) Bake until the top feels a bit firm and a toothpick inserted in the center comes out clean. Remove cake from oven and let it cool thoroughly in the pan.

Before serving, if desired, lay an 8-inch round lacy paper doily on top and lightly sift powdered sugar over the top; let cake sit for about 2 minutes, then gently lift the doily off to reveal the lacy powdered sugar pattern left on the cake top. *Makes one 9-inch round loaf cake.*

OLD-TIME MOLASSES CRISPS

Since these thin crisp cookies keep indefinitely in a covered jar, they have always been a perfect ready-made treat to take to a quickly-planned party at church or school.

1 cup light molasses, at room temperature	5 cups sifted all-purpose flour
1 cup sugar	2 eggs, beaten to a froth
½ cup butter or margarine, softened	1 teaspoon ground cinnamon
½ cup lard, at room temperature (butter or margarine may be substituted, but lard makes a very crisp product)	½ teaspoon baking soda
	½ teaspoon salt
	½ teaspoon ground ginger
	½ teaspoon ground cloves

In a large saucepan, blend together the molasses, sugar, butter, and lard. Cook just below a boil until all ingredients are liquified, stirring constantly. Remove from heat.

Place 2 *cups* of the flour in a large bowl. Add the hot molasses mixture and beat until smooth. Add the eggs, beating until well blended; let cool.

Meanwhile, into a large bowl sift the *remaining 3 cups* flour with the cinnamon, baking soda, salt, ginger, and cloves. When the egg mixture is cool, blend it into the flour mixture until smooth. Place dough in a bowl, cover, and refrigerate until quite cold before rolling out.

Preheat oven to 350°F. Remove chilled dough from refrigerator. On a lightly floured surface, roll the dough out until it's as thin as heavy wrapping paper or a very thin pie crust. Cut dough out with a 2-inch cookie cutter; place rounds about 1 inch apart on a lightly greased cookie sheet and bake until set and lightly browned, about 8 minutes.

Remove from pan with a floured pancake turner. Let cool on a piece of kraft paper (an opened brown grocery bag will do) placed on a flat surface. When thoroughly cooled, store in an airtight container until ready to serve. *Makes about 8 dozen cookies.*

EVA MAE'S FAVORITE MINCEMEAT

This simple-to-make, not-too-rich mincemeat makes four nine-inch pies. It also may be used in tarts, breads, turnovers (such as Mincemeat Turnovers, see below), and Aunt Mae's Mincemeat-Custard Pie (page 320).

1 pound boneless round beef or venison, cubed
2 pounds apples, pared, cored, and quartered (Northern Spy, McIntosh, or Jonathan preferred)
2½ cups dried apples or 1 cup currants
2½ cups dark raisins

¼ pound candied citron
¼ pound candied orange peel
¼ pound beef suet, ground
2 cups, packed, light brown sugar
1 cup apple cider
1 tablespoon ground cinnamon
1 tablespoon freshly grated nutmeg
2 teaspoons ground cloves

Place the beef cubes in a large saucepan. Cover with boiling water; cover pan and cook until the cubes are tender. Remove from heat and set uncovered in a cool place. When the meat is cool, remove it from the pan and set aside. Reserve 1 cup of the broth to finish the mincemeat.

Put the beef cubes through the coarse blade of a food grinder; set aside. Grind the fresh apples, dried apples, raisins, citron, and orange peel through the medium-coarse blade of the food grinder into a large bowl. Add the reserved ground beef and the suet, sugar, cider, and the reserved 1 cup broth to the bowl; blend together. Add the cinnamon, nutmeg, and cloves, mixing thoroughly.

Now wash the large saucepan; place the mincemeat mixture in the pan and simmer over low heat until thick, about 45 minutes to 1 hour, stirring often to prevent sticking and scorching. Let cool, then refrigerate.   *Makes about 12 cups mincemeat.*

MINCEMEAT TURNOVERS

Just before Christmas, when the winter social life started "buzzin'," and folks were "doin' chores early" and "off an' gone to some affair or another," women began to make up little platefuls of goodies out of the special things they had put away for the holidays—the year's mincemeat, pickles, a new kind of cookie, a little tutti-fruitti—just testing the recipes on their families before they staked their whole reputation as cooks on one big meal or a dozen Christmas-basket pies.

These turnovers, first tried out on the family, then maybe on a "special friend," were designed to test the flakiness of the crust and the richness of the mincemeat flavor. Once tested, the mincemeat was used in all sorts of rich tasting baked goods, among them pies, cakes, cookies and tarts. I like to serve these turnovers with vanilla ice cream.

Plain Turnover Pastry Dough (recipe
  follows)
2½ cups Eva Mae's Favorite
    Mincemeat (page 29)

Prepare the pastry dough; refrigerate. If made ahead and chilled, set the mincemeat out to warm to room temperature.

Meanwhile, preheat oven to 450°F. When the dough is well chilled, remove from refrigerator and divide in half. Roll out one portion and cut into 4-inch squares. Place 1 *tablespoon* (maybe slightly more) mincemeat on each. Moisten the edges of dough with a little water; then fold dough over filling to form a triangle and seal edges together by firmly pressing with a fork or by fluting them with your fingertips. Repeat with remaining half of dough and mincemeat to make more turnovers. With a spatula, transfer turnovers to a large ungreased cookie sheet, about 2 inches apart. Prick tops with a fork. Bake until crust is golden brown, about 20 to 25 minutes. Remove from oven and let cool to room temperature on the cookie sheet before serving.

Makes about 1 dozen turnovers.

Plain Turnover Pastry Dough
  3 cups sifted all-purpose flour
  1 teaspoon salt
  1 cup cold butter or margarine, cut
    into small pieces
⅓ to ½ cup cold water

Sift togther the flour and salt into a large bowl; cut the butter in with a pastry cutter or 2 dinner knives, or work butter lightly into the flour with your fingertips, until mixture is reduced to small pea-size pieces. Gradually sprinkle the water over the flour mixture, mixing lightly with a fork; add only enough water to hold the pastry together. Turn onto a floured surface and shape into a soft ball. Cover with plastic wrap or aluminum foil and refrigerate until well chilled before rolling out.

Makes enough dough for about 1 dozen turnovers.

JANE WATSON HOPPING

BRIGHTEST AND BEST OF THE SONS OF THE MORNING

Brightest and best of the sons of the morning,
    Dawn on our darkness and lend us Thine aid;
Star of the East, the horizon adorning,
    Guide where our infant Redeemer is laid.

Cold on His cradle the dewdrops are shining;
    Low lies His head with the beasts of the stall;
Angels adore Him in slumber reclining,
    Maker and Monarch and Saviour of all.

Say, shall we yield Him, in costly devotion,
    Odors of Edom and offerings divine,
Gems of the mountain and pearls of the ocean,
    Myrrh from the forest, or gold from the mine?

Vainly we offer each ample oblation,
    Vainly with gifts would His favor secure;
Richer by far is the heart's adoration,
    Dearer to God are the prayers of the poor.

—John P. Harding

🌿 THIN ICE

When Mother was a child, Will Bates was already bent and crippled with age. She and the other children were a bit shy with him but loved to hear him tell about his eleventh year, about staying on the farm miles from town with his grandparents "clear to Christmas." His rambling winter tale always started, "By November we was 'ready' for Christmas":

"Me and Grandma cleaned the house; we didn't have any need for hired girls to help us get ready for Christmas. We gathered the greenery for decorating the rooms and put it in the cold parlor to keep it fresh until the big day came. Almost every night we could hear Grandpa in

the barn or sheds and we knew that he was up to Santa's business, hammering away or cutting out something.

"I stayed all summer into the fall, and through Christmas. As it got colder and colder and as storms came through, I couldn't wait until the ice froze thick over the fields and Grandma would let me go skating across the countryside. At least four or five times I had my skates all cleaned up and ready. Then one day Grandma thought the ice was thick enough and let me go—with a stern warning to stay away from cricks and ponds that might not have froze enough.

"Those times was wonderful times for boys and girls—there wasn't much of anything to hurt you except when you fell down. Neighbors were friendly, and if you stopped by they'd ask you in to warm up and have a bite to eat. I skated nearly twelve miles that day through the fields and down a back road, then up the county road to Junction City and back home again."

At which point the old man would often lapse into silent reverie and, as Mother said, left them to finish the tale to their own liking. They had all heard about his eleventh year so often they knew all about the mincemeat pies he and his grandmother had made and left in a frozen row on a shelf in a storeroom, waiting to be brought into the kitchen and heated for company that might come to call or for Christmas dinner. And they knew about the huge turkey he and his grandmother had dressed and seasoned before they tucked it into a great black roasting pan.

Each of them had visions of his grandma's pantry all filled with potatoes and squashes, apples and onions, nuts, and everything a person could think of. The half-grown boys especially used to dream about that pantry; it gave them such a glow just thinking about it.

We knew that his parents came on the train for Christmas and that the only way they could get out to the farm was in a sleigh. We liked to think about them all wrapped in blankets, the sleigh bells jingling, everybody shouting, laughing, hugging, and talking all at once.

That was the year Will Bates's father shook his hand and told him that he was proud of him and the way he'd helped his grandparents with the farm work. That was the year he first felt like a man.

WILL'S FAVORITE APPLESAUCE FRUITCAKE

¾ cup butter
2 cups, packed, dark brown sugar
3 eggs
1½ cups unsweetened applesauce
3 cups sifted all-purpose flour
1 tablespoon baking powder
1 tablespoon ground cinnamon
1½ teaspoons baking soda
1 teaspoon salt
1 teaspoon ground nutmeg
½ teaspoon ground ginger
½ teaspoon ground cloves
6 cups mixed candied and dried fruits (any combination available)
2 cups mixed raisins and currants
1½ cups mixed nuts (use your favorites)

Preheat oven to 325°F. Cream the butter and sugar together until light and creamy. Add the eggs one at a time, beating after each addition. Stir in the applesauce.

Sift together the flour, baking powder, cinnamon, baking soda, salt, nutmeg, ginger, and cloves. In a large bowl, combine the candied and dried fruits, raisins and currants mixture, and nuts. Measure out about ½ cup of the flour mixture and toss the fruit-nut mixture with it. Gradually add the remaining flour to the applesauce mixture, stirring until well blended. Pour this batter over the fruit-nut mixture and fold together. Grease and flour three 5x9-inch loaf pans. (Note: Smaller bread pans may be used; be sure to adjust the baking time accordingly.) Pour one third of the batter into each pan; tap the pans gently on a flat surface once or twice to settle the batter. Bake until a toothpick inserted in the center comes out clean, about 1 hour and 45 minutes. Remove from oven and let sit for about 10 minutes, then loosening sides carefully with a knife, if necessary, remove from the pan. Place right side up on a wire rack to cool thoroughly, then wrap in waxed paper or aluminum foil and let age for about 1 week in the refrigerator. Serve in thin slices.

Makes three loaves of fruitcake.

EASY-TO-MAKE COCONUT SNOWBALLS

WHEN MOTHER MADE AN ANGEL CAKE

In fall and early winter, Mother's spring-hatched laying hens provided enough eggs for household use and for angel cakes. On blustery cold days, she would yield to our begging and make tender snowballs—broken balls of angel cake, lightly glazed and rolled in coconut.

Just as soon as Grandpa realized that Mama was beating egg whites into stiff peaks, he would come in out of the weather, set down to watch, and now and then give a bit of advice, as she folded in the sprinkled-on sugar and the sifted flour. While we all waited for the cake to bake, Grandpa would make a pot of coffee, bring in more wood for the cookstove, and pull his chair up close to the table.

The baked, cooled cake was barely torn into pieces, glazed and coated, before Grandpa initiated the festivities, pouring milk and coffee for all. Sometimes we sang carols while we ate sweet and airy snowballs to our hearts' content.

About 1 pound grated coconut, plain or toasted
Angel Cake (recipe follows)

Thin Powdered Sugar Frosting (recipe follows)

Place the coconut in a shallow bowl. Break the angel cake into small chunks. With a fork, dip each chunk into the frosting; drain well and roll immediately in the coconut. Dry on waxed paper or aluminum foil. Serve to eager family or guests; do not store for later use.

Makes about 2 dozen snowballs, depending on the size of the chunks.

Angel Cake

1¼ cups egg whites, at room temperature
1 teaspoon cream of tartar
¼ teaspoon salt

½ teaspoon vanilla extract
½ teaspoon lemon extract
1½ cups sugar, sifted
1 cup twice-sifted cake flour

Preheat oven to 300°F. Beat the egg whites in a large bowl until frothy. Sprinkle the cream of tartar and salt over them and add the vanilla and lemon extracts. Continue beating just until stiff peaks form; do not overbeat. Gradually fold in the sugar, about 2 tablespoons at a time.

Next, sift about ¼ cup of the flour at a time over the surface of the egg whites, folding it in between additions. Turn the batter into an ungreased 9-inch tube pan. Bake until light brown, about 1 hour. Invert pan onto a wire rack; let cake stay in the inverted pan until cool, about 1 hour.

When cake is cool, loosen sides carefully with a spatula and turn out onto a cake platter. *Makes 1 tube cake.*

Thin Powdered-Sugar Frosting
2 cups powdered sugar
About 6 tablespoons milk
1 teaspoon vanilla extract

Place the sugar in a medium-size bowl. Add the vanilla, then just enough milk, 1 tablespoon at a time, to make a fairly runny frosting, stirring until light and smooth. (*Note:* It's best to make this frosting one batch at a time. If you find you want a little more frosting for the snowballs, make an extra half-batch separate from the first batch.)

Makes enough frosting for 1 tube cake or
about 2 dozen Easy-to-Make Coconut Snowballs.

A CHRISTMAS DELIGHT

Served with hot coffee and a crispy little wafer or two, this elegant dessert—a favorite of Will's mother—can top off a very special dinner or provide a treat when holiday visitors come to call. Top it with slivered or finely sliced almonds or pecans if you like.

1 cup soft, finely chopped pitted
dates
1 8-ounce jar maraschino cherries,
finely cut, reserve syrup
Preserved Green Figs, finely cut,
reserve syrup (recipe follows)
1 cup ground roasted almonds
A few grains of salt
½ cup sugar
½ cup water
Brandy, to taste
2 quarts vanilla ice cream

In a small bowl, combine the dates, drained cherries, and preserved figs. Add the syrup from the jars and just enough boiling water to cover. (*Note:* The fruit should take up liquid and flavors should blend.) Let stand overnight.

The next day, prepare the syrup as follows: Boil sugar and water together for 5 minutes. To the fruit, add the almonds and sugar syrup, then add brandy to taste. Spoon over serving-size portions of ice cream, or, if you wish, soften the 2 quarts of ice cream slightly, then stir the fruit and syrup through the ice cream just enough to marble it. Freeze until firm before serving. *Makes 10 to 12 servings.*

Preserved Green Figs

4 pounds light green figs
3½ pounds granulated sugar

¼ cup lemon juice
2 sliced lemons

Wash firm-ripe figs; put in a large saucepan and cover with hot water, boil 15 to 20 minutes; then drain. Cut off both stems and blossom ends.

Add sugar and lemon juice to 8 cups boiling water. Stir to dissolve sugar before adding figs. Boil until the figs are clear, and the syrup begins to thicken. (*Note:* If the syrup becomes too thick before the figs are done, add a little boiling water. If the figs are clear but the syrup is thin, remove the figs and boil the syrup until it thickens.) Remove preserves from heat; set them overnight in a cool place.

The following day, pack preserved figs into hot scrubbed and sterilized pint jars. Seal with hot lids and sterilized rings. Process the pints for 30 minutes in a water-bath canner at simmering (180–185°F). Remove from water bath, cool, check the seal, and store in a cool, dry, dark place. (*Note:* A sealed jar should have a concaved lid.)

LONG AFORE I KNOWED WHO "SANTY-CLAUS" WUZ!

No matter how much mothers talk about angels on high and Baby Jesus, shepherds, and stars, some boys—like a few we know—can't dream of anything but Ol' Saint Nick, the presents he will bring, and Christmas dinner with all the goodies that abound.

WHO SANTY-CLAUS WUZ

Jes' a little bit o' feller—I remember still—
Ust to almost cry fer Christmas, like a youngster will.
Fourth o' July's nothin' to it!—New Year's ain't a smell!
Easter-Sunday—Circus-day, jes' all dead in the shell!
Lawzy, though! at night, you know, to set around an' hear
The old folks work the story off about the sledge an' deer.
An' "Santy" skootin' round the roof, all wrapt in fur an' fuzz—
Long afore I knowed who "Santy-Claus" wuz!

Ust to wait, an' set up late, a week er two ahead;
Couldn't hardly keep awake, ner wouldn't go to bed;
Kittle stewin' on the fire, an' Mother settin' here
Darnin's socks, an' rockin' in the skreeky rockin'-cheer;
Pap gap', an' wonder where it wuz the money went,

An' quar'l with his frosted heels, an' spill his liniment;
An' me a-dreamin' sleigh-bells when the clock 'ud whir an' buzz,
Long afore I knowed who "Santy-Claus" wuz!

Size the fire-place up an' figger how "Ole Santy" could
Manage to come down the chimbly, like they said he would;
Wisht 'at I could hide an' see him—wunderd what he'd say
Ef he ketched a feller layin' fer him thataway!
But I bet on him, an' liked him, same as ef he had
Turned to pat me on the back an' say, "Look here, my lad,
Here's my pack,—jes' he'p yourse'f, like all good boys does!"
Long afore I knowed who "Santy-Claus" wuz!

Wisht that yarn was true about him, as it 'peared to be—
Truth made out o' lies like that-un's good enough fer me!—
Wisht I still wuz so confidin' I could je' go wild
Over hangin' up my stockin's, like the little child
Climbin' in my lap to-night, an' beggin' me to tell
'Bout them reindeers, and "Old Santy" that she loves so well
I'm half sorry fer this little-girl-sweetheart of his—
Long afore She knows who "Santy-Claus" is!

—James Whitcomb Riley

❧ HE SPRANG TO HIS SLEIGH, TO HIS TEAM GAVE A WHISTLE

When Raymond, my husband, was a little boy, he went with his parents, brother Walter, and Grandma White to a Christmas program at the Newcastle Grammar School. There was singing by all the grades, and skits, readings, and poems, which he wiggled through. And then, wonder of wonders, Santa Claus himself gave away free candy, popcorn balls, and oranges right out of his bulging sack. The excitement was electric, Raymond was entranced. Then when Santa stood at the door and cried

out, "Happy Christmas to all, and to all a goodnight!" he wiggled out of his chair, ran out the door behind Santa, lost sight of him and searched everywhere for sleigh tracks, but magically there were none. Santa was gone.

RAYMOND'S FAVORITE GRAHAM CRACKER FUDGE

This delicious easy-to-make fudge was quite popular in the late thirties and during the forties. And in our old-fashioned family it still remains "a must" in winter. During the weeks before Christmas more than one candymaker stirs up a batch, much to all the men and boys' delight.

2 ounces unsweetened baking chocolate, cut into shavings	2 cups sugar
	1/4 teaspoon salt
1 cup evaporated milk	1 tablespoon butter or margarine

24 marshmallows, cut into bite-size
   pieces (or use bite-size pieces,
   which are available in today's
   markets)

3 cups graham cracker crumbs,
   finely ground
1 cup pecans or walnuts (preferred)
1 teaspoon vanilla extract

Grease an 8x8-inch cake pan: set aside.

Combine the chocolate and milk in a medium-size heavy-bottomed saucepan; heat over very low heat until chocolate melts; stirring occasionally. Add the sugar and salt, stirring until they dissolve. Continue cooking until mixture reaches the soft-ball stage (234°F to 240°F on a candy thermometer). Remove from heat and add the butter (it will melt as the syrup cools). Let cool slightly, then add the marshmallows, graham cracker crumbs, walnuts, and vanilla; mixing well. Press into the prepared cake pan. Refrigerate overnight. Cut into sixty-four 1-inch squares. These squares will keep well for a week or more if stored in an airtight container with waxed paper between the layers.

Makes 64 1-inch squares.

OLD-FASHIONED SPICE CAKE
WITH EASY-TO-MAKE LEMON BUTTER GLAZE

This was one of Aunt Mable's holiday cakes. Perhaps the recipe came from the years when she cooked at home and fancy things like slivered almonds, candied citron, and cherries were unaffordable. At any rate, this fragrant, flavorful old-time cake, with glaze streaming off it, spoke of Christmas to us all for many years. I like to make it into a loaf cake and glaze it lightly, but it may be baked in layers and frosted with a Creamy Orange Frosting.

2 cups all-purpose flour
1 cup, packed, light brown sugar
1 teaspoon ground cinnamon
1 teaspoon baking soda
½ teaspoon salt
½ teaspoon freshly grated nutmeg
¼ teaspoon ground cloves
2 eggs

1 cup light cream
½ cup melted butter
1 teaspoon finely grated lemon peel
Juice from 1 lemon
Easy-to-Make Lemon Butter Glaze
   (page 70) or Creamy Orange
   Frosting (page 123)

Preheat oven to 350°F. Sift together the flour, sugar, cinnamon, baking soda, salt, nutmeg, and cloves. In a large bowl, whip the eggs into the cream; slowly add the flour mixture, stirring to blend. Stir in the butter, lemon peel, and lemon juice. Pour the batter into a greased and lightly floured 5x9-inch loaf pan. Bake until done, about 1 hour. Remove from oven and let cake cool in the pan, then glaze it.

Makes 1 loaf cake or 12 servings.

MRS. D's APPLESAUCE CAKE

When I was in high school, my mother's father and my father's father and his wife and two children all lived with us on the homeplace. To help earn a little extra money, Mother worked outside our home at housecleaning for a short while because that was the only job she could take that allowed her enough free time to meet her responsibilities at home—caring for family members and working on the homeplace, tending cattle, chickens, and the like. Very quickly she found two older women she liked to work for; she felt needed and, as she has often said, she learned about living and growing old from them.

One of the jobs she liked very much was to help Mrs. D spruce up her house and make cakes or cookies for friends who came over for tea, to play cards, or for Christmas. This was a popular cake for such an occasion.

2 cups sifted all-purpose flour
3 tablespoons unsweetened cocoa powder
1 tablespoon cornstarch
2 teaspoons baking soda
1 teaspoon ground cinnamon
½ teaspoon salt

½ teaspoon freshly grated nutmeg
½ teaspoon ground cloves
1½ cups butter, melted
1 cup sugar
1½ cups raw mashed apples
1 recipe Sweetened Whipped Cream (page 60) optional

Preheat oven to 350°F. Lightly grease a 13x9x2-inch baking pan; set aside.

Into a large bowl, sift together the flour, cocoa, cornstarch, baking soda, cinnamon, salt, nutmeg, and cloves; set aside. In a second large bowl, cream together the butter and sugar; stir in the apples. Make a well in the flour mixture and place in it the apple mixture; stir only enough to blend. Pour batter into the prepared baking pan. Bake until cake springs back when lightly pressed and sides have pulled away from the pan, about 45 to 50 minutes. Serve warm, cut into 3-inch squares and topped with a dollop of Sweetened Whipped Cream or serve at room temperature, thinly sliced.   *Makes 1 large sheet cake.*

COCOA COOKIES WITH COCOA GLAZE

These good, sturdy cookies have always been a favorite with men and boys at our "Christmas doin's." Effie, a good farm cook, always brought a great pile of them, which disappeared readily as large work-gnarled hands gathered them up three or four at a time. And before the day was over, several men and a few boys would sidle up to her to remark, "Effie, there's nothing wrong with these cookies except they don't keep." And they were right—Effie always went home with empty trays.

5 cups sifted all-purpose flour	1 cup unsweetened cocoa powder
1 tablespoon baking powder	About ⅓ cup boiling water
1 teaspoon salt	1 cup milk
1 cup butter, softened	1 teaspoon ground cinnamon
1¾ cups, packed, light brown sugar	1 teaspoon vanilla extract
3 eggs, well beaten	Cocoa Glaze (recipe follows)

Preheat oven to 375°F. Sift together the flour, baking powder, and salt; set aside.

In a large bowl, cream together the butter and sugar. Add the eggs, mixing well. Place the cocoa in a small bowl; add just enough boiling water to make a paste; add this paste to the sugar-butter mixture, beating well. Stir in the milk, cinnamon, and vanilla. Add the flour-mixture and stir into a stiff dough. Roll out very thin and cut into cookies with a small round cookie cutter (dip the cutter into flour so the cookies don't stick to it). Place the cookies about 2 inches apart on a greased cookie sheet and bake until lightly browned, about 10 to 15 minutes. Remove from oven and immediately transfer to a wire rack or a piece of brown kraft paper (an opened grocery bag will do) to cool. When cool, make the glaze and spread it lightly on the cookies. Once the glaze is hard, the cookies may be stored on a platter, lightly covered with a clean kitchen towel, until ready to serve.   *Makes about 3 dozen cookies.*

Cocoa Glaze

5 tablespoons butter
¼ cup milk
About 1 to 2 tablespoons boiling
  water

¼ cup plus 2 tablespoons
  unsweetened cocoa powder
1 teaspoon vanilla extract
1 cup powdered sugar

In the top of a double boiler, combine the butter and milk and cook just until butter melts and milk is hot. Remove from heat. Add just enough boiling water to the cocoa to make a paste. Add this paste to the butter mixture, stirring to blend. Stir in the vanilla, then the sugar. If the glaze is too thick, add a little more warm milk.

Makes enough glaze for about 3 dozen cookies.

MARJORIE'S ALMANAC

Little fairy snow-flakes
  Dancing in the flue;
Old Mr. Santa Claus,
  What is keeping you?
Twilight and firelight
  Shadows come and go;
Merry chime of sleigh-bells

Tinkling through the snow;
Mother knitting stockings
(Pussy's got the ball),—
Don't you think that winter's
Pleasanter than all?

—Thomas Bailey Aldrich

AND THE SNOW DRIFTED DOWN, ALL AROUND, ALL AROUND

Deep in farm country you can smell a snow storm in the crisp pure air. At first the flakes fall gently, riding in on every little breeze; they don't stick. Then slowly a downlike comforter spreads over farm machinery, and stacks of used lumber, and settles on old shake-roofed barns and outbuildings. Soft caps build on the tops of fence posts and glittering white garlands bear the limbs of pine, cedar, and fir trees to the ground.

As the sky darkens the fast-falling flakes whiten the air, veiling the farm house, and hiding gardens and orchards, until the old familiar place —the bustling workplace of summer—becomes a fairy land, softened, beautiful.

When the storm passes in the night, silence envelops the country-side; even the animals are quiet. Looking out of an upstairs window, one is filled with the awe-inspiring power of nature that has brightened the landscape, bathing all in a heavenly glow.

DELICIOUS LIGHT FRUITCAKE

Stirred up on cold snowy days early in December and tucked away tightly wrapped to mellow a bit, this simple fruitcake is easy to make and requires a minimum of costly ingredients. It has always been a favorite in our family. Baked in a tube pan and coated with a fruit glaze, it looks very festive on the sideboard and pleases the palate of everyone.

2½ cups all-purpose flour
1 teaspoon baking powder
½ teaspoon salt
1 cup slivered almonds
1½ cups candied cherries, cut in half
1 cup candied citron, chopped
½ cup candied orange peel, chopped
1 cup butter or margarine, softened

1 cup sugar
5 eggs
1½ teaspoons finely grated lemon peel
1 tablespoon strained lemon juice
Simple Powdered Sugar Glaze (page 24), optional
Additional bits of the almonds and candied fruits, for garnishing cake, optional

Preheat oven to 300°F. (*Note:* All fruitcakes are baked in a slow oven.) Grease thoroughly either a 9-inch tube pan or 9x5x3-inch loaf pan, line the pan with waxed or heavy kraft paper (a brown grocery bag will do); grease the paper and dust it with flour, tipping the pan upside down to remove any extra flour; set aside. (Fruitcakes are tender and heavy which makes them difficult to turn out unless you prepare the baking pan this way.)

Into a medium-size bowl, sift together 2 *cups* of the flour with the baking powder and salt; set aside. In a second medium-size bowl, combine the almonds and candied fruits; the remaining ½ cup flour and set aside.

Cream the butter in a large bowl. Gradually add the sugar, working until both are creamy. Add the eggs, one at a time, beating well after each addition. Stir in the lemon peel and lemon juice. Then add the flour and mix to form a rather thick batter. Fold in the nuts and candied fruit mixture; when blended, turn into the prepared cake pan. Bake until lightly browned and firm to the touch, about 1 hour and 45 minutes. Cool in the pan on a wire rack and serve as is or, if desired, you may gently remove the cake from the pan when the cake is just barely warm enough to melt a glaze; immediately frost with Simple Powdered Sugar Glaze and decorate the top with bits of almonds and candied fruits. Store leftover cake, tightly wrapped in aluminum foil, in the refrigerator.

Makes 1 tube cake or 1 loaf cake.

THE CHILDREN'S ALMOND BRITTLE

At Christmas, when the youngest children wanted to help make candy, old-time mothers let them make this recipe, all the while keeping a careful eye on the proceedings.

2 cups sugar
1 teaspoon vanilla extract
1 cup whole almonds, cut in half
    lengthwise

Butter a heatproof platter and set aside. Heat the sugar in a heavy iron skillet over high heat, stirring constantly, just until dissolved. Immediately remove from heat and add the vanilla and almonds. Pour onto a heatproof buttered platter; when cool, break into pieces.

Makes about ½ to ¾ pound.

WELSH NECTAR

3 lemons
2 gallons boiling water

2 pounds sugar
1 pound finely chopped raisins

Thinly slice the rind from the lemons; set peeled lemons aside. Place the peelings in a crock or large vessel which will hold 2 or more gallons of liquid. Pour the water over them. When cool, squeeze and strain the juice from the lemons into the water. Add the sugar and raisins. Cover with several layers of cloth (a folded dishtowel will do) and let stand for 4 to 5 days in a cool place, stirring everyday. Then strain through a jelly bag or several thicknesses of cheesecloth and bottle for immediate use.

Makes 2 gallons.

                          JANE WATSON HOPPING

🌿 RUN, RUN, AS FAST AS YOU CAN

When Ada's grandchildren were small, she read to them by the hour. Their favorite story was about the little gingerbread boy because when the story was finished their grandma would usually get up and bake them some little gingerbread boys:

Once upon a time there was a little girl and a little boy.

They hadn't any little brothers, nor even any little sisters, and they thought they would like a little brother to play with. So they made a little boy of gingerbread.

They made little red candy boots, a little yellow candy hat, and a brown candy coat for him.

Then they rolled him out and put him in a big pan and put the pan in the oven.

Then they shut the oven door and said, "Bake, Oven! Bake! And we shall have a little brother to play with."

When they thought it was time for the Gingerbread Boy to be done, they opened the oven door.

Out he jumped through the door, and away he ran through the street.

The little boy and the little girl ran after him as fast as they could, but the Gingerbread Boy laughed and shouted.

> *Run! Run!*
> *As fast as you can!*
> *You can't catch me,*
> *I'm the Gingerbread Man.*

LITTLE GINGERBREAD BOYS

Initially, Ada baked these gingerbread boys to hang on the Christmas tree, but the children and grandchildren and even their friends begged for more, until she could count the number of cookies she had made by the dozens and dozens.

2½ cups sifted flour
  2 teaspoon ground ginger
½ teaspoon salt
½ cup butter (preferred) or
    margarine
½ cup sugar
½ cup light molasses, at room
    temperature

½ teaspoon baking soda
¼ cup hot water
Red Hots (cinnamon candies), for
    decorative buttons
Dark seedless raisins, for eyes
1 recipe Simple Powdered Sugar
    Glaze (page 24)

Into a medium-size bowl, sift together the flour, ginger, and salt; set aside. Melt the butter in a large saucepan over low heat. Remove from heat and stir in the sugar, then the molasses. In a cup, dissolve the baking soda in the hot water. Alternately add the flour mixture and dissolved baking soda to the molasses mixture; begin with the flour and end with the baking soda. When a medium-firm dough (one that feels firm to the touch and yet rolls out easily) has formed, cover and refrigerate until well chilled, about 3 hours.

Preheat oven to 350°F. Remove the chilled dough from the refrigerator and turn onto a floured surface. Using a small portion at a time, roll out the dough ⅛ inch thick. Cut out with a gingerboy cookie cutter. (Note: Handle the dough as little as possible and work quickly so the warmth of your hands doesn't soften it too much.) Place the cookies about 2 inches apart on a greased cookie sheet. Press red hots in place for buttons, and add raisins for the eyes.

Bake until lightly browned, about 10 to 12 minutes. Remove from oven and let cool about 3 minutes on the cookie sheet, then lift onto wire racks to finish cooling.

Meanwhile, prepare the frosting. When the cookies are thoroughly cooled, spoon the frosting into a pastry bag fitted with a small nozzle and pipe on collars, boots, cuffs, and belts. Let the frosting harden. Store in an airtight container until ready to serve.   *Makes about 2 dozen cookies.*

JANE WATSON HOPPING

SPICY MULLED CIDER

On old homesteads apple trees and orchards were planted first, often before the house was built. Such trees yielded tons of red, green, yellow, and striped fruit. For cider, farmers mixed sweet and tart apples with a heady fragrance and flavor to give the cider a rich earthy taste.

1 *quart apple cider*
2 *tablespoons light honey*
1/4 *teaspoon ground cinnamon*
1/8 *teaspoon freshly ground nutmeg*
1/8 *teaspoon ground ginger*
1/8 *teaspoon ground cloves*

4 to 6 *cinnamon sticks, each about*
  6 *inches long*
4 to 6 *center slices of unpeeled*
  orange
8 to 12 *whole cloves*

In a medium-size saucepan, combine the cider, honey, and the ground spices. Heat over high heat until the honey completely dissolves. Serve immediately or reduce heat to low to keep warm until ready to serve. To serve, pour the cider into mugs and garnish with cinnamon sticks and orange slices stuck with cloves. *Makes 4 to 6 servings.*

THE MELLOW LIGHT
OF CANDLES SMALL

Not so many years ago, Christmas was very much a homemade family affair. Aunt Mable recalls simple gifts: a new fangled measuring cup with writing on the side; hand-turned rolling pins for the cook, one a lightweight, golden-colored sugar pine for easy rolling, another of heavy yew or myrtle wood for pie crusts and noodles; an array of wooden spoons handcarved from cherry, apple, maple, and oak; a toy train and a rocking horse for the little ones; a cradle for the new baby; knitted stockings, sweaters, and caps—all the product of many hours lovingly spent.

Those plain warm, human times, also joyfully remembered by James Whitcomb Riley in his nostalgic poem, "A Feel in the Chris'mas-Air," touch our hearts with gladness.

From *A FEEL IN THE CHRIS'MAS-AIR*

They's a kind o' feel in the air, to me,
When the Chris'mas-times sets in,
That's about as much of a mystery
As ever I've run ag'in'!—
Fer instance, now, whilse I gain in weight
And gineral health, I swear
They's a goneness somers I can't quite state—
A kind o' feel in the air!

Two little darlings and friend

They's a feel in the Chris'mas-air goes right
To the spot where a man lives at!—
It gives a feller a' appetite—
They ain't no doubt about that!—
And yit they's somepin'—I don't know what—
That follers me, here and there,
And ha'nts and worries and spares me not—
A kind o' feel in the air!

Is it the racket the children raise?—
W'y, no!—God bless 'em!—no!—
Is it the eyes and the cheeks ablaze—
Like my own wuz, long ago?—
Is it the bleat o' the whistle and beat
O' the little toy-drum and blare
O' the horn?—No! no!—it is jest the sweet—
The sad-sweet feel in the air.

—James Whitcomb Riley

ABOUT AN OLD-FASHIONED SCHOOL TEACHER

Right after Aunt Mable graduated from the twelvth grade she took a job teaching in a small country school. Many times during her long life she told us that those were delightful years in which she had had the privilege of opening children's minds to the wonders about them: the power in ciphering, the enrichment of reading, the beauty of good penmanship, and the use of language.

Later in her life, when she was perhaps fifty years of age, she learned that a janitor was needed at the local grammar school. Long years had passed since she had taught school, times had changed radically, but she longed to be with the children, lesson books, and teachers, so she applied for the job and got it. During the years that she worked at the school, she kept it scrupulously clean and did many extra things to provide pleasant surroundings for those going about the business of education. And as people in the community said, both pupils and teachers alike thought the world of "Mrs. Porter."

We who were the children in her family learned much from her about the environment we lived in. Through her vision we saw the sunrise with enlightened eyes; the brilliant blues, greens, and sable black of the peacock feather; the identifying colored veins in the rocks at our feet. She taught us about bird and animal life, about plants, and about the stars.

And not least, she shared with us the beautiful old Christmas cards in her card collection while she told us tales about Christmases of long ago, of superstition, merrymaking, of kings and carols.

AUNT MABLE'S IMITATION BOAR'S HEAD PORK ROAST WITH HONEY BUTTER GLAZE

When we were children Aunt Mable would serve a pork roast at the family gathering just before Christmas and then tell us about the great halls of old-time warlords in England, about huge Christmas banquets, about a roasted boar's head decorated with garlands of rosemary and bay and with an apple thrust between its teeth, brought ceremoniously and slowly in processional through the hall on a gold or silver platter to the sound of trumpets and much revelry.

1 (5-pound) boneless pork loin roast
2 teaspoons salt
1 teaspoon black pepper
2 teaspoons dried oregano leaves

Honey Butter Glaze (recipe follows)
Cranberry Apple Relish (recipe follows)

Preheat oven to 350°F. Season the roast with the salt and pepper; pulverize the oregano between your thumb and forefinger as you sprinkle it over the fat side of the roast. Place the roast fat side up in a roasting pan fitted with a rack. Roast uncovered until an internal temperature as tested on a meat thermometer reads 185°F, or about 35 minutes to the pound. During the last 30 minutes of baking period, glaze lightly once or twice. Serve with Cranberry Apple Relish.   *Makes 8 to 10 servings.*

Honey Butter Glaze

½ cup honey
½ cup water
1 tablespoon butter
Freshly grated nutmeg (about ½
  teaspoon)

In a small saucepan, heat honey, water, and butter together. Spoon over meat and grate fresh nutmeg over the top.   *Makes about 1 cup.*

Cranberry Apple Relish

2 cups apples, peeled, cored, and
  diced (Jonathan apples
  preferred)
4 cups fresh cranberries
1½ cups sugar
1 cup golden raisins

1 teaspoon salt
Grated rind of 1 lemon
Juice of 1 lemon, strained
1 teaspoon ginger
¼ cup water, more if needed

In a large saucepan, combine apples, cranberries, sugar, raisins, salt, lemon rind and juice, ginger, and ¼ cup water. Bring to a boil; lower heat, cover, and simmer until cranberries and apples are tender, about 8 to 10 minutes. Remove from the heat and cool. Turn into a glass jar that will hold at least 6 cups of relish. Cover and chill. Serve with pork (also delicious with goose or lamb).   *Makes about 5 cups.*

A WINTERTIME VEGETABLE MEDLEY

On old-time farms, root vegetables, which stored well, were regulars on the supper table. They were used in every conceivable way: cooked plain, in stews and the like, and in desserts. This simple vegetable dish makes a perfect accompaniment to almost any supper.

1 cup water
1½ teaspoons salt
3 cups peeled and slivered potatoes
3 cups scraped and slivered carrots
1 cup peeled and slivered celeriac

½ cup minced fresh parsley
6 tablespoons butter or margarine,
  melted
⅛ teaspoon black pepper

Combine the water and salt in a large saucepan and bring to a boil. Add the potatoes, carrots, and celeriac and cook just until tender, about 10 to 12 minutes; don't overcook. Drain. Add the parsley, butter, and pepper, tossing until well blended. Serve piping hot.

Makes 6 to 8 servings.

ADA'S JELLIED TOMATO SALAD
WITH HOMEMADE LEMON MAYONNAISE

In about 1936 the use of gelatin in salads became very popular in our family. The women devised, searched for, and traded recipes in which oranges, apples, peaches, and even tomatoes were used to brighten up winter menus.

2½ cups canned whole tomatoes
 1 rib celery, finely chopped
 ½ teaspoon salt
 1 envelope (1 tablespoon)
   unflavored gelatin
 ¼ cup cold water

1 tablespoon strained lemon juice
1 tablespoon minced chives or
   scallions
4 to 6 large lettuce leaves
Homemade Lemon Mayonnaise
(recipe follows)

In a medium-size saucepan, combine the tomatoes, celery, and salt. Simmer until flavors are blended, about 10 minutes. Meanwhile, sprinkle the gelatin over the cold water; let soften about 5 minutes, then stir.

Once the tomato mixture has finished cooking, remove from heat. Add the gelatin and lemon juice, stirring until gelatin dissolves. Strain; discard coarse tomato pulp and celery left in strainer. Add the chives to the strained liquid. Pour into 4 to 6 small molds. Chill until firm. Just before serving, unmold each salad onto a lettuce leaf and top with a dollop of homemade lemon mayonnaise.   *Makes 4 to 6 servings.*

Homemade Lemon Mayonnaise
 1 egg yolk
 ⅛ teaspoon salt
 ⅛ teaspoon ground white pepper
   (black may be substituted)

⅛ teaspoon paprika
⅛ teaspoon dry mustard
1½ tablespoons strained lemon juice
1 cup salad oil

In a small straight-sided bowl, combine the egg yolk, salt, pepper, paprika, and mustard; beat together. Add the lemon juice and beat again. Very gradually add the oil, beginning with one drop at a time (and never adding more than about 1 teaspoon at a time), beating hard between additions. When the last of the oil has been added, the mixture should be thick and creamy. Chill slightly before serving. (*Note:* Occasionally homemade mayonnaise will curdle, losing its thick smooth texture. To restore the creamy texture, add a scant *tablespoon* of oil to an additional egg yolk, then little by little add *half* the mixture to the curdled mayonnaise; discard the remaining half egg yolk.)   *Makes about 1½ cups.*

EFFIE'S SCONES

Delicious served piping hot, buttered lavishly and spread with strawberry or raspberry jam, Effie's scones were always a welcome childhood treat. Now I make them for my children and grandchildren in my own kitchen. Grandpa Miller liked to eat these scones plain or with just a smidgen of butter tucked inside, that way they reminded him of his long-passed friend Angus Crawford who had loved scones with a passion.

2⅓ cups all-purpose flour
2½ teaspoons baking powder
  1 tablespoon sugar, plus about 2
    tablespoons more for sprinkling
    over scones just before baking

½ teaspoon salt
6 tablespoons chilled butter or
  margarine
2 eggs
3 tablespoons milk or light cream

Note: Prepare scones shortly before dinner is ready so they can be served piping hot. Notice that the baking time is short, only 10 to 15 minutes.

Preheat oven to 450°F. In a large bowl, sift together the flour, baking powder, the 1 tablespoon sugar, and the salt. Cut the butter into the dry ingredients with a pastry cutter or 2 dinner knives, or rub it in gently with your fingertips, until a coarse mealy texture is obtained.

Separate 1 of the eggs and place the yolk in a small bowl; reserve about 1 *tablespoon* of the white. Add the other *whole* egg to the egg yolk and beat until frothy. Add the egg yolk mixture and milk to the flour mixture, mixing well. Turn dough onto a lightly floured surface and roll ½ inch thick. Cut dough into 3-inch squares, then cut each square into 2 triangles. Arrange the triangles on a greased baking sheet. Beat the reserved egg white until frothy and brush tops of triangles with it. Sprinkle with the 2 tablespoons sugar. Bake until light golden brown, about 10 to 15 minutes. Serve immediately.   *Makes about 10 scones.*

EFFIE'S CHOCOLATE YULE LOG
FILLED WITH SWEETENED WHIPPED CREAM

At Christmastime in 1927, Effie saw a recipe for a chocolate yule log with a French name she couldn't pronounce and thought it was "pretty fancy Christmas fare." But since she didn't cut it out of the newspaper and couldn't quite remember how the recipe went, she made this chocolate roll and always swore that it was every bit as good as that one would have been.

4 eggs, separated and at room
  temperature

½ cup sugar
¼ cup cold water

1 cup all-purpose flour
¼ cup unsweetened cocoa powder
1 teaspoon baking powder
½ teaspoon salt

Sweetened Whipped Cream (recipe follows)
Sifted powdered sugar

Preheat oven to 400°F. Grease a 15x10x2-inch baking sheet (or a jelly roll pan) and line it with waxed paper, then grease the paper; set aside.

With a whisk or rotary beater, whip the egg whites into soft mounds. Gradually add the sugar, beating just until stiff peaks form; do not overbeat. Lightly beat together the egg yolks and water, then gently fold into the egg whites, being careful not to reduce the volume of the whites. Into a medium-size bowl, sift together the flour, cocoa, baking powder, and salt, then gently fold into the egg white mixture. Pour the batter into the pan, spreading it out evenly. Bake until done and barely browned (the cake will spring back when lightly pressed), 15 to 20 minutes. Remove from oven and immediately cut off 1 inch from all four sides. Turn out onto a damp cloth that's been wrung dry. Peel off the paper.

Next, prepare the Sweetened Whipped Cream; spread over the warm cake and roll the cake lengthwise into a log, using the cloth to lift and help turn the cake.

When the log has been made, wrap the dish towel around it to hold it together until it cools. Once completely cool, carefully unwrap. Let the surface dry out a little (if it is a bit sticky) then sprinkle the top with powdered sugar, or for a lacy delicate coating, lay a paper lace doily over the top and sift powdered sugar over it. Serve in thin slices.

Makes about 10 to 12 servings.

Sweetened Whipped Cream
1 cup heavy cream
½ teaspoon vanilla extract
2 to 4 tablespoons powdered sugar

With a rotary beater or whisk, beat the cream until thick and foamy. Add the vanilla, then powdered sugar to taste, beating until stiff enough to spread. (*Note:* There is a fine line between stiff enough to spread like frosting and whipped cream that's overbeaten and tastes like butterfat. Don't overwhip or the cream will turn into butter.) *Makes about 2 cups.*

OLD-FASHIONED MINCEMEAT CAKE WITH FUDGE FROSTING

Aunt Clary who loved this cake thought it could pass for a "fancy" fruitcake. In the fall she made Eva Mae's Favorite Mincemeat for her winter baking and for use in this cake.

1 cup, packed, light brown sugar
½ cup butter or margarine
1 cup Eva Mae's Favorite
    Mincemeat (page 29)
½ cup buttermilk
1 teaspoon baking soda

2 egg yolks, well beaten
1 teaspoon vanilla extract
2 cups all-purpose flour
1 teaspoon ground cinnamon
1 teaspoon ground allspice
Fudge Frosting (recipe follows)

Preheat oven to 350°F. Grease and flour a 13x9x2-inch baking pan; set aside. In a large bowl, cream together the sugar and butter; stir in the mincemeat. In a medium-size bowl, blend together the buttermilk, baking soda, egg yolks, and vanilla. In a separate medium-size bowl, sift together the flour, cinnamon, and allspice. Add the buttermilk mixture to the sugar-butter mixture, then add the flour-spice mixture, beating lightly until well blended and smooth. Pour batter into the prepared pan and bake until a toothpick inserted into the center comes out clean, 45 to 50 minutes. Remove from oven and set aside to cool in the pan. Once the cake is thoroughly cooled, make the frosting and ice the cake while the frosting is still warm. Serve with freshly made coffee.

Makes 1 large sheet cake or about 18 generous
2x3-inch servings (or more smaller ones).

Fudge Frosting

½ cup granulated sugar
2 tablespoons unsweetened cocoa
    powder
2 tablespoons butter or margarine
¼ cup milk

1 tablespoon light corn syrup
⅛ teaspoon salt
½ teaspoon vanilla extract
About ¾ cup powdered sugar

In a medium saucepan, combine the granulated sugar and cocoa, blending well. Add the butter, milk, corn syrup, and salt. Bring to a boil, stirring frequently, then boil vigorously for 3 minutes, stirring only occasionally. Remove from heat and let cool to lukewarm. Beat in the vanilla and enough powdered sugar to make the frosting thick and creamy. *Makes enough to ice 1 large sheet cake.*

🌿 Of Elves and Sugarplums

Aunt Mable taught us that the legend of our Santa Claus had grown out of the life of a real man, Saint Nicholas, who had lived a long time ago. This young, kind, and generous bishop was highly respected for the wondrous works he did converting unbelievers to Christianity. He also became well loved by the people.

As time passed, almost a thousand years after his death, he became the patron saint of children and of travelers. And through the centuries his feast day—celebrated by European people on the sixth of December—slowly became attached to the Christmas holidays; he became the giver of gifts to all good children.

When the Dutch came to the New World and settled in New Amsterdam (New York City), they continued to celebrate Saint Nicholas's feast day. English settlers nearby were so taken by the lovely celebrations and the emphasis on children that they, too, soon celebrated the festivities of the Dutch. English children, however, could not pronounce the Dutch name for Saint Nicholas correctly. When filled with holiday excitement they ran the name together and cried out "Santa Claus, Santa Claus, Santa Claus!"

Then, when our grandmother was a little girl, Clement Clarke Moore wrote, as a loving surprise for his own children, a poem titled "A Visit From Saint Nicholas." From that moment on, our American Santa Claus—dressed in fur from head to foot, tarnished with ashes and soot, carrying a bundle of toys on his back—became our Jolly Old Elf.

> *His eyes, how they twinkled! his dimples how merry!*
> *His cheeks were like roses, his nose like a cherry;*
> *His droll little mouth was drawn up like a bow,*
> *And the beard on his chin was as white as the snow.*

And each year since, our emotions have been sparked by his "Merry Christmas to all, and to all a good night!" And we, knowing full well the difference between myth and reality, smile and tell our children glowing tales about a warm-heated gift-giver from the north pole who spends his life bringing joy to others. Like the famed Hoosier poet, James Whitcomb Riley, we still worship at the shrine of innocence:

JANE WATSON HOPPING

TO SANTA CLAUS

Most tangible of all the gods that be,
O Santa Claus—our own since Infancy!—
As first we scampered to thee—now, as then,
Take us as children to thy heart again.

Be wholly good to us, just as of old;
As a pleased father, let thine arms infold
Us, homed within the haven of thy love,
And all the cheer and wholesomeness thereof.

Thou lone reality, when O so long
Life's unrealities have wrought us wrong:
Ambition hath allured us,—fame likewise,
And all that promised honor in men's eyes.

Throughout the world's evasions, wiles, and shifts,
Thou only bidest stable as thy gifts:—

A grateful king re-ruleth from thy lap,
Crowned with a little tinseled soldier-cap:

A mighty general—a nation's pride—
Thou givest again a rocking-horse to ride,
And wildly glad he groweth as the grim
Old jurist with the drum thou givest him:

The sculptor's chisel, at thy mirth's command,
Is as a whistle in his boyish hand;
The painter's model fadeth utterly,
And there thou standest,—and he painteth thee:—

Most like a winter pippin, sound and fine
And tingling-red that ripe old face of thine,
Set in thy frosty beard of cheek and chin
As midst the snows the thaws of spring set in.

Ho! Santa Claus—our own since Infancy—
Most tangible of all the gods that be!—
As first we scampered to thee—now, as then,
Take us as children to thy heart again.

—James Whitcomb Riley

OLD-FASHIONED SUGARPLUMS

When we were children Aunt Mable used to recite poetry for us. At Christmas I would beg her over and over again to "tell me about the Sugarplum Tree." And she, always a teacher, would say, "Remember, this is a poem by Eugene Field." The part I loved best was:

Have you ever heard of a Sugarplum Tree?
'Tis a marvel of great renoun!
It blooms on the shore of the Lollipop Sea
In the garden of Shut-Eye Town.

½ pound glacéed (candied) or dried
   black figs (see Note)
½ pound glacéed (candied) or dried
   apricots (see Note)
½ pound whole almonds

Note: Glacéed or candied fruit is readily found in specialty food shops at Christmas. To make sugarplums you may also stuff dates, prunes, or peaches. Original sugarplums were candied stuffed figs and green plums.
   With a sharp knife, cut a slit in the side of the figs and apricots to

form a pocket and insert an almond into each pocket; work the fruit until the nut is well embedded, then with your fingertips squeeze the pocket closed. Wrap in plain or colored aluminum foil, tie a ribbon around the tiny package, and hang as an ornament on the Christmas tree (place at a distance from the lights so the lights don't dry out the fruit). Or, arrange the unwrapped fruit on a glass plate and cover with plastic wrap, then decorate with ribbons and give as a gift.

Makes 1½ pounds sugarplums.

AUNT CLARY'S APPLE TEA

Aunt Clary thought this was a wintertime comfort tea and loved to make it in December about Christmastime and well into cold January. (I've always wondered if it was not an ancient scurvey-prevention tea.)

4 to 6 Baldwin, Rome Beauty, or
    Winesap apples
⅓ to ½ cup sugar

*Finely grated zest from 1 lemon (a
    good teaspoonful; be sure not to get
    the bitter white pith into the zest)*
6 to 8 cups boiling water
Lemon juice, to taste

Wash and core the apples, leaving the skin on. Cut into slices and arrange in a large casserole dish; add the sugar and lemon zest and pour boiling water over all. Cover and let steep 15 minutes. Strain the mixture and serve the liquid hot or cold, adding lemon juice to taste. (Note: The strained solids may be made into a fine applesauce for serving with meat by putting them through a colander; sweeten to taste and season with ground cinnamon, ginger, and nutmeg.) *Makes 6 to 8 servings.*

SHEILA'S CHERRY BLISS

When served on a pale green glass plate, this candy catches everyone's eye.

2 cups sugar
½ cup heavy cream
½ cup butter
½ teaspoon pink food coloring or ¼
    teaspoon red food coloring

½ cup candied cherries, chopped
1 teaspoon rose extract

Combine the sugar, cream, and butter in a medium-sized, lightly greased heavy kettle. Cook over medium heat until mixture reaches the hard-ball stage (250°F to 268°F on a candy thermometer). (Note: To test doneness, drop ¼ teaspoon hot syrup into a cup of ice water. If the syrup separates into hard threads when it hits the water, but can thereafter be shaped into a hard ball with the fingers, it's done.) Remove from heat and cool to about 120°F. Add the food coloring and beat until the candy just begins to grain and become thick. Add the cherries and rose extract. Pour into a buttered 8x8x1½-inch pan. Let cool at room temperature until firm, then cut into 1-inch pieces. Use fresh; don't store.

Makes about 1 pound of candy.

COLLEEN JANE'S PECAN DATE SEAFOAM CANDY

Even an amateur candymaker can have terrific success with this easy-to-make, light-textured candy. At our house we serve it as soon as it has cooled, or shortly thereafter. And we add it to plates and boxes of candies that we give to neighbors and friends.

3 cups sugar	Pinch of salt
½ cup light corn syrup	1 cup coarsely chopped dates
2 to 3 tablespoons water	1 cup coarsely chopped pecans
2 egg whites, at room temperature	

In a large saucepan, combine the sugar, corn syrup, and water. Cook over medium-high heat until the mixture reaches a soft-ball stage (234°F to 240°F on a candy thermometer). Meanwhile, beat the egg whites until stiff peaks form; add the salt and whip a few seconds more. When the syrup is at the soft-ball stage, pour it over the egg whites in a thin stream beating continuously until the candy holds its shape when dropped from a spoon. Fold in the dates and pecans. Pour into a buttered 9x9-inch pan. When it begins to harden, cut into squares.

Makes about 2 pounds.

Gillett, Wisconsin
Dec. 4, 1908

Dear Santa Claus,

I want to tell you about a family who live in the woods a long way from the main road. The woods are so thick that I am afraid you would miss the little log house unless you were shown how to go there.

The family came over from Russia not long ago, and there are three children. The little girl never had a doll in her life. One of the boys, Alexis, likes birds, and last summer he caught a wild one and made a cage for it and tamed it. The other boy, Feodor, likes plants, and sticks every flower he gets into the ground to see whether it will grow. Some of them do, too. Their chimney is only a stovepipe, but I think you could slip in at the door, because it has no lock. Please leave a doll for the little girl, a parrot in a cage for Alexis, and some packages of all kinds of flower seeds for Feodor.

You needn't bother to bring anything to me.

Your friend,
John Franklin.

CHRISTMAS COMPANY'S COMING

When my husband Raymond was young, the back door at his house was never locked. Neighbors and friends came onto the porch, tapped once or twice, called out "Anybody home?" and walked in to share steaming cups of black coffee and a little gossip. The traffic increased to a steady flow during the Christmas season. Soon all over the house tables were weighted down with cookies, nuts, and candies, and streams of Christmas cards festooned the archways and windows. By mid-December a large Christmas tree flocked with homemade snow awaited the gift-giver himself.

AN OLD-FASHIONED WELCOME

There's nothing cheers a fellow up just like a
  hearty greeting,
A handclasp and an honest smile that flash the
  joy of meeting;
And when at friendly doors you ring, somehow
  it seems to free you
From all life's doubts to hear them say: "Come
  in! We're glad to see you!"

At first the portal slips ajar in answer to your
  ringing.
And then your eyes meet friendly eyes, and wide
  the door goes flinging;
And something seems to stir the soul, however
  troubled you be,
If but the cheery host exclaims: "Come in!
  We're glad to see you!"

—Edgar A. Guest

OLIVE'S CHRISTMAS SNOW

Each year during the late forties and early fifties my mother-in-law flocked her Christmas tree with homemade snow, which lay quite naturally along the tops of the boughs. Dusted with a clear confettilike glitter, it sparkled in the softly lighted room, reflecting the green, red, blue, and gold of the lights on the tree.

½ cup lukewarm water
½ cup plus about 2 slightly rounded
  tablespoons gentle soap flakes
  (Ivory Snow preferred)
Plain silver glitter, optional

CAUTION: Make certain that children in the home realize the snow is made of soap and should not be handled or played with.

In a medium-size mixing bowl combine water and soap flakes or granules. (Note: Only gentle flakes or granules will whip up to a meringuelike consistency.) Stir to dissolve, then whip by hand or with an electric beater until homemade snow looks like stiff meringue and holds its shape when spread along the branches of an evergreen tree. Dust with glitter if you wish. The moist snow will dry out overnight and cling tightly to the branches.   *Makes about 3 cups.*

MOLASSES OATMEAL BREAD WITH EASY-TO-MAKE LEMON BUTTER GLAZE

Old-time women made this bread right along with breakfast. Before they served everyone at the table their oatmeal they dipped enough out of the pot for their breadmaking. Made with molasses and generously spiced, then coated with a lemon butter glaze, this bread was a welcome treat by mid-morning.

1 cup very hot water
2 tablespoons molasses
½ cup, packed, light or dark brown
   sugar
3 tablespoons dry or granulated
   yeast
2 eggs, well beaten
½ cup or more raisins
⅓ cup vegetable oil (olive oil
   preferred) or pork lard
¼ cup Homemade Candied Orange
   Peel (recipe follows)

2 teaspoons salt
1 teaspoon ground cinnamon
½ teaspoon ground nutmeg
2 cups cooked Breakfast Oats
   (recipe follows)
About 4 cups flour, plus flour for
   rolling and kneading dough
4 tablespoons or more butter, plus 1
   tablespoon for softening bread
   crust
Easy-to-Make Lemon Butter Glaze
   (recipe follows)

In a large bowl, combine the very hot water with the molasses and ¼ *cup* of the sugar; stir to dissolve sweeteners. When the mixture is lukewarm (105°F to 115°F), stir in the yeast; let sit until frothy, about 10 minutes. Then add the eggs, raisins, oil, orange peel, salt, cinnamon, and nutmeg; stirring to blend. Add the breakfast oats, stirring until thoroughly blended. Next, add *3 cups* of the flour, stirring to make a very soft dough. Add enough of the *remaining 1 cup* flour to make a soft pliable dough that will readily turn out onto a floured surface. Using additional flour as necessary, knead into a soft dough that will not stick to your hands. Pat dough into a 2-inch thick rectangle, then spread with 4 tablespoons or more butter and sprinkle on the *remaining ¼ cup* sugar. Roll up the dough over the butter and sugar (like a jelly roll), and place in a greased and floured 10-inch tube pan. Let rise until doubled in size, abut 1 hour.

   Meanwhile, preheat oven to 400°F. When dough has doubled in bulk, bake at 400° for 15 minutes; then reduce oven setting to 350° and continue baking until top and bottom of bread is nicely browned, about

1 hour longer. Turn out onto a large plate, then place right side up. Rub the top with the 1 tablespoon butter to soften the crust; let bread cool to lukewarm, then make the glaze and spread a very thin coating of it over the loaf.   *Makes 1 loaf.*

Breakfast Oats

1 quart water
1/4 cup, packed, light brown sugar
1 tablespoon butter or olive oil
1 teaspoon salt
1 1/2 cups rolled oats (quick-cooking preferred)

1/2 cup bran
1 teaspoon ground cinnamon
1/2 teaspoon freshly grated nutmeg
1/4 teaspoon ground ginger
About 1/2 cup dark or golden raisins
Milk or cream, for serving over oats

Bring the water to a boil in a medium-size saucepan; add the sugar, butter, and salt. When boiling rapidly, add the oats; reduce heat and simmer for 3 minutes, stirring only if oats seem to be sticking (occasionally draw a spoon through them without stirring). Remove from heat. Stir in the bran, then the cinnamon, nutmeg, and ginger, then fold in the raisins. Serve immediately or, if making for the Molasses Oatmeal Bread, set aside *2 cups* for the bread and eat the rest with milk or cream over it.   *Makes about 8 cups.*

Easy-to-Make Lemon Butter Glaze

3/4 cup powdered sugar
1 tablespoon butter

1/2 teaspoon lemon juice
About 1 to 2 teaspoons water

In a small bowl, combine the sugar, butter, and lemon juice. Stir in just enough water, 1 teaspoon at a time, to make a light and creamy glaze. Spread evenly over warm bread.   *Makes enough to glaze 1 loaf of bread.*

Homemade Candied Orange Peel

Peel from 2 or 3 oranges
3 tablespoons lemon juice
Boiling water

1 cup sugar
1 cup warm water

Cut orange peel into strips with scissors. Boil until tender with lemon juice and enough hot water to cover. In another saucepan, boil sugar and water until syrup drops slowly from a spoon and spins a thread (268°F). Add the cooked, drained orange peel to the syrup and boil 2 to 3 minutes; then stir until the sugar granulates and clings to the peel. Turn into a sieve, shake off loose sugar, and store candied peel in an airtight container.   *Makes about 1 1/2 cups.*

IRISH POTATO CAKE
WITH CHOCOLATE GLAZE

Mace, a spice that is made from the dried outer covering of the nutmeg and usually ground, is not used nearly often enough in cakes. It has a distinctive flavor and there is nothing quite like it for this cake.

Enough Irish potatoes to yield 1 cup
  mashed (must be hot)
1 cup grated sweet chocolate (about
  4 ounces)
1 cup butter or margarine
1 cup sugar
4 eggs, separated and at room
  temperature
½ cup milk
2 cups all-purpose flour
1 teaspoon baking powder

½ teaspoon salt
½ teaspoon ground cinnamon
¼ teaspoon ground mace
¼ teaspoon freshly grated nutmeg
¼ teaspoon ground cloves
1 cup chopped walnuts
1 cup raisins
Chocolate Glaze (recipe follows),
  sifted powdered sugar, or Sweetened
  Whipped Cream (page 60)

Peel, cook, and mash the potatoes; measure out 1 cup. While still hot, add the chocolate, beating just until well blended. Set aside in a warm place.

Preheat oven to 350°F. Grease and flour a 13x9x2-inch baking pan or a large deep 10-inch round loaf pan. In a large bowl, cream together the butter and sugar. Add the egg yolks and beat until fluffy. Stir in the milk, then beat hot potatoes with chocolate. Add potato-chocolate mixture. Next, sift together the flour with the baking powder, salt, cinnamon, mace, nutmeg, and cloves; stir into the butter mixture. Beat the egg whites until stiff peaks form, then lightly fold them in (gently so as not to reduce volume). Fold in the walnuts and raisins. Turn the batter into the prepared baking pan and bake until a toothpick inserted in the center comes out clean, about 45 to 50 minutes. Remove from oven and

cool in the pan. Once cake is thoroughly cool, glaze lightly with Chocolate Glaze or, if you prefer, dust with powdered sugar or serve with dollops of Sweetened Whipped Cream.

Makes 1 cake or about 12 servings.

Chocolate Glaze
2 ounces unsweetened chocolate
3 tablespoons butter or margarine
1 cup powdered sugar

½ teaspoon vanilla extract
2 tablespoons hot water

In a medium-size saucepan, melt the chocolate and butter over low heat. Remove from heat and stir in the powdered sugar and vanilla. Stir in just enough hot water, about 1 teaspoon at a time, to make glaze smooth, shiny, and of an easy spreading consistency.

Makes enough to glaze 1 sheet cake or loaf cake.

🌿 LABORS OF LOVE

When I was a child, and even long before that, country men and women alike were very creative about making the things they needed. Money might be in short supply, but not skills. Like my dear, talented friend Emma—who would not have considered herself artistic—folks in those days saw raw materials for projects everywhere about them, from which they made not only "needed things" but gifts for birthdays and especially for Christmas.

Women made quilts and children's clothes, aprons, and blouses out of colored cotton, flour, and feed sacks; patterns were passed from hand to hand for making an apron out of a man's dress shirt, taking advantage of the back which was never worn as much as the rest of the shirt. Nimble fingers kept crochet hooks and knitting needles flying, chairs were graced with handmade doilies, and simple dresses were made lovely by bits of tatted lace.

Men made furniture, bowls, stirring spoons, and buttons for the women, and little dish cupboards, wagons and wooden pins for the girls. Hunting men worked in bone and hides, making bone buttons, rugs, leather hinges. Such folks were known for the skill of their hands.

<img_1 /> SHEILA'S FANCY APRON FOR CHRISTMAS DAY

Old-time women wore aprons for every occasion: those made out of the backs of men's dress shirts for everyday cooking and cover-up aprons made out of worn and faded dresses for dirty work; neat starched white aprons or fancy little ones of checked gingham worked in all sorts of cross-stitch embroidery designs for company cooking; and special-occasion aprons like this hand-crocheted Christmas apron.

MATERIALS

500 yards size 50 crochet thread, white, ecru, or colored
Size 11 crochet hook
1½ yards of ¼-inch ribbon
Note: Stitches should be tight to give body to the apron (loose stitches make the work baggy).

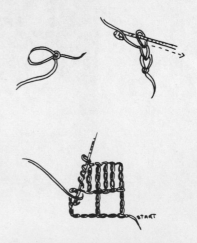

Crochet a foundation chain of 217 *chain stitches*. Treble crochet in 5th stitch from the hook. Then treble crochet in the next 2 foundation chain stitches, making a *filet square*. Chain 2 stitches, then skip 2 foundation chain stitches, and treble crochet in the next foundation stitch to make an *open mesh square*. Repeat until there are 71 alternating filet and open mesh squares, ending with filet square.

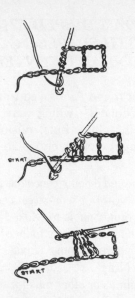

Once the foundation has been established, use the visual guide to complete the pattern. *Left and right filet squares* (triangles) will be needed for the deer's hooves, tips of horns, and tail, and for snow banks and various other parts of the design.

When the apron panel is finished, edge with either Snow Flower Lace (page 18) or Woodland Ferns (page 19), hand stitching the lace on all 4 sides of the panel. Then weave the ribbon through the open mesh squares at the top of the panel, thus making the ties for the apron.

ADA'S DIPPED CHOCOLATES
WITH SIMPLE-TO-MAKE
FONDANT CENTERS

Our friend Ada loved to make fancy Christmas candy, especially dipped chocolates—which were delicious! The centers might be nougats, caramels, jellies, nuts, raisins, or fondants, depending on her mood. She bought dipping chocolate from the local candy store.

1 pound dipping chocolate (see
Note) or semi-sweet chocolate
1 pound Simple-to-Make Fondant
Centers (recipe follows) or 2
pounds of other candies (see
Note)
Walnuts or other nuts for tops of
candy, optional

Note: Commercial dipping chocolate is sold in large hard bars; pieces are broken off, then weighed out for selling. When using dipping chocolate, allow one pound for dipping three pounds of fondant; two pounds for other types of candy. Nuts and raisins may be rolled around in whatever chocolate remains in the pan after the dipping and dropped onto a waxed paper off the tip of a spoon.

If using the fondant centers, prepare them a day ahead. For dipping they should be firm, but not chilled, neither should they be warm enough to be soft.

Plan to dip the candy in a cool room (under 60°F) that is dry and draft free. Drafts, steam (such as from food cooking on top of the stove), and humidity will affect the color and gloss of dipping chocolate; other coatings and melted semisweet chocolate bars are not so temperamental. Professional candy dippers temper dipping chocolate by heating it to 130°F and stirring it at temperatures of more than 100° so the cocoa butter will not separate out. Tempered chocolate is easier to work with.

When candies of different types are to be dipped in the same coating, begin with the lightest and most delicate centers while the coating is fresh and in prime condition, then work toward the coarser materials, ending with nuts or raisins. Work as quickly as possible.

To dip the candy, scrub with soap and water and dry thoroughly a window screen and place it on a table with a part of the screen projecting over the edge. Cover that part with waxed paper. Heat the dipping chocolate to about 95°F. Spear a piece of candy on the sharp end of a darning needle. Dip it in the melted chocolate, then quickly run the head of the needle through the waxed paper and the screen so the chocolate is deposited on the paper without being touched by your hands. If desired, immediately arrange a nut on top of the candy.

Makes about 2 pounds of candy.

Simple-to-Make Fondant Centers
1 egg white
1½ teaspoons water
2½ cups powdered sugar, sifted,
    plus ¼ cup for kneading

For plain fondant, beat the egg white and water in a medium-size bowl until well blended. Add enough powdered sugar to make fondant that is firm and not sticky. Turn mixture out on a flat surface lightly dusted with powdered sugar and knead until smooth.

To make the plain fondant mixture into Vanilla Fondant, knead in *1 tablespoon softened butter* and *1 teaspoon vanilla extract.* For Chocolate Fondant, knead 2 squares of melted unsweetened chocolate into *1 cup* of plain fondant, and flavor with ½ *teaspoon vanilla.* Other flavors like orange or strawberry may be made by adding *1 tablespoon softened butter,* orange or strawberry extract (or whatever flavoring you like), and a drop or two of food coloring.

An unusual (and good!) fondant is made by adding *1 tablespoon softened butter, 1 teaspoon brandy or rum extract* and ¼ *to ½ cup very finely chopped nutmeats.*

Immediately put plain or flavored fondant wrapped in waxed paper in a covered container to age overnight at room temperature.

Makes 1 pound of fondant.

🌿 LOVE OFFERINGS

For this Christmas book our dear friends Helen and Esther Boardman—made beautiful by long and gentle lives of service to humanity and the teaching of a philosophy of peace and love—have shared with us this poem from Myra Brooks Welch's book of poems which bears the same name as the poem, "The Touch of the Master's Hand," and a few memories from their dedicated lives:

'Twas battered and scarred, and the auctioneer
Thought it scarcely worth his while
To waste much time on the old violin,
But he held it up with a smile.

"What am I bid, good folks," he cried,
"Who'll start the bidding for me?"
"A dollar, a dollar"; then, "Two! Only two?
Two dollars, and who'll make it three?

Three dollars, once; three dollars, twice;
Going for three—" but no,
From the room, far back, a gray-haired man
Came forward and picked up the bow;

Then, wiping the dust from the old violin,
And tightening the loose strings,
He played a melody pure and sweet
As a caroling angel sings.

The music ceased, and the auctioneer,
With a voice that was quiet and low,
Said: "What am I bid for the old violin?"
And he held it up with the bow.

"A thousand dollars, and who'll make it two?
Two thousand! And who'll make it three?
Three thousand, once, three thousand, twice,
And going, and gone," said he.

The people cheered, but some of them cried,
"We do not quite understand
What changed its worth." Swift came the reply:
"The touch of a master's hand."

And many a man with life out of tune,
And battered and scarred with sin,
Is auctioned cheap to the thoughtless crowd,
Much like the old violin.

A "mess of pottage," a glass of wine;
A game—and he travels on.
He is "going" once, and "going" twice,
He's "going" and almost "gone."

But the Master comes, and the foolish crowd
Never can quite understand
The worth of a soul and the change that's wrought
By the touch of the Master's hand.

HELEN AND ESTHER'S GUMDROP COOKIES

The Boardman sisters often talk of home and family. In winter as the holiday season approached, they loved to recall their childhood Christmases:

"At Christmas when we were children, our parents' large oak table would be stretched out with extra leaves in it until it filled our little kitchen. For us the holiday season was always filled with love, merriment, and company. Our mother was a good cook, so we had a delicious Christmas dinner: turkey and dressing, baked sweet potatoes and Irish potatoes too, orange cranberry relish, homemade bread, mince and pumpkin pies, old-fashioned plum pudding, candies, and many other dishes made with recipes" . . . such as this one from Helen and Esther, saved just for that season of the year.

2 cups gumdrops
1 cup butter, softened
2 cups, packed, light brown sugar
2 eggs, well beaten

½ cup blinky (sour) milk or
    buttermilk
3½ cups all-purpose flour
1 teaspoon baking soda
1 teaspoon salt

Cut the gumdrops into small pieces; set aside. In a large bowl, blend the butter and sugar together. Add the eggs and beat a few strokes. Stir in the milk. Into a medium-size bowl, sift together the flour, baking powder, and salt and add to the buttermilk mixture. When thoroughly combined, fold in the gumdrops. Refrigerate for at least 1 hour before baking. Drop the chilled dough by rounded teaspoonfuls onto a lightly greased cookie sheet, about 2 inches apart. Bake in a preheated 400°F oven until lightly browned, 8 to 10 minutes. Remove from the oven and immediately lift off the cookie sheet and place on a wire rack to cool. Store in an airtight container. *Makes about 6 dozen cookies.*

ESTHER'S AFTER-DINNER PEPPERMINT WAFERS

These little wafers are lovely for Christmas teas or for taking to various family get-togethers.

2 cups sugar
½ cup milk
¼ cup light corn syrup
¼ teaspoon cream of tartar

8 to 12 drops oil of peppermint or
    peppermint extract
Green food coloring, optional

In a large heavy pan, combine the sugar, milk, corn syrup, and cream of tartar. Cook over low heat until sugar dissolves, stirring constantly; then increase heat to high and cook and stir slowly until mixture boils. Cover for about 3 minutes and continue boiling so sugar crystals on the sides of pan can wash down with the steam. Uncover and continue cooking without stirring until mixture reaches the soft-ball stage (234°F to 240°F). Remove from heat. Cool slightly, then beat until creamy. Add 8 to 12 drops of oil of peppermint or peppermint extract. Drop syrup by teaspoonfuls onto a piece of foil; or drop only half the syrup onto a piece of foil, tint the second half lightly with green food coloring, and drop it onto a second piece of foil. Leave enough room so that wafers do not touch each other. When mints are thoroughly cool, serve immediately or store on a plate covered with a napkin until ready to serve.

Makes about 1¼ pounds of candy.

OUR SISTER MARGARET'S PINEAPPLE AND COTTAGE CHEESE SALAD

Helen and Esther's sister Margaret, much younger than they and dearly loved, grew up to be a good cook like their mother. Through the years they recall having spent many happy times at her home, enjoying good meals and sharing with her the pleasures which her children and grandchildren have given them all.

6 *large lettuce leaves*
6 *slices canned unsweetened*
   pineapple

2 *cups cottage cheese*
Λ *small jar Maraschino cherries,*
   drained

Set out 6 salad plates and arrange a lettuce leaf on each. Place the pineapple on the lettuce and fill center of each with ⅓ *cup* of the cottage cheese; garnish with cherry. Margaret's colorful, quick and easy-to-make salad is excellent and festive for the holidays. *Makes 6 servings.*

CHILDREN BRING US LAUGHTER, AND CHILDREN BRING US TEARS

There is nothing more joyful than children playing in the snow, eyes sparkling, noses red, feeling out the season, reveling through the days before Christmas. And like an epidemic they infect everyone in sight with their boisterous spirits.

HIS CHRISTMAS SLED

I watch him with his Christmas sled;
   He hitches on behind
A passing sleigh, with glad hooray,
   And whistles down the wind;
He hears the horses champ their bits,
   And bells that jingle-jingle—
You Woolly Cap! you Scarlet Mitts!
   You miniature "Kriss Kringle"!

I almost catch your secret joy—
  Your chucklings of delight,
The while you whiz where glory is
  Eternally in sight!
With you I catch my breath, as swift
  Your jaunty sled goes gliding
O'er glassy track and shallow drift,
  As I behind were riding!

He winks at twinklings of the frost,
  And on his airy race,
Its tingles beat to redder heat
  The rapture of his face:—

The colder, keener is the air,
  The less he cares a feather.
But, there! he's gone! and I gaze on
  The wintriest of weather!

Ah, Boy! still speeding o'er the track
  Where none returns again,
To sigh for you, or cry for you,
  Or die for you were vain.—
And so, speed on! the while I pray
  All nipping frosts forsake you—
Ride still ahead of grief, but may
  All glad things overtake you!

—Edgar A. Guest

ON ANY ORDENARY MAN IN A HIGH STATE OF LAUGHTURE AND DELIGHT

Let the old man laugh and be
Blest therefor eternally!

As it's give' me to perceive,
I most certin'y believe
When a man's jest glad plum' through,
God's pleased with him, same as you.

—James Whitcomb Riley

JANE WATSON HOPPING

My father

🌿 LET THE OLD MEN LAUGH

Daddy's friend John Watts was an avid storyteller who loved the capriciousness of human nature. He'd say:

The world's too serious, ain't near as playful as it used to be. People don't "jaw" at folks or "pull their leg" like we used to do. Seems to me like not so long ago everybody laughed a whole lot easier—at life, each other, and thereselves—than they do now.

Folks in those days learned early about "joshin'." They knew that a little "funnin" was the grease that made the social wheels turn. Somehow, they was blessed with a natural sense of humor and even little children knew when folks was just teasin' 'em and when they was trying to say mean things to 'em while they laughed like it was some big joke.

My Pa, he loved to tease me about Christmas. He'd tell me if I didn't cut out my mischief makin', I'd be getting switches in my Christmas stocking. Mama, she'd laugh at that and start to singing: "You better watch out, you better not cry,/ You better not pout, I'm tellin' you why,/ Santa Claus is coming to town." Then she'd laugh til I got to laughin' at her laughin' at me.

Sometimes my Grandpa, he'd say, "Johnny, if you didn't find trouble, it would up and find you!" And I was a kid who couldn't climb a tree without tearin' my britches, or walk home from school without steppin' in the mud. If I took off my shoes to walk on home barefoot, I'd lose one of 'em for sure.

Sometimes, if I tried their patience too hard, Pa would have to have a "good talk" with me. Though, about halfway through the talk, Pa, he'd remember things he'd done when he was a boy and get to talkin' about that. And if Grandpa got rung on into it, he could really remember what Pa was like when he was young. I tell you, that really cooled things down a whole lot. First thing you know we was all laughin' at each other's stories.

TOASTED ANGELS

Uncle Bud brought this Christmas breakfast-dish recipe home with him from "the war to end all wars." As he used to say, a boy in France told him about it on a miserable night in 1917 as they huddled together talking about family and home.

For each serving, wrap one large oyster in a thin slice of bacon. Fasten the bacon tightly with a wooden toothpick. Sprinkle with paprika and add a drop of lemon juice. Broil until the bacon is crisp. Serve over hot buttered toast.

OLD MAN PARKER'S VEGETABLE GOOSE

Old Man Parker was a friendly, harmless, eccentric sort of man. He lived alone in a small shack on his two or three acres. In summer he raised beautiful flowers all over the property: hollyhocks, stock, roses, and sunflowers almost eight feet high. His garden overflowed with string beans, tomatoes, cantaloupes, berries, and sturdy life-giving foods like potatoes and squash. From his little orchard, he harvested luscious fruits like apricots, cherries, and figs.

Then at Christmas, he gave away home-dried apricots and figs, and fresh oranges, nuts, apples, and cabbages to the neighbors for Christmas presents. He called this dish Vegetable Goose because, like a goose, it's stuffed.

1 round fat baking squash, *about 2 quarts in size. (A small golden delicious or Hubbard squash will do nicely. For a larger squash double the stuffing recipe.)*
4 *green onions, chopped*
1½ *cups mashed potatoes, still hot*
1 *tablespoon melted butter, plus about 1 tablespoon more melted butter for brushing on and basting squash*
½ *teaspoon salt*
¼ *teaspoon black pepper*
¼ *teaspoon dried sweet marjoram leaves*
1 *egg, well beaten*

Parboil the squash in a large kettle of unsalted water until it begins to get tender. Drain and place in cold water; let cool. Peel, then cut a slice off the top to make a lid and remove the seeds.

Preheat oven to 375°F. In a medium-size bowl, combine the onions, potatoes, 1 tablespoon butter, salt, pepper, and marjoram. Add the egg and then mix lightly together until blended. Fill the squash and replace the top. Brush the outside of the squash with melted butter. You can also lightly salt and pepper the surface, if you wish.

If the squash will fit, place it in a greased round casserole dish. If not, put it in a greased 13x9x2-inch baking pan suitable for serving it in, since it is quite difficult to transfer to a serving dish once it is baked.

Bake just until lightly browned and cooked through, about 35 to 40 minutes, basting now and again with melted butter. (When done, the

squash should be tender but not so well done that the dish is sagging.) Serve piping hot with a well-seasoned salad and whole-wheat rolls, such as Effie's Honey Whole-Wheat Rolls Plus. (Old Man Parker drank icy goats' milk with this dish.)

UNCLE BUD'S OLD-FASHIONED VINEGAR PIE WITH LARD PASTRY CRUST

During the winter in the old days, farm women had plenty of lard or butter for making pie crusts, eggs and flour for thickening fillings, and vinegar for all sorts of purposes, everything from washing windows to making this old-fashioned vinegar pie, which has won adherents for hundreds of years.

Note: Old-time pies were thickened with flour, but cornstarch makes a clearer filling.

Lard Pastry Crust (recipe follows)
3 eggs, separated
1⅓ cups sugar
¼ cup cornstarch (see Note)
2 cups boiling water
¼ cup cider vinegar
1 tablespoon butter or margarine
1 teaspoon lemon extract
A drop or 2 yellow food coloring, optional
⅓ teaspoon salt, a pinch of which goes into the meringue

Preheat oven to 400°F. Bake the pie crust before preparing the filling; set the baked crust aside to cool.

Place the egg yolks in a small bowl and the whites in a medium-size bowl. Beat the yolks until thick; set aside for the filling. Set aside egg whites at room temperature for the meringue.

In a 2-quart saucepan, combine 1 cup of the sugar and ⅓ teaspoon salt minus a pinch with the cornstarch, blending well. Gradually add the boiling water, stirring constantly until filling is smooth and partially thickened. Stir in the egg yolks. Bring the filling to a boil over medium heat, stirring constantly; continue boiling and stirring for 1 minute. Remove from heat and add the vinegar, butter, and lemon extract. (Note: If you wish, you may add a drop or two of yellow food coloring at this point. Old-timers wouldn't do this; they expected to see a clear pale pie colored only by the egg yolk.) Set filling aside to cool.

Meanwhile, reheat oven to 400°F and prepare the meringue as follows: In a deep medium-size bowl with straight sides, beat the egg whites until soft mounds form. Gradually add the remaining ⅓ cup sugar and a pinch of salt; continue beating just until stiff peaks form.

Pour the cooled filling into the baked pie crust. Spread some of the meringue around the edge of the filling, making sure it touches the crust all around, then fill in the center; use the back of a spoon to swirl the meringue into high and low patterns. Bake until lightly browned, about 15 to 20 minutes. Let cool (do not refrigerate) before serving. Serve within 2 hours after baking, or after 2 hours chill until ready to serve.

Makes one 9-inch pie.

Lard Pastry Crust

1 cup all-purpose flour	⅓ cup lard
½ teaspoon salt	2 to 3 tablespoons cold water

In a medium-size bowl, combine the flour and salt, mixing well. Using a pastry cutter or 2 dinner knives, cut in the lard until the mixture is reduced to granules the size of peas. (*Note:* Do not rub the lard into the flour with your hands; it has a low melting point and, if warmed, will soak into the flour, making the crust less flaky.) Sprinkle 2 to 3 table-spoons cold water over the flour-lard mixture, 1 tablespoon at a time, stirring gently with a fork until dough is moistened and almost clings to the sides of the bowl; add 2 to 3 teaspoons additional water, if needed.

Turn dough onto a lightly floured surface and knead 1 or 2 times to form a ball. Wrap in aluminum foil or waxed paper and refrigerate until chilled, about 30 minutes. When chilled, remove from refrigerator and roll out on a floured surface to about ⅛ inch thick. Line a 9-inch pie pan with it, leaving about 1½ inches overhanging rim. Carefully tuck the overhang under between the pastry and pan; crimp edges with the tines of a fork, then prick dough all over the bottom and sides. Bake until crust is crisp, slightly puffed, and light golden brown, about 15 to 20 minutes. Remove from oven and let cool before filling.

Makes one 9-inch pie crust.

🌿 Soon You'll Be a Man, My Son

Not so long ago, on cold December evenings before Christmas, people brought out poems like Rudyard Kipling's "If," which were highly prized by men and women who wholeheartedly believed the lines he penned:

> *If you can keep your head when all about you*
> *Are losing theirs and blaming it on you;*
> *If you can trust yourself when all men doubt you,*
> *But make allowance for their doubting too:*

Our little lads—from a friend's family album

If you can wait and not be tired by waiting,
    Or, being lied about, don't deal in lies,
Or being hated don't give way to hating,
    And yet don't look too good, nor talk too wise;

If you can dream—and not make dreams your master;
    If you can think—and not make thoughts your aim,
If you can meet with Triumph and Disaster
    And treat those two impostors just the same:
If you can bear to hear the truth you've spoken
    Twisted by knaves to make a trap for fools,
Or watch the things you gave your life to, broken,
    And stoop and build 'em up with worn-out tools;

If you can make one heap of all your winnings
  And risk it on one turn of pitch-and-toss,
And lose, and start again at your beginnings,
  And never breathe a word about your loss:
If you can force your heart and nerve and sinew
  To serve your turn long after they are gone,
And so hold on when there is nothing in you
  Except the Will which says to them: "Hold on!"

If you can talk with crowds and keep your virtue,
  Or walk with Kings—nor lose the common touch,
If neither foes nor loving friends can hurt you,
  If all men count with you, but none too much:
If you can fill the unforgiving minute
  With sixty seconds' worth of distance run,
Yours is the Earth and everything that's in it,
  And—which is more—you'll be a Man, my son!

Along with such high-minded, impressive literary works went the gentle schooling of mothers and grandmothers who thought it was their duty to help a child—boy or girl—to develop character—meaning moral strength, self-discipline, and fortitude. Many a small boy or girl snuggled on a soft lap and was held gently but firmly in a mother's arms as she talked about not ever hitting children who were smaller, about doing unto others as you would have them do unto you. If a grandmother was nearby, and often she was, she might lay down her knitting and remind the child that no matter how young he was, he must take responsibility for his behavior. Should the father come in from doing chores or splitting wood, he might take his child outside with him, ostensibly to cut wood, but while they worked he might explain that the mother and grandmother were only trying to teach him how to be a man of worth.

MARYLAND FRIED CHICKEN
WITH CREAM GRAVY

Grandpa and Grandma Meekins were married in Maryland, their home state in the late 1800s, and were among those who settled near Columbus, Ohio, the land of milk and honey. At pre-Christmas dinners when all the children came home, she always served this favorite chicken dish.

1 (2½-to-3 pound) drawn fryer,
   cut into serving pieces
About ⅓ cup all-purpose flour for
   dusting meat
1½ teaspoons salt
¼ teaspoon black pepper
1 egg, beaten to a froth
¼ cup milk

1 cup fine dried breadcrumbs
   (whole-wheat preferred), sifted
½ cup pork lard or vegetable oil
Cream Gravy (recipe follows)
1 recipe Easy-to-Make Riced
   White Potatoes (page 93),
   optional

Preheat oven to 350°F. On a pie plate, blend together the flour, salt, and pepper; dredge the chicken pieces in this mixture and lay them out on a piece of waxed paper; reserve leftover flour for the gravy. Combine the egg and milk in a bowl and dip chicken in it, then roll in the bread-crumbs. Heat the lard in a large Dutch oven until hot. Brown the chicken pieces in the hot lard on both sides. Transfer to a platter. (*Note:* The chicken at this point should be browned but not cooked through.)

Return all chicken pieces to the Dutch oven. Cover and bake until tender, about 1 hour, turning once or twice; if the Dutch oven seems too dry during the baking process, add *1 to 2 tablespoons hot water.* Transfer chicken to a platter; set aside in a warm place while making the Cream Gravy with some of the pan drippings.   *Makes about 4 servings.*

Cream Gravy
Serve this gravy spooned over the chicken or serve Easy-To-Make Riced White Potatoes as a side dish topped with this gravy.

¼ cup pan drippings from cooking
   chicken
¼ cup flour, left over from
   dredging chicken
1 cup homemade chicken broth
   (see Note)

1½ cups light cream (or milk, if you
   wish)
Salt and black pepper
1 tablespoon minced fresh parsley,
   optional
1 tablespoon sherry, optional

Note: For homemade chicken broth, cook the neck, back, and wing tips covered with at least 2 cups of lightly salted water for about 30 minutes; strain.

Drain off all but ¼ cup of pan drippings from the Dutch oven. Add the flour and cook over low heat until flour is lightly browned, stirring until mixture is smooth and loosening browned bits from the bottom of the pan. Add the broth and cream. Cook until gravy thickens, stirring constantly. Season to taste with salt and pepper. Add the parsley and sherry if desired; if the gravy seems too thick, stir in a little boiling water.   *Makes about 4 servings.*

EASY-TO-MAKE
RICED WHITE POTATOES

Riced potatoes are very fluffy. They should never be stirred or packed
down. Mother, an old-time cook, always let them drop gently into the
serving bowl as they came out of the ricer. Serve these with cream gravy
spooned over them as a side dish with Maryland Fried Chicken (page
91).

4 medium-size white (Irish) potatoes, pared and cut in half	2 or more cups of boiling water
	Salt and black pepper

Put the potato halves in a large saucepan with 1 inch of boiling water;
cover and boil until potatoes are tender, about 30 to 35 minutes; don't
overcook or they will be watery and mushy. Drain water off, then place
saucepan, uncovered, over very low heat and cook, gently and constantly shaking the pan, until the potatoes dry a little and become mealy,
about 2 minutes. Remove from heat and sprinkle potatoes with salt and
pepper. While still hot, force the potatoes through a potato ricer into a
heated serving dish; do *not* stir or pack down. Serve immediately.

Makes 3 to 4 servings.

AUNT MABLE'S SPICED PEARS

Aunt Mable's pantry was a sight to behold. She was very precise about
everything she did, including her canning and preserving. Every quart
or pint of fruit, vegetables, pickles, or preserves was so perfectly packed
into the jars that everyone commented on it, and all would agree that
she could easily steal away all the prizes at the county fair—which she
often did.

1 quart undrained home-canned pears (or use store-bought pears packed in medium or light syrup, which will do nicely)	1 (3-inch) stick of cinnamon
	1 teaspoon lemon juice
	1 strip of lemon peel

In a 2-quart saucepan, combine the pears and their juice or syrup with
the cinnamon, lemon juice, and lemon peel. Simmer only long enough
to enhance the flavors and heat the fruit, about 5 minutes. Remove the
pears from the cooking liquid and serve them hot in small bowls alongside poultry, pork, or lamb. (*Note:* Combine the pear cooking liquid
with orange juice or apple cider to make a pleasant drink; if the drink is
too sweet, add 2 or more cups of cold tea.)

Makes 3 to 4 servings of spiced pears.

FARM COUNTRY MAPLE CREAM

In farm country where Ayrshire, Brown Swiss, Guernsey, Holstein, and Jersey cows poured forth frothy buckets of warm milk—night and morning—and where spring houses overflowed with butter, cheese, and skim and whole milk, cooks took every opportunity to add milk to a meal.

Easy-to-make desserts like the following were popular in winter because they could easily be chilled in pantries or store rooms.

1 envelope (1 tablespoon)
  unflavored gelatin
¼ cup cold water
2 eggs, separated and at room
  temperature
¼ cup plus 2 tablespoons, packed,
  light brown sugar

1 cup milk mixed with ½ cup heavy
  cream or 1½ cups milk
½ teaspoon vanilla extract
⅛ teaspoon salt
⅛ teaspoon maple flavoring

Sprinkle the gelatin over the cold water; set aside for about 5 minutes to soften.

In the top of a double boiler, beat the egg yolks lightly, then slowly stir in *2 tablespoons* of the sugar and the 1 cup milk-cream mixture (or 1½ cups milk). Cook over hot (not boiling) water, stirring constantly, until mixture thickens enough to coat a spoon. Add the gelatin, stirring until it dissolves. Refrigerate until set, then beat with a rotary beater or electric mixer until smooth; set aside. Whip the egg whites into soft peaks; slowly add to them the *remaining ¼ cup* sugar and the vanilla, salt, and maple flavoring and continue beating until stiff but not dry peaks form. Fold into the gelatin mixture. Refrigerate until well chilled before serving. *Makes about 4 servings.*

                         JANE WATSON HOPPING

SHEILA'S SOUTHERN
CORN MUFFINS

This family-sized or company-sized recipe for corn muffins delights everyone. They are crisp and flavorful and just right for serving with pork or chicken. Uncle Bud says, "Why eat potatoes when you can eat good old cornmeal muffins?"

2 eggs, lightly beaten
2 cups blinky (sour) milk or
   buttermilk
3 tablespoons butter or margarine,
   melted
1 teaspoon salt

About 2½ cups sifted water-ground
   cornmeal
1 tablespoon baking powder
1 teaspoon baking soda
1 teaspoon cold water

Preheat oven to 425°F. While preheating oven, heat the muffin tins until quite warm, then take them out and grease them generously. Set aside until needed.

Place the eggs in a large bowl; stir in the milk, butter, and salt. Slowly stir in 1 cup cornmeal or just enough to make a thin batter; beat well. Sift the baking powder over batter. Dissolve the soda in the cold water and add to the batter; stir until well blended. Add just enough more cornmeal to make a medium-thick batter (you will need to use 1 cup or more). Fill the muffin cups two-thirds full. Bake until golden brown and crusty, 15 to 20 minutes. Serve piping hot.

Makes about 1½ to 2 dozen muffins.

FOLKS AT LONESOMEVILLE

Pore-folks lives at Lonesomeville—
  Lawzy! but they're pore
Houses with no winders in,
  And hardly any door:
Chimbly all tore down, and no
  Smoke in that at all—
Ist a stovepipe through a hole
  In the kitchen wall!

Pump 'at's got no handle on;
  And no wood-shed—And, wooh!—
Mighty cold there, choppin' wood,
  Like pore-folks has to do!—
Winter-time, and snow and sleet
  Ist fairly fit to kill!—
Hope to goodness Santy Claus
  Goes to Lonesomeville!

—James Whitcomb Riley

HOPE TO GOODNESS *SANTY CLAUS* GOES TO LONESOMEVILLE

Because the poor have always been with us, old-fashioned schools had their annual candy sale well before Christmas to raise money for sweaters, coats, shoes, and books for children that had none. Women dusted off recipes, robbed their teapots and baking powder cans for money, and began to stir up sticky mixtures that would be transformed into candy, letting the children help whenever possible so that they could share in the spirit of giving.

When pounds of fudge, divinity, nougats, even homemade marshmallows, taffy, and the like were ready, the festive candy sale began. The tables were decorated with holly or wild red berries, various classes sang jolly carols like "Deck the Halls" and recited poetry like:

> Twas the night before Christmas, when all through
>   the house
> Not a creature was stirring, not even a mouse;
> The stockings were hung by the chimney with care,
> In hopes that Saint Nicholas soon would be there. . . .

Candy sold for a penny a piece or twenty-five cents a plateful. And when the joyous day was over and the money counted, folks went home with a rich feeling of warmth crowding around their hearts, knowing that because they cared, teachers during the holiday would filter through the community and gently persuade proud fathers, who ached because they couldn't seem to provide enough, to accept the coats or shoes or books for the sake of their children.

EFFIE'S STAINED-GLASS CHRISTMAS CANDIES

Cooked to "just the right temperature," Effie's clear, brightly-colored candies were beautiful to look at and delicious to suck on and crunch between the teeth. When she took them to the school candy sale the children were fascinated by the color, and people being what they are, it wasn't long until the hard, clear, colorful candy was named "Effie's Stained-Glass Christmas Candy."

2 cups sugar
½ cup light corn syrup
½ cup hot water
Food coloring of your choice, 2 to 3
  drops, more if you wish (see Note)

Flavoring agent of your choice (such
  as 2 to 3 drops of peppermint oil or
  cinnamon oil; see Note)

Note: Oil-based food coloring and oil-based flavoring oils were the secret ingredients in Effie's candy; use them if possible. The flavoring oils—peppermint oil, cinnamon oil and such—are often available at the drug store. Both food coloring and food flavoring oils are found in specialty food shops.

Lightly grease a large flat heatproof platter and also the inner walls of a large heavy saucepan. In the saucepan, combine the sugar, syrup, and water. Bring to a boil, stirring just until sugar dissolves and mixture begins to boil, then cook, without stirring, to the hard-crack stage (300°F to 310°F), watching the thermometer carefully so that the syrup doesn't get too hot. (*Note:* As the temperature of the syrup approaches 310°F, the syrup will begin to darken which would spoil the clear bright color you want. Once the thermometer reads about 300°, begin to test the candy as follows: Drop ¼ teaspoon of the hot syrup into a cup of ice water; if ready, the syrup should separate into hard threads which, when removed from the ice water, remain brittle and break easily.) Promptly stir in the food coloring and flavoring, then remove from heat and pour candy onto the platter.

When the candy is cool enough to be handled, quickly (the candy hardens rapidly) cut into 1-inch strips, beginning on the outside edges; use buttered kitchen shears or a pair of scissors for this. Then cut or break strips into 1-inch pieces.   *Makes about 1 pound of candy.*

EASY-TO-MAKE CHOCOLATE FUDGE WITH ROASTED PECANS AND CANDIED CHERRIES

In the old-days this favorite Christmas candy contained cream of tartar (an acid) to keep it from becoming grainy. With the more modern use of corn syrup in place of the cream of tartar, it could (and still can) be considered one of the "never fail" candies. However it was made, Uncle Ben loved it with nuts and candied cherries in it, the cherries being a fairly recent addition, one he had never even heard of in childhood.

Butter, for greasing cakepan and
  saucepan
2 cups sugar
2 ounces unsweetened chocolate,
  grated
½ cup light corn syrup

⅔ cup milk or light cream
⅛ teaspoon salt
2 tablespoons butter
1 tablespoon vanilla extract
½ cup roasted pecans
½ cup candied cherries, halved

Butter an 8x8x1½-inch baking pan; also butter the sides of a large heavy saucepan.

In the saucepan, combine the sugar, chocolate, syrup, milk, and salt. Bring to a boil, stirring just until sugar dissolves, then cook, without stirring, until mixture reaches soft-ball stage (234°F to 240°F); don't overcook. Remove from heat and add the butter but *don't* stir yet and *don't* jostle the pan. Let the fudge cool to about 120°, then add the vanilla and start beating vigorously without stopping until the candy becomes very thick and starts to lose its gloss. Quickly add the pecans and cherries, if using, and pour into the buttered baking pan. Score while warm and cut when firm.

Makes about 1 pound, or slightly more with pecans and cherries.

BROWN SUGAR CARAMELS

Mother sometimes made these for Christmas as well as Halloween and New Year's Eve. She said the recipe was perhaps the first candy recipe she remembers writing down (she learned in childhood to make divinity and fudge by just watching).

½ cup butter, plus butter for
    greasing baking pan
2 cups, packed, light brown sugar
¼ teaspoon salt

1 cup light corn syrup
1¾ cups light cream
1 tablespoon vanilla extract

Lightly butter an 8x8x1½-inch baking pan; set aside.

Melt the butter in a large saucepan. Add the sugar and salt; blend well. Add the syrup, stirring until smooth. Gradually add the cream, stirring constantly. Cook over medium heat until mixture reaches the firm-ball stage (242°F to 248°F). (To test doneness, drop ¼ teaspoon of the hot syrup into a cup of ice water; if ready, a firm ball will form that will hold its shape when taken out of the ice water and won't flatten unless pressed with your fingers.) Immediately remove the candy from heat and stir in the vanilla. Pour into the prepared baking pan (the candy should be about ½ to ¾ inch thick). Cool and cut into 1-inch squares. Wrap in aluminum foil or waxed paper and store in an airtight container until ready to serve. *Makes about 1 pound of candy.*

AUNT MAE'S SALTWATER TAFFY

Aunt Mae believed that the first saltwater taffy was made with water from the ocean. And even though Ada read to her an account of how the legendary candymaker only used saltwater once when he ran out of fresh water—which worked just fine—Aunt Mae preferred her own version of the story.

2 cups sugar
1½ cups water
1 cup light corn syrup
1½ teaspoons salt

2 tablespoons butter, plus about 1
tablespoon more for rubbing on
your hands
1 tablespoon vanilla extract

About ½ cup cornstarch, for cutting
  taffy out

Grease a large flat heatproof platter or a marble slab; also grease the sides of a large heavy saucepan.

In the saucepan, combine the sugar, water, syrup, and salt. Cook slowly over medium heat, stirring constantly until the sugar has dissolved; then continue cooking without stirring until mixture reaches the hard-ball stage (250°F to 268°F). (To test doneness, drop ¼ teaspoon of the hot syrup into a cup of ice water. If done, the syrup will separate into hard threads when it hits the water, but can thereafter be shaped into a hard ball with your fingers, one that will roll about on a chilled buttered salad plate.) Immediately remove from heat and add the 2 tablespoons butter and the vanilla. Pour the syrup out onto the greased platter or slab and let cool until it can be handled. Rub at least 1 tablespoon of butter on your hands, then shape the candy into a ball and begin to pull it, folding it back again on itself. Work at this until the taffy is light in color and has become hard to pull; this will take from 5 to 20 minutes. Next, pull the taffy into a rope; gently let it fall onto a surface liberally sprinkled with cornstarch. Cut into bite-size pieces. Let the taffy rest for a few hours, then wrap each piece in waxed paper or aluminum foil and store in an airtight container.

Makes about 1 pound of candy.

A happy Christmas.

'TWAS THE NIGHT BEFORE CHRISTMAS

When our children Randy and Colleen were small, they would get so excited about the coming of Christmas morning that we would tuck them into bed early. Then Dad would settle down on the floor beside them and tell about Christmas when he was a boy, about the time he knew that presents were hidden in his Mother's closet and was about to peek when he heard Santa's voice telling him to "Stay out of there!"

And then they loved the following story about Santa's visit to my house when I was about six or seven years old: On Christmas Eve my sister Sheila and I waited impatiently as the darkness settled in for our father to come home from work so that we could open our presents. Then much to our surprise we heard Santa arrive, bells jingling, his reindeer stamping their hooves, and Santa's soft footsteps sneaking their way across the porch that led to our parlor, then finally, strange rattling-package noises! Then there was a slamming of our door, jolly laughter—"Ho! Ho! Ho!" and a great booming cry, "Merry Christmas to All and to All a Good Night!"

JEST 'FORE CHRISTMAS

Father calls me William, sister calls me Will.
Mother calls me Willie, but the fellers call me Bill!
Mighty glad I ain't a girl—ruther be a boy,
Without them sashes, curls, an' things that's worn by
   Fauntleroy!
Love to chawnk green apples an' go swimmin' in the lake—
Hate to take the castor-ile they give for belly-ache!
'Most all the time, the whole year round, there ain't no
   flies on me,
But jest 'fore Christmas I'm as good as I kin be!

Got a yeller dog named Sport, sick him on the cat;
First thing she knows she doesn't know where she is at!
Got a clipper sled, an' when us kids goes out to slide,
'Long comes the grocery cart, an' we all hook a ride!
But sometimes when the grocery man is worrited an' cross,
He reaches at us with his whip, an' larrups up his hoss,
An' then I laff an' holler, "Oh, ye never teched me!"
But jest 'fore Christmas I'm as good as I kin be!

Gran'ma says she hopes that when I git to be a man,
I'll be a missionarer like her oldest brother, Dan,
As was et up by the cannibals that live in Ceylon's Isle,
Where every prospeck pleases, an' only man is vile!
But gran'ma she has never been to see a Wild West show,
Nor read the life of Daniel Boone, or else I guess she'd know
That Buff'lo Bill an' cowboys is good enough for me!
Excep' jest 'fore Christmas, when I'm as good as I kin be!

And then old Sport he hangs around, so solemn-like an' still,
His eyes they seem a-sayin': "What's the matter, little Bill?"
The old cat sneaks down off her perch an' wonders what's
    become
Of them two enemies of hern that used to make things hum!
But I am so perlite an' tend so earnestly to biz,
That mother says to father: "How improved our Willie is!"
But father, havin' been a boy hisself, suspicions me
When, jest 'fore Christmas, I'm as good as I kin be!

For Christmas, with its lots an' lots of candies, cakes an'
    toys,
Was made, they say, for proper kids an' not for naughty
    boys;
So wash yer face an' bresh yer hair, an' mind yer p's and q's,
And don't bust out yer pantaloons, and don't wear out
    yer shoes;
Say "Yessum" to the ladies, and "Yessur" to the men,
An' when they's company, don't pass yer plate for pie again;
But, thinkin' of the things yer'd like to see upon that tree,
Jest 'fore Christmas be as good as yer kin be!

—Eugene Field

🎄 A CHRISTMAS CHANGE OF HEART

Farms of the past were yeasty, heady playgrounds for children of all ilk. Besides learning to do "women's work," girls grew up to be tomboys, climbing trees with their brothers, riding like the wind on a fast horse, throwing a "mean" snowball. Boys hooted and hollered and ran through the fields and woods like "wild Indians."

City mothers might be horrified at what they saw in such farm children—lack of manners, decorum, and assorted other civilized qualities—but what they might overlook was the self-confidence, bravery, creativity, individuality, sense of humor, openness, and social warmth that such a life instilled in the young.

WILLIE'S BEST-EVER CAKE WITH WHIPPED SNOW FROSTING

This old-fashioned one-two-three-four cake was a "special-treat cake" at our house when we were young. Mother usually frosted it with a whipped snow frosting.

2 cups sugar	3 cups twice-sifted cake flour
1 cup butter	1 teaspoon vanilla extract
4 eggs, separated and at room temperature	1 cup milk
1 tablespoon baking powder	Whipped Snow Frosting (recipe follows)
¼ teaspoon salt	

Preheat oven to 350°F. Grease and flour three 9-inch cake pans. In a large bowl, cream the sugar and butter together until light and fluffy; add the egg yolks, 1 at a time, beating well after each addition. Add the baking powder and salt to the flour. Add the vanilla to the sugar-butter mixture, then alternately add the flour mixture and milk, beating until

JANE WATSON HOPPING

smooth after each addition. Now beat the egg whites until stiff peaks form; fold them into the batter. Pour the batter into the pans and bake until light golden-brown, about 25 to 30 minutes. Remove from oven and let cake cool in the pans for about 10 minutes; then turn out on a wire rack to finish cooling. Frost when completely cool.

Makes one 3-layer cake.

Whipped Snow Frosting

1 cup light corn syrup	Pinch of salt
3 egg whites, at room temperature	1 teaspoon vanilla extract

In a small saucepan, bring the corn syrup to a boil. Meanwhile, beat the egg whites with the salt until stiff but not dry. Slowly pour the hot syrup over the egg whites, beating constantly. Continue beating until the frosting is fluffy and will hang in peaks. Stir in the vanilla.

Makes enough frosting to fill and frost one 3-layer cake.

ADA'S GOLDEN DELICIOUS SQUASH DROPS

Yielding nearly one hundred cookies, this recipe was a favorite in the days of big families and large Christmas gatherings.

2 cups, packed, light brown sugar	2 teaspoons baking powder
1 cup butter or margarine	2 teaspoons baking soda
2 eggs, lightly beaten	1 teaspoon ground ginger
2 cups pureed or finely chopped cooked squash	1 teaspoon ground cloves
	2 cups chopped walnuts
4⅓ cups all-purpose flour	2 cups dark raisins
2 tablespoons cinnamon	

Preheat oven to 350°F. In a large bowl, cream the sugar and butter together until fluffy. Beat in the eggs. Add the squash and stir to blend. In a separate large bowl, sift together 4 *cups* of the flour with the cinnamon, baking powder, baking soda, ginger, cloves, and salt. Then add the flour mixture to the sugar-butter mixture; blend until a thick batter is formed. Dust the walnuts and raisins with the *remaining* ⅓ *cup* flour. Drop by teaspoonfuls onto a lightly greased cookie sheet. Bake until light brown, about 12 minutes. Immediately transfer from pan with a spatula to cool on a wire rack. When cool, store in an airtight container until ready to serve. The cookies will remain fresh for about 1 week in storage.

Makes about 9 dozen cookies.

WILLIE'S FAVORITE CUSTARD PIE

When Willie was a little boy he often teased his mother into making a custard pie with this tad of verse:

> The moon in the sky is a custard-pie,
>   An' the clouds is the cream pour'd o'er it
> An' all o' the glittering stars in the sky
>   Is the powdered sugar for it.

Plain Pastry Dough (recipe follows)
 4 eggs, lightly beaten
½ cup sugar
½ teaspoon salt
3 cups milk, scalded

½ teaspoon vanilla extract
Dusting of freshly grated nutmeg
 (about ⅛ teaspoon)
1 recipe Sweetened Whipped Cream
 (page 60)

Prepare the pie dough; chill for at least 30 minutes.

Preheat oven to 450°F. In a large bowl, combine the eggs, sugar, and salt. Slowly add the milk and vanilla; stir to blend. Remove the pie dough from the refrigerator and roll out on a lightly floured surface to about ⅛ inch thick. Line a 9-inch pie pan with it and trim, leaving 1 inch overlapping rim; tuck the edges under between the dough and the pan and flute with your thumbs and forefingers or with the tines of a fork. Pour two thirds of the filling into the pan, then carefully set pan on the pulled-out oven rack; add remaining filling, dust top with nutmeg, and ease the rack back into place. Promptly close oven and bake for 10 minutes at 450° to set the custard, then reduce oven setting to 325° and continue baking until top of custard is light golden brown and a knife inserted into the center comes out clean, about 30 to 40 minutes. Remove from oven and let cool. Serve slightly warm or cooled to room temperature with a dollop of Sweetened Whipped Cream.

Makes one 9-inch pie.

Plain Pastry Dough

1½ cups all-purpose flour
 ½ teaspoon salt
 ½ cup butter or margarine

¼ to ⅓ cup cold water, depending
 on the dryness of the flour

In a medium-size bowl, combine the flour and salt, mixing well. Using a pastry blender or 2 dinner knives, cut in the butter until the mixture is reduced to granules the size of peas. Sprinkle 2 to 3 *tablespoons* cold water over the flour-butter mixture, 1 tablespoon at a time, stirring gently with a fork until dough is moistened and almost clings to the sides of the bowl (add *2 to 3 teaspoons* additional water if needed).

Turn dough onto a lightly floured surface and knead 1 or 2 times to form a ball. Wrap in aluminum foil or waxed paper and refrigerate until chilled, about 30 minutes.

Pretty Lights

From the time our son Randy was only two years old, he just loved Christmas. He searched through catalogs for "presents" and walked around, around, and around the Christmas tree. He would stick out one chubby little finger and touch, so gently, the shiny ornaments and he would sit in the shelter of the tree and wait for Dad to come home and turn on the pretty lights.

Then one day, in a state of pure passion, he took hold of a branch. Down came the tree, ornaments and all. Randy's big blue eyes turned stormy as he wailed to me, "I broke it!" Dad came in and comforted him and set up the tree. We took the breakable ornaments off and redecorated it with ribbons, candy canes, cookies, and unbreakable balls—we didn't mind a bit, for the greatest gift we had ever received was our first baby, Randy.

From *THE OLD HOME FOLKS*

The Child-heart is so strange a little thing—
So mild—so timorously shy and small—
When grown-up hearts throb, it goes scampering
Behind the wall, nor dares peer out at all—

—James Whitcomb Riley

BRANDY SNAPS

These delicious crisp little cookies are lovely for a holiday tea party or for little boys and girls who just love cookies.

½ cup butter, chilled
1 cup all-purpose flour
1 cup powdered sugar
2 eggs, well beaten

2 teaspoons brandy
¼ cup granulated sugar, for dipping
cookies

Preheat oven to 425°F. Cut the butter into the flour (as you would for pastry) with a pastry cutter or 2 table knives. Add the powdered sugar, eggs, and brandy; beat the batter vigorously. Cover and chill for 30 minutes. Meanwhile, lightly grease a large cookie sheet.

When the dough is thoroughly chilled, shape it by rounded teaspoonfuls into balls; dip tops in granulated sugar and place, sugar side up and about 3 inches apart on the cookie sheet. Bake just until set, about 5 minutes. Immediately transfer from the pan to cool on an opened brown grocery bag or on kraft paper. When thoroughly cooled, store in an airtight container until ready to serve.   *Makes about 2 dozen snaps.*

AUNT PEG'S SILVER CAKE
WITH SNOWY LEMON FROSTING

At Christmas Aunt Peg loved the carol "Silver Bells," and Uncle Ben loved her Silver Cake with Snowy Lemon Frosting.

3 cups sifted cake flour
1 tablespoon baking powder
½ cup butter
1½ cups sugar
1 cup milk

½ teaspoon lemon extract
4 egg whites, stiffly beaten
Snowy Lemon Frosting (recipe follows)

Preheat oven to 375°F. Grease two 9-inch cake pans. Sift together the flour and baking powder 3 times. In a large bowl, cream the butter until light; gradually add the sugar, beating until fluffy. Alternately add the milk and dry ingredients to the butter-sugar mixture, beating well after each addition. Stir in the lemon extract, then fold in the egg whites quickly and thoroughly. Divide the dough evenly between the 2 cake pans. Bake 30 minutes. Remove from oven and let cool. When thoroughly cool, spread the frosting between the layers and over the top and sides of the cake. *Makes one 2-layer cake.*

Snowy Lemon Frosting

2 egg whites
1½ cups sugar
3 tablespoons water

2 tablespoons lemon juice
¼ teaspoon finely grated lemon peel

In the top of a double boiler, combine the egg whites, sugar, water, and lemon juice. Beat with a rotary beater until well blended. Place over rapidly boiling water and cook until the frosting stands in peaks, about 7 minutes, beating constantly. Remove from over boiling water; add the lemon peel and continue beating until thick enough to spread.
Makes enough for frosting one 2-layer cake.

LIGHT-AS-DOWN ANGEL PIE
IN A LEMON PASTRY CRUST

A crispy crust sets off the light-as-down filling in this pie.

Lemon Pastry Crust (recipe follows)

1 cup sugar	1 teaspoon vanilla extract
1/3 cup cornstarch	1 cup heavy cream
1 1/2 cups boiling water	1/3 cup shredded coconut, toasted

Bake the pie crust before preparing the filling; set aside to cool.

In the top of a double boiler, combine the sugar and cornstarch, mixing well. Add the boiling water and cook until thick, stirring occasionally. Remove from heat, and stir in the vanilla. Let cool at room temperature until the heat is almost out of the filling, then put in the refrigerator to finish cooling.

Meanwhile, beat the cream until stiff, but be careful not to overwhip. Remove the filling from the refrigerator and fold in the cream. Turn into the baked pie crust and top with coconut. Refrigerate for about 2 hours before serving.   *Makes one 9-inch pie.*

Lemon Pastry Crust

1 1/2 cups all-purpose flour, plus 1/2 cup for rolling dough	1 egg, well beaten
	2 tablespoons cold water
1/2 teaspoon salt	2 tablespoons lemon juice, strained
3/4 cup butter or margarine	

Into a large bowl, measure flour and salt; stir to blend. With a pastry cutter or 2 dinner knives, work the butter into the flour until it is granular, each grain being about the size of a pea. Into a small bowl, measure 2 *tablespoons* of the beaten egg and add the cold water and lemon juice. Stir well together. Gradually, *1 tablespoon at a time,* add the egg-water-lemon liquid to the flour mixture. Stir with a fork, moistening the dry ingredients until the mixture begins to hold together. Then turn out onto a lightly floured surface and, kneading only two or three times, shape the dough into a ball. Refrigerate until needed.

To bake the crust, preheat oven to 450°F. Turn chilled dough onto a floured surface and form into a ball; roll out and fit into a 9-inch pie pan; flute the edges. With a fork prick the sides and bottom of uncooked shell, or, if you wish, fill with dry beans to hold crust in place while cooking. Bake crust 15 minutes, then remove beans and continue baking crust until light brown, 5 or more minutes. Place on a wire rack to cool.   *Makes one 9-inch pie crust.*

🌿 A Sleigh Ride Revisited

When it snows, Mother likes to tell us how thrilling sleigh rides were in her youth:

"Dad would fill the sleigh with clean straw that still held the scent of summer in it and then cover it with heavy quilts. Then Grandpa, Grandma, Mother, Dad, my brothers and sisters, all ten of us, snug in heavy boots, coats, and scarves, wrapped in Grandma's woolen blankets, would pile into the sleigh and go gliding over country roads, white now with new-fallen snow, past meadows, scattered farm houses, and through the woods. Joyfully, as we dashed through the familiar countryside, we sang 'The Old Oaken Bucket,' 'Tenting Tonight,' and all the ancient carols, 'It Came upon the Midnight Clear,' 'Silent Night,' 'Hark! The Herald Angels Sing.' "

Jingle, jingle, sleigh bells ringing
In the frosty air,
Merry laughter, pure delight,
Peeling everywhere.

Horses prancing, heads held high,
Warm breath misting as they blow,
Snowflakes falling from the sky,
While we're speeding o'er the snow.

EFFIE'S FAVORITE PORK ROAST
WITH ROSEY PICKLED CRAB APPLES

Effie always cuts all the excess fat off her pork roast before seasoning it for cooking and puts the fat away for rendering into lard. She put this roast on a pan with a rack in it so the roast wouldn't sit in the excess fat drippings. All women of that time knew that pork had to be cooked well done; today trichinosis has practically been eliminated, but, to play safe, pork should still be cooked well done. No one had a thermometer in those days to check for doneness of pork, so the cook used an eye test: Well-done pork should look white or gray and the juices should run clear (all pink color in the juices and meat should be gone).

Mother marinated her pork roasts for several hours in milk or buttermilk to sweeten the taste before cooking. Both Mother and Effie thought pork roast should be served at pre-Christmas dinners, especially when folks were cold and hungry.

1 (5-pound) fresh boned pork loin roast (a boned roast from the middle of the loin is the choicest cut, because it yields tender meat that is easily carved)
1 tablespoon salt
1½ teaspoons black pepper
1 teaspoon dried sweet marjoram leaves

2 cloves of garlic, cut into slivers, optional
Rosey Pickled Crab Apples (recipe follows)
Sprigs of parsley, for garnish, optional

Preheat the oven to 350°F. Trim the roast so that only about 1 inch of fat remains on the surface. Score the fat. Rub the roast with the salt and pepper and place fat side up. Sprinkle the top with marjoram and, if desired, insert slivers of garlic into the meat. Place in a shallow roasting pan fat side up (put the ribs down). Bake until meat is cooked through, allow about 40 to 45 minutes per pound. When about three fourths of the cooking time is up, insert a meat thermometer into the thickest part of the meat (make sure the probe is not touching bone) and begin to check the temperature; pork will be well done and yet still moist at 170°F. Remove from oven and let the roast sit in the pan for about 10 minutes; then place on a serving platter and surround it with rosey pickled crab apples. Garnish with parsley sprigs, if you wish.

Makes 8 to 10 servings.

Rosey Pickled Crab Apples

4 quarts crab apples, uniform in size
  (choose sound ones)
2 cups cider vinegar
5 cups, packed, light brown sugar

2 sticks cinnamon
1 tablespoon whole cloves
1 tablespoon whole allspice

Wash the crab apples and cut off blossom ends; do not pare them. Make a spiced syrup by combining the vinegar, sugar, cinnamon, cloves, and allspice; simmer gently for about 20 minutes, then with a slotted spoon remove the whole spices. Add apples, a few at a time, to the syrup and cook gently (so as not to burst the skins) until apples are tender but not soft. Remove the apples from the syrup and immediately pack in hot, well scrubbed and sterilized jars, adding enough of the hot syrup to the jars to cover apples. Cover with new lids prepared according to manufacturer's directions and screw on sterilized metal rings. Label and date. Store in a cool, dark, and dry place.   *Makes 5 to 6 pints.*

SAVOY SALAD
WITH EASY-TO-MAKE MAYONNAISE

Savoy is a light to dark green crinkly sweet-flavored cabbage that grows in the fields as vigorously as its plain green and red cousins. We love using it during the Christmas season because it dresses up ordinary coleslaw recipes and gives them a festive air.

¼ cup chilled Easy-to-Make
  Mayonnaise (recipe follows)
4 cups finely shredded Savoy
  cabbage (about half a medium
  head)

¼ cup finely minced winter-growing
  chives (tender green onions may
  be substituted)
½ cup dairy sour cream
Salt
Black pepper

Combine the cabbage and chives in a large salad bowl. In a small bowl blend together the sour cream and mayonnaise; pour over the Savoy and toss. Taste and season with salt and pepper as desired.

Makes 6 to 8 servings.

Easy-to-Make Mayonnaise

Chill the salad oil, mixing bowl, and beaters (those used with an electric mixer or a rotary beater) in the refrigerator before making the mayonnaise.

2 egg yolks	Dash of black pepper
1 teaspoon dry mustard	Dash of paprika
1 teaspoon salt	1½ cups chilled salad oil
1 teaspoon powdered sugar	2 tablespoons vinegar
Dash of ground Cayenne pepper	

Place the egg yolks in a medium-size bowl of an electric mixer, or use a rotary beater; add all the other ingredients *except* the oil and vinegar; beat until well blended. While beating, alternately add the oil and vinegar, a little at a time, until the mixture begins to thicken; then add larger amounts of oil. Continue beating and adding oil and vinegar until of mayonnaise consistency. (*Note:* Should the mixture curdle, whip another egg yolk in a separate bowl and add to the curdled mayonnaise, or add the curdled mayonnaise to a tablespoon of water in another bowl and beat until smooth.) Pour into a clean glass jar and cover tightly. Store under refrigeration. Use as you like for salads or sandwiches.

Makes 1¾ cups.

FLUFFY BAKED IRISH POTATOES
WITH GOLDEN SOUR CREAM DRESSING

To feed his large family, Uncle Bud grew hundreds of pounds of potatoes —red and white ones, and a large round buttery golden-fleshed variety he called German potatoes. As children, we loved to go over to Uncle Bud and Aunt Sue's house in winter and help carry a basket or bucket of earthy nuggets in from the potato cellar.

It seemed to us that our cousins ate spuds at every meal—and perhaps they did. All we remember is the wonderful flavor of the golden-colored potato salad made with the German potatoes, the creamed red potatoes and pan-fried white spuds with bits of onion in them, potatoes stuffed and without stuffing, dressed and without dressing, potato ribbons, potato fritters, and these fluffy, light baked potatoes with golden sour cream dressing.

6 medium-size Irish potatoes (select smooth potatoes)

About 2 tablespoons softened butter, for greasing skins of potatoes

Golden Sour Cream Dressing (recipe follows)

Salt and black pepper, as desired

Preheat oven to 425°F. Scrub the potatoes and remove eyes and any blemishes. Take a little soft butter on your fingers and grease the potato skins. Place on an ungreased baking sheet and bake until tender, about 45 to 50 minutes. To test for doneness, wrap a towel around your hand and squeeze the potatoes; if done, they should feel soft. When done, immediately break open the skins to keep them from being soggy and serve promptly with dollops of the dressing and salt and pepper to taste.

Makes 6 servings.

Golden Sour Cream Dressing

2 hard-cooked egg yolks (For how to cook tender yolks, see Note in recipe for Delicious Stuffed Eggs, page 213.)

1 cup dairy sour cream

1 teaspoon strained lemon juice

1 teaspoon powdered sugar

Dash of salt

Dash of white pepper

Press the yolks through a sieve into a small bowl. Add the sour cream and beat until well blended. Add the sugar, lemon juice, salt, and pepper and beat well. Refrigerate if made ahead, but make at the last moment possible.

Makes about 1 rounded cup.

QUICK BUTTERMILK BUNS

When Mother needed buns in a hurry for holiday dinners, she made this easy-to-make recipe. In almost no time the house was perfumed with the yeasty fragrance of bread, and company and family alike began to hang around the kitchen.

1 package dry or granulated yeast

¼ cup lukewarm water (105°F to 115°F)

1 cup lukewarm buttermilk

1 tablespoon sugar

¼ teaspoon baking soda

5 tablespoons butter, softened
2½ cups all-purpose flour, plus
    about ½ cup for kneading

1 teaspoon baking powder
1 teaspoon salt

Preheat oven to 400°F. Grease a 13x9x2-inch baking pan; set aside. Sprinkle the yeast over the warm water; set aside to proof for about 10 minutes.

In a large bowl, combine the buttermilk, sugar, baking soda, and 3 *tablespoons* of the butter. Stir until butter melts and sugar dissolves. Add the yeast; stir to blend. Sift in the 2½ cups flour and the baking powder and salt; stir into a soft dough, then let stand about 10 minutes. Turn dough onto a lightly floured board and knead until smooth and elastic. Pinch off small rolls about the size of an egg and tuck them close together in the prepared pan; rub tops with 1 *tablespoon* butter. Wet a clean cloth with real warm water and wring dry, then cover the buns with it. Let buns rise until doubled in size. Remove towel and bake until lightly browned, about 15 to 20 minutes. Remove from oven and rub tops with the *remaining 1 tablespoon* butter. Serve immediately.

Makes about 2 dozen buns.

YULETIDE CARROT CAKE

My daughter Colleen loves this rich party cake.

2½ cups granulated sugar or 2½
    cups, packed, light brown
    sugar
1½ cups vegetable oil
4 egg yolks
5 tablespoons hot water
1 teaspoon lemon extract
2½ cups sifted all-purpose flour
2 teaspoons ground cinnamon
1 teaspoon ground nutmeg

½ teaspoon baking soda
½ teaspoon baking powder
½ teaspoon ground cloves
¼ teaspoon salt
1 cup chopped walnuts (or other
    nut meat)
1 cup golden raisins
1½ cups finely grated carrots
4 egg whites, stiffly beaten

Preheat oven to 350°F. Grease pan first, then fit waxed paper into the bottom of a 10-inch springform tube pan, then grease the paper. In a large bowl, blend together the sugar, oil, and egg yolks. Stir in the hot water and lemon extract. Sift together the flour, cinnamon, nutmeg, baking soda, baking powder, cloves, and salt. Combine the walnuts and raisins and shake enough of the flour mixture over them to lightly coat. Add the flour mixture to egg yolk mixture. Blend in the carrots and walnut-raisin mixture, then fold in the egg whites. Pour batter into the prepared tube pan. Bake 1 hour and 5 minutes to 1 hour and 25 minutes. (Test doneness by sticking a toothpick into the top of the cake; if it comes out clean the cake is done.) Remove from oven; let cool for 15 minutes in the pan, then unmold onto a cake plate. (If the cake does not readily turn loose from the pan, loosen it with a thin knife blade.) Remove paper from the bottom of the cake and using a second plate turn the cake top side up. Serve thin slices with a dollop of whipped cream or with ice cream.   *Makes one tube cake.*

CHRISTMAS CARD MAGIC

The Christmas cards and letters
*   with messages of cheer*
Renew the bonds of friendship
*   neglected through the year.*
They bring a sense of nearness,
*   a unity that gives*
A oneness of the spirit
*   in fellowship that lives.*

The crowded days of duties
*   return with stern demand,*
But somehow they are lightened
*   because we understand*
That others care and keep us
*   within their hearts and prayers,*
And we in turn remember,
*   so each a blessing shares.*

When Christmas rush is over
*   how good it seems to take*
Time to re-read and ponder;
*   then memories awake*
To bring us close together,
*   forgetting years have passed;*
O Christmas cards, your magic
*   makes Christmas spirit last.*

—Della Adams Leitner

Wish you a merry CHRISTMAS

Yuletide Greetings

By the late eighteen-hundreds, Christmas cards, which were originally the size of a gentleman's address card and inscribed simply with "A Merry Christmas and Happy New Year," had become quite elegant with paintings or drawings of holly branches, embossed figures, landscapes, and robins and wrens on them.

🎄 CHRISTMAS CARD MAGIC

Aunt Mable loved cards of all sorts, but especially very old Christmas cards. Most of those in her collection had comic robins, perky robins, and robins in the snow on them because she passionately loved birds. (All of her life she picked up any lovely blue, black, orange, or spotted feather she found and laid it on her windowsill to enjoy for a while and to share with us.)

She loved to send cards to people in all seasons, but especially at Christmas when she would combine a carefully chosen card and a loaf of one of her delicious sweet breads and take them as token gifts to friends, neighbors, and family.

PUMPKIN RAISIN BREAD
WITH NUTMEG GLAZE

On farms great piles of pumpkins are brought in out of the fields and stored for winter use; some are small, hard-fleshed, sweet pie-pumpkins. Others are giants easily weighing forty pounds, in some cases several hundred pounds, and are not only good for pies, cakes, and breads, but when pastures are barren and feed is dry—just hay and grain—are sometimes a succulent treat for cattle.

1½ cups, packed, light brown sugar
½ cup vegetable oil (olive oil
   preferred)
2 eggs, beaten
1 cup cooked pumpkin puree
   (canned pumpkin may be used)
1⅔ cups sifted all-purpose flour
2 teaspoons baking powder
1 teaspoon baking soda
½ teaspoon salt

½ teaspoon ground cinnamon
½ teaspoon freshly grated nutmeg
½ teaspoon ground ginger
¼ teaspoon ground cloves
½ cup chopped walnuts
½ cup dark raisins
Nutmeg Glaze (recipe follows),
   optional
Whipped cream, optional

Preheat oven to 325°F. Grease and flour a 10-inch tube pan.

In a large bowl, combine the sugar and oil; add the eggs and stir to blend. Add the pumpkin, beating until thoroughly mixed. Into a second large bowl, sift together the flour, baking powder, soda, and salt; add the cinnamon, nutmeg, ginger, and cloves. Stir the flour mixture into the pumpkin mixture, then fold in the walnuts and raisins. Spoon into the prepared pan. Bake until bread springs back when fairly lightly pressed and has developed a rich golden color, about 1 hour; the cooked bread should be firm on top. Remove from oven and let stand 10 to 15 minutes to cool slightly, then loosen from the pan with a spatula and turn out onto a large plate. Serve immediately or let cool completely before serving. Serve plain or glaze with Nutmeg Glaze. If desired, serve topped with whipped cream. *Makes 1 loaf.*

Nutmeg Glaze

1 tablespoon butter, softened	About 2 tablespoons apple cider
1 cup powdered sugar, a bit more if needed	A light grating of fresh nutmeg (no more than ⅛ teaspoon)

Stir the butter and sugar together; add enough cider to make a thin-consistency glaze. Add nutmeg to taste. Spread over lukewarm or cooled bread.

EASY-TO-MAKE ORANGE CAKE WITH ORANGE FILLING AND CREAMY ORANGE FROSTING

Grandpa White's oranges were ready to pick just before Christmas and all of us knew that we would be given a bagful or two for holiday use. With such abundance we, at our house, liked to make this orange-flavored cake with its delicious orange-flavored filling and frosting.

3 eggs, separated and at room temperature	1 cup strained orange juice
⅔ cup butter or margarine, softened	2 teaspoons finely grated orange zest (grate only the orange-colored outer layer of the rind)
1½ cups sugar	Orange Filling (recipe follows)
3 cups sifted all-purpose flour	Creamy Orange Frosting (recipe follows)
1 tablespoon baking powder	
1 teaspoon salt	

Preheat oven to 400°F. Grease and lightly flour three 9-inch cake pans; set aside.

In a large bowl, cream together the egg yolks, butter, and sugar. Sift the flour with the baking powder and salt. Alternately add the flour mixture and orange juice to the egg yolk mixture, blending well. Stir in the orange zest. Beat the egg whites until stiff moist peaks form, then fold them gently into the batter. Pour one third of the batter into each cake pan. Bake until light golden and tops spring back when lightly pressed, about 20 to 25 minutes. Remove from oven and cool in the pans for about 10 minutes, then turn out on a wire rack and cool thoroughly. When completely cool, spread chilled orange filling between the layers and frost the top and sides lightly with frosting.

Makes one 3-layer cake.

Orange Filling

2 *tablespoons butter*
¼ *cup sugar*
2 *eggs, beaten*
½ *cup orange juice*

1 *tablespoon finely grated orange zest (grate only the orange-colored outer layer of the rind)*
½ *teaspoon lemon extract*

Combine all the filling ingredients in the top of a double boiler. Cook over boiling water until well thickened, about 10 minutes, stirring constantly. Chill before using.   *Makes enough filling for one 3-layer cake.*

Creamy Orange Frosting

¼ *cup butter or margarine, at room temperature*
Few grains of salt
2 *tablespoons grated orange rind*
1 *unbeaten egg yolk*

2¼ *cups powdered sugar, sifted*
2 *tablespoons orange juice*
1 *tablespoon lemon juice*
Cream

Soften butter in a medium bowl. Then add salt, grated orange rind, and egg yolk; work with a wooden spoon until light and creamy. Gradually stir in about ⅓ *cup* powdered sugar. Add *remaining* sugar, orange and lemon juice, and, using a wooden spoon or an electric mixer, beat until smooth. Thin with only enough cream to develop a spreading consistency.   *Makes enough frosting to lightly cover a 3-layer cake.*

CHRISTMAS POUND CAKE STUDDED
WITH CANDIED CHERRIES

When I was growing up, any candied fruit used in this Christmas cake was homemade, candied in season as cherries ripened and as orange or lemon peels were saved when the orange and lemon pulp had been put to other uses. Sometimes the cake had homemade candied apricots, figs, or pears in it. Even so, this delicious cake was always eagerly awaited as part of the Christmas Day festivities.

½ cup golden raisins
½ cup finely chopped candied
   cherries
¼ cup finely chopped candied
   orange peel
¼ cup finely chopped candied
   lemon peel
½ cup slivered almonds
About 2¼ cups all-purpose flour
  1 cup butter or margarine,
   softened

1½ cups granulated sugar
  5 eggs
  1 teaspoon salt
½ teaspoon freshly grated nutmeg
1½ teaspons vanilla extract
½ cup powdered sugar
  1 tablespoon cold water
  6 candied cherries, cut in half for
   studding top of cakes
A few whole almonds, for garnishing
  top of cakes, optional

Preheat oven to 350°F. Grease two 9x5x2¼-inch loaf pans; set aside. Combine the raisins, finely chopped candied cherries, candied orange and lemon peel, and almonds into a medium-size bowl. Dust with 3 to 4 *tablespoons* of the flour and set aside.

    In a large bowl, cream the butter and granulated sugar together. Add the eggs, 1 at a time, beating thoroughly after each addition. Beat in 2 *cups* flour and the salt and nutmeg. Add the vanilla and beat vigorously. Fold in the raisin mixture. Divide the batter equally between the 2 loaf pans. Bake until cake is golden brown and firm to the touch, about 1 hour to 1 hour and 20 minutes. (*Note:* Don't be too quick to remove the cakes from the oven; test with a tooth pick and look to see if the cakes

                               JANE WATSON HOPPING

have shrunk away from the sides of the pans. If the cakes don't seem too brown, err in the direction of overbaking, not underbaking.)

When done, remove from oven. Let set 10 to 15 minutes to cool slightly. Then turn out of the pans and immediately set, tops up, on a wire rack to cool. When thoroughly cooled, make a glaze as follows: Mix the powdered sugar with the cold water. Using the glaze as a glue, garnish the top of each loaf with a portion of the candied cherry halves and the whole almonds, if desired, by dipping the cut side of each cherry half (or one side of the almond) in glaze and arranging it to form a pattern on top of the loaves. *Makes 2 loaf cakes.*

AUNT MABLE'S CRANBERRY BREAD WITH CRANBERRY ORANGE SAUCE

One Christmas, Aunt Mable made many loaves of cranberry bread to give to the family, friends, and good neighbors.

As I watched her work, she told me that the tart deep-colored little berries had been cultivated in this country for more than a hundred years on the low-lying bog land (in Massachusetts, Wisconsin, New Jersey, Washington, and Oregon), that they grow both round and oval in shape depending on the variety, and that while the little berries had been traditionally called cranberries, they had also been called "craneberries" because the slender stems on which they grew were curved like a crane's neck.

½ cup butter, softened
2 cups, packed, light brown sugar
2 eggs, beaten to a froth
1½ cups orange juice
1 tablespoon finely grated orange zest (grate only the bright-orange outer layer of the rind)
2 cups fresh cranberries, coarsely chopped
4 cups sifted all-purpose flour

1 tablespoon baking powder
1 teaspoon baking soda
1 teaspoon salt
½ teaspoon ground cinnamon
½ teaspoon freshly grated nutmeg
1 cup pecans, finely chopped
⅔ cup dark raisins
Cranberry Orange Sauce (recipe follows), optional

Preheat oven to 350°F. Grease two 9x5x2¾-inch loaf pans; set aside.

In a large bowl, cream the butter until soft. Add the sugar and eggs; stir together. Add the orange juice and zest, stirring to blend, then add the cranberries. In a second large bowl, sift the flour with the baking powder, baking soda, salt, cinnamon, and nutmeg. Stir the dry ingredients into the cranberry mixture. When thoroughly blended, fold in the pecans and raisins. Turn into the prepared baking pans and bake until loaves are richly colored and firm to the touch, 55 to 60 minutes. Remove from oven and let loaves sit in pans for about 10 minutes; then loosen bread with a spatula and turn out onto a wire rack to cool. Serve as is, warm or cold, or serve lukewarm with Cranberry Orange Sauce.

Makes 2 loaves.

Cranberry Orange Sauce

1½ cups orange juice
1½ cups sugar
  1 cup fresh cranberries, coarsely
    chopped

2 tablespoons finely grated orange
  zest (grate only the bright-
  orange outer layer of the rind)
2½ tablespoons cornstarch
2 tablespoons water
½ teaspoon freshly grated nutmeg

In a saucepan, combine the orange juice, sugar, cranberries, and orange zest. Bring just to the boiling point over high heat, then cook for about 1 minute or until the berries are a bit tender and have given up their juice, stirring occasionally. Remove from heat. In a small bowl, mix together the cornstarch and water; stir into the cooked cranberries. Cook sauce over medium heat only as long as it takes to thicken the sauce (the sauce will be clear), then stir the nutmeg into the sauce and remove from heat. Transfer sauce to a small bowl; let cool to lukewarm. Serve over slices of cranberry bread. *Makes about 3 cups.*

BUCKTHORN

JANE WATSON HOPPING

IT TAKES A HEAP O' LIVIN' IN A HOUSE T' MAKE IT HOME

In 1895 Edgar Albert Guest began to work on the *Detroit Free Press* where his talent for down-home verse captured the hearts of the readers. Among his widely syndicated rhymes one finds the following poem, "A Heap O' Livin'," sometimes simply called "Home":

> It takes a heap o' livin' in a house t' make it home,
> A heap o' sun an' shadder, an' ye sometimes have t' roam
> Afore ye really 'preciate the things ye lef' behind,
> An' hunger fer 'em somehow, with 'em allus on yer mind.
> It don't make any differunce how rich ye get t' be,
> How much yer chairs an' tables cost, how great yer luxury;
> It ain't home t' ye, though it be the palace of a king,
> Until somehow yer soul is sort o' wrapped 'round everything.
>
> Home ain't a place that gold can buy or get up in a minute;
> Afore it's home there's got t' be a heap o' livin' in it;
> Within the walls there's got t' be some babies born, and then
> Right there ye've got t' bring 'em up t' women good, an' men;
> And gradjerly, as time goes on, ye find ye wouldn't part
> With anything they ever used—they're grown into yer heart:
> The old high chairs, the playthings, too, the little shoes they wore
> Ye hoard; an' if ye could ye'd keep the thumbmarks on the door.
>
> Ye've got t' weep t' make it home, ye've got t' sit an' sigh
> An' watch beside a loved one's bed, an' know that Death is nigh;
> An' in the stillness o' the night t' see Death's angel come,
> An' close the eyes o' her that smiled, an' leave her sweet voice dumb.
> Fer these are scenes that grip the heart, an' when yer tears are dried,
> Ye find the home is dearer than it was, an' sanctified;
> An' tuggin' at ye always are the pleasant memories
> O' her that was an' is no more—ye can't escape from these.
>
> Ye've got t' sing an' dance fer years, ye've got t' romp an' play.
> An' learn t' love the things ye have by usin' 'em each day;
> Even the roses 'round the porch must blossom year by year
> Afore they 'come a part o' ye, suggestin' someone dear
> Who used t' love 'em long ago, an' trained 'em jes' t' run
> The way they do, so's they would get the early mornin' sun;
> Ye've got t' love each brick an' stone from cellar up t' dome:
> It takes a heap o' livin' in a house t' make it home.

AUNT MABLE'S ROAST CHICKEN
WITH POTATOES AND CARROTS

Born and reared on the farm, Aunt Mable even into her old age never gave up the country ways. Her gardens and flowers were lovely in summer, and in late fall and early winter she butchered year-old hens for the stock pot and year-old roosters for the roasting pan.

1 (3½- to 4-pound) roasting chicken
   (On farms, a young rooster is
   generally used as a roasting
   chicken, and a large hen is used
   for boiling. Any size chicken may
   be roasted but this size will make
   4 to 6 nice servings.)
Salt
Black pepper
A sprinkling of dried oregano leaves,
  finely crushed

2 cups water
About ¼ cup dried onions or 1 small
  chopped fresh onion or 1 package
  dried onion soup mix
4 to 6 potatoes
4 to 6 carrots
Cornstarch, for making pan gravy
Cold water, for making pan gravy

Preheat oven to 400°F. Remove the neck and giblets from the chicken; discard the liver or save to cook another time. Wash the chicken and remove all excess fat. Salt and pepper the chicken, inside and out. Sprinkle lightly with oregano and place in the center of a large roasting pan; pour the water around the edges. Add the dried onions (or the fresh onion or dried onion soup mix). Cover and bake until chicken is almost done; a meat thermometer inserted into the breast should read about 165°F.

While the chicken is roasting, peel the potatoes; remove blemishes and eyes and cut each in half lengthwise. Peel the carrots; cut in half crosswise, then cut the thicker pieces in half lengthwise (which will make the cooking time for the carrots and potatoes about the same).

Once the chicken's internal temperature is about 165°F, check the broth in the pan and add ½ cup water needed (there should be at least 2 inches of broth in the pan). Then arrange the carrots in the roasting pan, laying them in the broth; put the potatoes over them (potatoes will steam done). Salt and pepper the vegetables and sprinkle on a bit more oregano. Cover and continue baking until the vegetables are tender when pierced with a fork, about 30 minutes.

Remove chicken to a serving platter; set aside to keep warm. Spoon the vegetables into a dish, cover, and set aside to keep warm. Skim the fat off the pan juices; dilute to taste with water. Then thicken with cornstarch that's been dissolved in cold water. (*Note:* For a medium gravy, dissolve 1½ *tablespoons* cornstarch in 3 tablespoons cold water and add to each pint of measured broth.) Serve immediately.

Makes about 4 to 6 servings.

ADA'S HEAVENLY HASH SALAD

This salad became popular with our family in about 1936 when marshmallows, canned pineapple, and store-bought mayonnaise became available on the market and when the "close-money times" of the thirties had eased enough so that some of us at least could afford such luxuries. As times got better, it quickly became a favorite Christmas salad.

1 cup marshmallows, cut into
  quarters (or use tiny whole
  marshmallows that are available
  these days)
1 cup small cubed pineapples,
  drained
½ cup chopped almonds

½ cup mayonnaise (preferably Easy-
  to-Make Mayonnaise, page
  116)
½ cup heavy cream, whipped and
  lightly sweetened with 1
  tablespoon sugar

Combine all the ingredients except the whipped cream in a large bowl; refrigerate for several hours. When ready to serve, fold in the whipped cream. *Makes 4 to 6 servings.*

DELICIOUS BRAN MUFFINS
WITH AUNT MAE'S DRIED-APRICOT JAM

Aunt Mae served these muffins with tea in the afternoon. The old-fashioned jam recipe is one that has been passed down through her family. Make the jam at least several days before serving.

Aunt Mae's Dried Apricot Jam   ¾ teaspoon salt
  (recipe follows)   ¼ cup molasses
  1 cup whole-wheat flour   1 egg, well beaten
¾ cup bran   ⅔ cup milk
  1 tablespoon baking powder   4 tablespoons butter, melted

Preheat oven to 425°F. Grease a 12-cup muffin pan; set aside.

In a medium-size bowl, combine the flour, bran, baking powder, and salt; stir to blend. In a small bowl, combine the molasses, egg, milk, and butter and add to the dry ingredients, stirring just until barely blended; do not overmix. Spoon the batter into the prepared muffin cups. Bake until browned and firm to the touch, about 25 minutes. Serve piping hot with dried-apricot jam.   *Makes 1 dozen muffins.*

Aunt Mae's Dried-Apricot Jam
This jam reminds us of preserves. Dad and Randy think it is fine flavored, and Colleen and I like it because it is an economical spread.

1 pound dried pitless apricots
3 pints water
4 pounds sugar (9⅓ cups)

Wash the apricots and soak overnight in the water either at room temperature or in the refrigerator.

The following day bring the reconstituted apricots and the water in which they were soaked to a boil in a large saucepan; cook over medium heat for 20 minutes, stirring frequently so the fruit doesn't settle and stick to the bottom of the pan. Add the sugar, stirring until dissolved. Continue cooking 15 minutes longer; watch that the syrup doesn't boil up and run over.

Immediately ladle into hot freshly scrubbed and sterilized pint jars; fill to ¼ inch from the top. Wipe rims with a clean cloth. Put on brand new lids which have been heated in a pan of boiling water according to manufacturer's instructions. Screw on clean, sterilized metal rings until fairly tight. Set aside to cool. When cool, test for an airtight seal. To do this, press center of lid down, if it is curved down and stays down, the jar is sealed. (If the lid has not sealed, remove ring and lid; wash lid and wipe off top of jar with clean damp cloth, then put the lid back on, then the ring. Simmer in a boiling waterbath for 10 minutes.) Store in a cool, dark, and dry place to preserve color and quality.

Makes about 5 or 6 pints.

AN EASY-TO-MAKE CARROT PUDDING WITH LEMON SAUCE

Aunty thought this carrot pudding was fancier than the older recipes we all used because it called for grated lemon peel, white seedless raisins, and cake flour. It was delicious, but not really so different from the old recipes that often called for sweetener like sorghum, molasses, or honey instead of brown sugar, plain old dark raisins instead of white seedless, and any flour we had on hand.

6 tablespoons suet, finely ground
  (Purchase clean white suet at
  the butcher's or ask for it at the
  meat counter at your grocery
  store.)
½ cup, packed, dark brown sugar
1 egg
1 tablespoon water
1 cup finely grated carrots
1 cup white seedless raisins
2 teaspoons finely grated lemon
  peel

1¼ cups sifted cake flour
1 teaspoon baking powder
1 teaspoon ground cinnamon
1 teaspoon grated nutmeg
½ teaspoon baking soda
¼ teaspoon ground cloves
½ teaspoon salt
¼ teaspoon ground ginger
Lemon Sauce (recipe follows)

Work the suet with a spoon until soft. Add the sugar, stirring together. Beat the egg with the water and add to the suet-sugar mixture; stir until blended. Stir in the carrots, raisins, and lemon peel. Sift the flour with the baking powder, cinnamon, nutmeg, baking soda, salt, cloves, and ginger. Gradually add the dry ingredients to the suet-sugar mixture, stirring well. Turn into a greased and floured 1½-quart pudding mold or can; fill no more than two-thirds full; cover.

Set the mold in a deep saucepan with a wire rack fitted in the bottom. Pour enough boiling water in the saucepan to come about half-way up the sides of the mold. Cover saucepan and slowly bring to a boil, then reduce heat to maintain water at a simmer and steam for 2 hours. Unmold onto a serving platter. When pudding is almost cool, serve topped with Lemon Sauce. *Makes 10 to 12 servings.*

Lemon Sauce

1 cup sugar	½ cup water
½ cup butter or margarine	½ cup strained lemon juice
1 tablespoon cornstarch	Finely grated rind from 1 lemon

Combine the sugar and butter in the top of a double boiler. In a small bowl, dissolve the cornstarch in the water and lemon juice; add to the sugar-butter mixture. Stir in the lemon rind. Bring the sauce to a boil over medium heat, stirring almost constantly until sugar dissolves, butter melts, and ingredients are well blended. Continue cooking until sauce is clear and thick, about 15 to 20 minutes more. Serve while still hot or when lukewarm. *Makes about 2 cups.*

OLD-FASHIONED "APRICOTLETS"

These delicious little "fruitlets" were one of Johanna's special treats given to us all at Christmas. Sometimes she used dried peaches, pears, or apples instead of apricots.

2 cups dried pitted apricots	½ cup cold water
2 cups sugar	¼ cup slivered almonds
1 tablespoon cornstarch	Powdered or granulated sugar
⅛ teaspoon salt	
2 packages (2 tablespoons) unflavored gelatin	

Line an 8x8-inch cake pan with waxed paper or aluminum foil; set aside. Put the apricots in a medium bowl, pour hot water over them to cover; set aside to reconstitute (to take up the water). Soak for about an hour or more until apricots are soft, then cook them in a saucepan using very little water until they are tender; take care not to let them burn. Puree the fruit in a blender, then cook until very thick. Add the sugar, cornstarch, and salt and continue cooking down until mixture is thick.

Meanwhile, soften the gelatin in the cold water at least 2 minutes. Add the gelatin to the apricot mixture and stir until the gelatin has dissolved. Continue cooking mixture until it is very thick again. Remove from heat and add the almonds. Pour apricotlets into the prepared pan. Allow candy to stand 24 hours, then cut into 1-inch squares or 2x1-inch rectangles. Roll in powdered or granulated sugar. Let them stand until the surface has dried. Store in an airtight container.

Makes a little over a pound of candy.

🌿 THE FIRST SNOWFALL

In the old days, well-brought-up children were encouraged to have compassion for older folks and the infirm. We learned to run little errands or do small chores for our grandfather, who lived with us. My special job was to go into the garden to help pick tomatoes, because he was color-blind and could not tell by feeling them which tomatoes were beginning to turn red and which were still green.

My husband's mother took a different tack: On cold winter nights when he was small, Olive would settle him down in bed beside her and recite for him poetry she had learned by heart, like the following poem, "Somebody's Mother" by Mary Dow Brine.

> The woman was old and ragged and gray
> And bent with the chill of the winter's day.
> The street was wet with a recent snow
> And the woman's feet were aged and slow.
>
> She stood at the crossing and waited long,
> Alone, uncared for, amid the throng
> Of human beings who passed her by,
> Nor heeded the glance of her anxious eye.
>
> Down the street, with laughter and shout,
> Glad in the freedom of "school let out,"
> Came the boys like a flock of sheep,
> Hailing the snow piled white and deep.
>
> Past the woman so old and gray
> Hastened the children on their way,
> Nor offered a helping hand to her—
> So meek, so timid, afraid to stir
> Lest the carriage wheels or the horses' feet
> Should crowd her down in the slippery street.
>
> At last came one of the merry troop,
> The gayest laddie of all the group;
> He paused beside her and whispered low:
> "I'll help you cross, if you wish to go."
>
> Her aged hand on his strong young arm
> She placed, and so, without hurt or harm,
> He guided the trembling feet along,
> Proud that his own were firm and strong,
>
> Then back again to his friends he went,
> His young heart happy and well content.

"She's somebody's mother, boys, you know,
For all she's aged and poor and slow,
And I hope some fellow will lend a hand
To help my mother, you understand,
If ever she's poor and old and gray,
When her own dear boy is far away."

And "somebody's mother" bowed low her head
In her home that night, and the prayer she said
Was, "God be kind to the noble boy,
Who is somebody's son, and pride and joy!"

OLD WOMEN'S FAVORITE: DUTCH APPLE CAKE

On old-time farms and in town homes too, pantries and apple sheds were well stocked with Winesaps, Jonathans, Northern Spys, Arkansas Blacks, Wolf Rivers, and other apples for wintertime use. Women and girls alike made applesauce, pies, puddings, and other apple dishes in an attempt to use up the embarrassment of riches. Old women particularly loved to make this Dutch Apple Cake, which was often served warm for breakfast, as a bedtime snack, or even for Christmas company.

Butter, for greasing baking pan
 1 cup sifted all-purpose flour
 1 teaspoon baking powder
¼ teaspoon salt
 2 eggs
 1 teaspoon vanilla extract
 1 cup sugar

½ cup milk
 1 tablespoon butter
 4 apples, pared and cut into eighths
½ cup sugar
 1 scant teaspoon ground cinnamon
Heavy cream or whipped cream, for
 topping

Preheat oven to 375°F. Butter an 8x8x2-inch baking pan. Sift the flour, baking powder, and salt into a medium-size bowl. In a large bowl, beat the eggs and vanilla together until thick; gradually stir in the sugar until well blended. In a small saucepan, heat the milk and butter together just until butter melts. Then alternately add the flour mixture and the heated milk to the egg-vanilla mixture; stir until smooth. Turn batter into the prepared pan and spread it out evenly. Press the apple slices into the batter; arrange them together, making three or four rows. Combine the sugar and cinnamon and sprinkle over the top. Bake until apples are tender and the batter is lightly browned and done through, about 30 to 35 minutes. (Test with a toothpick; when the toothpick comes out clean the cake is done.) Cool the cake in the pan to room temperature or serve straight from the oven. Cut into squares; serve topped with a tablespoon of heavy cream or a spoonful of Sweetened Whipped Cream (page 60).   *Makes 4 to 6 servings.*

SODA BISCUITS:
AN OLD-TIME BASIC RECIPE

When I was a girl, you could ask any woman you knew if she would tell you how to make soda biscuits. She might kindly take the time to give you her recipe and a few tips to go along with it, or if she was a feisty old lady, she might ask you, "How come if you're ten or twelve years old you don't know how to do it yerself?"

*2 cups all-purpose flour, plus ½
   cup for rolling out dough
½ teaspoon baking soda
½ teaspoon salt*

*4 tablespoons cold butter or pork
   lard
¾ cup blinky (sour) milk or
   buttermilk*

Preheat oven to 475°F. In a large bowl, combine the flour, baking soda, and salt. Cut the butter or lard into the dry ingredients with a pastry cutter or 2 dinner knives until the mixture is reduced to bits as fine as coarse cornmeal. (*Note:* If using lard, do not rub it into the flour mixture with your hands; lard has a low melting point and, if warmed, will soak into the flour, making the biscuits less flaky.) Add enough milk to make a soft dough (it may take a tablespoon more or less depending on the dryness of the flour). Turn onto a smooth floured surface and lightly knead a few times. Roll ½ inch thick and cut into biscuits with a floured biscuit cutter. Place biscuits on an ungreased cookie sheet and prick with a fork. Bake until light brown, 12 to 15 minutes. Serve piping hot.

Makes 1 dozen biscuits.

Glazed Cinnamon Buns
Preheat oven to 475°F. Generously grease a cookie sheet. Roll *1 recipe Soda Biscuits* dough into a 12x8-inch rectangle that is ¼ inch thick. Generously spread with *soft butter*; sprinkle with *½ cup light brown sugar* and *1 teaspoon cinnamon*. Sprinkle with a few *raisins* or *nuts*, if you wish. Roll like a jelly roll and cut into 1-inch slices; place on a baking sheet, cut side down. Bake until light brown, 15 to 20 minutes. Remove from oven and set aside in the pan to cool slightly. When warm, glaze with powdered sugar glaze.

For the glaze, measure *1½ cups powdered sugar* into a small bowl. Add *3 tablespoons heavy cream* and *1 teaspoon vanilla extract*. Stir until creamy and light enough to spread (add more cream if necessary). With a spatula immediately spread over the warm cinnamon rolls. (*Note:*

Glazes made with cream harden rather quickly and firm up when rolls are cool.) *Makes 1 dozen cinnamon buns.*

Easy-to-Make Dinner Rolls

Preheat oven to 475°F. Grease a cookie sheet. Roll *1 recipe Soda Biscuits dough* into a 12x8-inch rectangle that is ¼ inch thick. Cut into rolls with a floured 2-inch cutter. Fold in half, pressing edges firmly together. Place slightly apart on the prepared cookie sheet. Brush with *melted butter;* cover and let stand in a warm place for about 20 minutes. Bake for 10 minutes, then brush again with melted butter and continue baking 10 to 15 minutes more. Remove from oven, brush lightly with more butter and serve immediately. *Makes about 1 dozen rolls.*

AUNT CHARITY'S ROSE LEAVES

These crisp little cookies were a favorite with the women of the Christian Missionary Society of Aunt Charity's little church. Many plans were made over tea and these cookies to support missionaries in the field and provide for the needy at Christmastime.

⅓ cup butter or margarine, softened
   at room temperature
2 *cups sugar*
2 *eggs, well beaten*
¼ *teaspoon salt*
1 *teaspon rose extract*
2 *cups all-purpose flour*

Note: Rose extract can be obtained in specialty shops which feature novelty food items.

Preheat oven to 350°F. In a large bowl cream the butter until light; gradually add 1 cup of the sugar, beating until fluffy. Stir in the eggs. Add the salt and rose extract, stirring to blend. Add the flour, mixing well into a soft dough. Cover and refrigerate until chilled, for 30 minutes to 1 hour.

Sprinkle a generous amount of the remaining sugar over a surface suitable for rolling out dough. Cut the chilled dough into thirds; leave 1 portion out to roll and refrigerate the remaining 2 portions. Roll out the portion very thin, adding more sugar if needed to keep dough from sticking. Use small fancy cookie cutters (rose leaves if you can find them) to cut out the cookies. Place on a greased cookie sheet and bake until lightly browned, 8 to 10 minutes. Remove from oven, let cool for a minute or so, then transfer to a wire rack or to an opened brown grocery bag to finish cooling. Repeat with remaining dough portions to make more cookies. Store in an airtight container until ready to serve.

Makes about 4 dozen rose leaves.

EFFIE'S SOFT BUTTTERMILK MOLASSES DROPS WITH RAISINS

Nothing could be better with icy-cold milk than warm and soft old-fashioned molasses drops. Grandpa loved them "too hot to handle," right out of the oven. Freddie wanted his cold so he could "dunk 'um."

1 *cup butter or margarine, softened*	1 *teaspoon salt*
1 *cup sugar*	1 *teaspoon ground ginger*
1 *egg, well beaten*	¼ *teaspoon ground cloves*
½ *cup molasses*	¼ *teaspoon freshly grated nutmeg*
3 *cups all-purpose flour*	1 *cup buttermilk*
1 *tablespoon ground cinnamon*	⅔ *cup golden raisins*
2 *teaspoons baking soda*	

Preheat oven to 375°F. Grease a cookie sheet. In a large bowl, cream the butter until light. Gradually add the sugar, beating until fluffy. Stir in the egg and molasses. In a medium-size bowl, sift together the flour, cinnamon, baking soda, salt, ginger, cloves, and nutmeg. Then alternately add the flour mixture and buttermilk to the butter-sugar mixture, stirring well between additions to make a soft dough. Stir in the raisins. Drop by teaspoonfuls, 2 to 3 inches apart, on the greased cookie sheet. Bake until cookies are well risen, firm to the touch, and browned, about 10 minutes. Remove from the oven and let sit on the cookie sheet for about 3 minutes, then transfer to a wire rack or an opened brown grocery bag to cool. These cookies will keep for about a week if stored in an airtight container.

Makes 6 to 7 dozen cookies.

AUNT CLARY'S "HANDY ANDY"

When Aunty was a girl, rice and raisins were put together in a muslin sack, the top was fastened shut, and the sack was immersed in boiling salt water and simmered until the rice was tender and swelled enough to fill the sack. The sack of cooked rice and raisins, called "Handy Andy," was then set aside in the pantry to chill. After it firmed up and was ready for use, it was removed in one cohesive chunk from the sack, sliced as needed, and served for breakfast or snacks with cream and sugar. The remaining Handy Andy was put back in the sack by some cooks, or by others put in a bowl and covered with a clean dish cloth and returned to the pantry, which would be cool or cold, depending on the time of year. (Such ready-to-eat rice kept quite well for three days or more.)

8 to 10 cups hot water
2 cups long-grained white rice
1 teaspoon salt

Boiling water, for rinsing rice
2 cups raisins (dark preferred)

Bring the hot water to a boil in a large saucepan. Gradually add the rice and salt, stirring only enough to separate the grains. Boil covered for 15 to 20 minutes or until the grains are tender (they should be soft when pressed between your thumb and forefinger). Drain the rice into a strainer; then rinse by passing boiling hot water through the cooked rice to remove excess starch. Add the raisins which will take up some of the moisture and pack both in a bowl. Set aside uncovered to cool; then cover and refrigerate until well chilled and firm. This will last several days if kept refrigerated. *Makes about 8 cups or 10 to 12 breakfast servings.*

ANGELS WE HAVE HEARD ON HIGH

Angels we have heard on high,
Sweetly singing o'er the plains,
And the mountains in reply,
Echoing their joyous strains.

REFRAIN

Gloria in excelsis Deo,
Gloria in excelsis Deo.

Shepherds, why this jubilee?
Why your joyous strains prolong?
What the gladsome tidings be
Which inspire your heav'nly song?

REFRAIN

Come to Bethlehem and see
Him whose birth the angels sing;
Come, adore on bended knee,
Christ the Lord, the newborn King.

REFRAIN

See Him in a manger laid,
Whom the choir of angels praise;
Mary, Joseph, lend your aid,
While our hearts in love we raise.

REFRAIN

FAR FLUNG FROM JUDEAN HILLS

One Sunday morning before Christmas, when my children were small, I settled them down to play with favorite toys and to spend some time with their father while I took a long walk through the pasture and up into the woods.

On a knoll high above the homeplace, I stopped to gaze at mist that hung like freshly carded wool among the mountains surrounding the fingerling valley in which we live and to watch gray-blue clouds scurry across the sky. A cold wind came up, so I threaded my way quickly into the heart of the woods. As I walked among the leaves my tred was almost silent; there was a holiness about the place, as though I was moving through God's first cathedral. In protected spots, white hoarfrost still clung to leaves and mossy ground. My lungs ached a bit with the cold.

As I made my way deeper and deeper in among the trees, my thoughts moved slowly over the natural beauty that surrounded me; probed into the meaning of Christmas and the impact of Christ's birth on mankind; and into the strengths and weaknesses of my own life.

Then a startled wide-eyed doe sprang out of a thicket of wintered madrone. Enraptured, my heart leapt with her. And suddenly I felt as though all disappointments, large and small tragedies, the unfairness of things, and everyday worries were washed away.

🌿 A WILDERNESS CHRISTMAS

In small mountain valleys, above Fish Lake, there are many old cattle ranches, on which ancient houses still stand, sturdy and weather-tight. Originally built of home-cut materials, then roofed with hand-split shakes, these are family seats that have sheltered the same clan through the years.

At Christmas we sometimes go up into the high country, over snowy roads, through avenues lined by giant white-garlanded pine trees to visit our friends, whose lives mirror those of their ancestors. Raymond always stops the car on the rise above their ranch so we can fill our souls with the simplicity of yesteryear. We watch the smoke rise from the low, wide chimneys and know that there is a silent invitation to join the good-hearted family gathered around the glowing, fir-scented fire inside.

We know that the latch string is out, hot coffee is on the stove. The old home, simply furnished, dressed up with holly berries, evergreen boughs, and paper chains, awaits our arrival, so we leave our vantage point high on the snow-covered hill, and make our way into the past, where warm hands reach out to greet us, and loving folk pull us inside:

> *Where the fragrance of the cookin' fire*
> *Perfumes the warm sweet air,*
> *And the womens' laps is filled with babies,*
> *All with golden hair.*

HOMESTEAD ON A HILL TOP

When we were growing up, Mother used to tell us that she, like other country people, had deep roots. And she would talk to us in parables about many things, about family, solidarity, patience, and personal strength, Christian giving, and about Grandpa's English walnut grove.

How, when Grandpa was about fifty years of age, he had first planted whole black walnuts, shell and all, knowing that the root system of this nut could withstand the ravages of time, wind storms, and drought.

Then, when Grandpa was about sixty and the black walnut trees had grown trunks a little thicker than his arm, he topped them and grafted English walnut whips onto the hardy root stock.

The grafts took, and in another ten years, when Grandpa was seventy, his trees were large, with their limbs and leaves forming a canopy over the ground where the golden-shelled nuts dropped.

When Grandpa was in his eighties, he would walk in winter among the trees, slowly, but pleasured by the great trunks, which were rough and black-brown at the bottom, where the black walnut rootstock provided support for the tree, and up above where the great framework of smooth, gray-barked English walnut limbs soared into the sky, perhaps thirty or forty feet.

MA'S BONELESS
BEEF LOIN CUTLETS

When Jack Riley was a little boy on the farm, his mother always celebrated the fall butchering by cooking a good-size platter of beef loin
cutlets (filets mignons). Just a little fella and even more innocent of
fancy French cuts of meat than his mother, Jackie thought it would be
great to "eat them steaks all the time."

When he was a man—full grown and gone from home—his Ma
always managed somehow to talk his Pa into saving something back to
butcher at Christmas time, so she could have a big platter of beef loin
cutlets for when Jack came home.

4 tablespoons fat (butter or
   margarine preferred)
Salt
Black pepper

8 small boneless beef loin cutlets
   (about 4 ounces each), pounded
   to a 1-inch thickness
½ cup milk
⅔ cup all-purpose flour
1 cup dry breadcrumbs

Melt the fat in a heavy skillet. Meanwhile, salt and pepper the cutlets.
Pour the milk into an 8- or 9-inch pie pan; place the flour in another
pan. Dip the meat in the milk, then dredge in the flour, then back into
the milk, then into the breadcrumbs, giving each piece a nice coating.
Place the cutlets, uncrowded, in the hot fat and brown on one side
until the blood rises to the surface, then turn each piece over and brown
on the other side. (Note: breaded meat is not turned twice since it causes
the coating to fall off.) Serve immediately.   Makes 4 man-size servings.

MA'S OLD-FASHIONED POTATO SALAD
WITH HOMEMADE MARINADE
AND BOILED DRESSING

In the old days people called potatoes the "poor man's bread" because
for a field of potatoes the yield was high, much higher than grain of any
kind. The great crops of potatoes, some tubers weighing a pound a piece,
were staple fare, eaten almost everyday.

10 medium-size red potatoes
Homemade Marinade (recipe
   follows)
Boiled Dressing (recipe follows)
   1 cup finely chopped celery
   1 cup chopped sweet pickles

6 hard-cooked eggs, chopped (for
   how to achieve a tender yolk,
   see Note in recipe for Delicious
   Stuffed Eggs, page 213)
1 tablespoon minced fresh parsley

Put the potatoes in a large Dutch oven and cover with boiling water. Return water to a boil. Reduce heat, cover pan, and simmer for 30 minutes or until potatoes are fork tender but not mushy. Drain and set aside to cool until you can handle them.

While the potatoes are cooling, prepare the marinade; set aside. Peel the warm potatoes and cut them into ¼ inch cubes. Place in a large mixing bowl and pour the marinade over the cubes so they will absorb the flavor; gently stir to coat cubes, being careful not to mash them. Cover and refrigerate for several hours, gently stirring now and then to redistribute the marinade.

Now prepare the boiled dressing; cover and refrigerate until ready to use.

Once the potatoes have marinated several hours, but a few hours before serving, assemble the salad by adding the celery, pickles, eggs, and parsley to the undrained marinated potatoes; then add the boiled dressing and stir gently. Refrigerate a few hours so the flavors have time to blend. (*Note:* Today we know that potato salad should always be kept cold to prevent spoilage. It is not really a leave-on-the-table dish; once everyone has been served, return the salad to the refrigerator.

Makes 8 to 10 servings.

Homemade Marinade

½ cup salad oil (*olive oil preferred*)
¼ cup chopped green onions or mild
  sweet onions
¼ cup cider vinegar

2 teaspoons salt
2 teaspoons dry mustard
¼ teaspoon ground cayenne pepper
¼ teaspoon black pepper

Stir all the marinade ingredients together to blend.

Makes 6 to 8 servings.

Boiled Dressing

3 tablespoons sugar
1 tablespoon all-purpose flour
1 tablespoon salt
1¼ cups milk
3 egg yolks
¼ cup cider vinegar

2 tablespoons butter
1 tablespoon finely grated fresh
  horseradish or prepared
  horseradish
1 tablespoon prepared mustard

In a saucepan, combine the sugar, flour, and salt. Place over medium heat and gradually add the milk, stirring constantly until mixture begins to boil; boil about 1 minute, then remove from heat. In a medium-size bowl, beat the egg yolks until light, then gradually add the hot milk mixture, stirring all the while. Return mixture to the saucepan; place over low heat and gradually bring the dressing almost to a boil. Remove from heat. Add the vinegar, butter, horseradish, and mustard. Cover and refrigerate. *Makes about 1½ cups.*

CABBAGE AND FRUIT SALAD WITH ORANGE CREAM DRESSING

In the old days, early December through mid-winter was the time for using vegetables like cabbage, which was stored about the farm in cool places where it would not freeze, apples, which were always stored in great supply in an apple shed, and oranges, which were harvested just before Christmas. This favorite old-time salad takes advantage of such bounty.

About ¾ cup, more if you wish, Orange Cream Dressing (recipe follows)
2 cups shredded white cabbage
1 cup chopped apples (Golden Delicious preferred)

1 cup seeded and cubed orange pulp
½ cup finely chopped celery (cut from the white tender center of the head of celery)
Dash of salt

First prepare the cooked portion of the Orange Cream Dressing; set aside to cool at room temperature.

Combine the cabbage, apples, oranges, and celery in a salad bowl. Now finish the dressing. Add the dash of salt to the salad, then immediately add ¾ cup or more of the dressing, folding until well blended.

Refrigerate until chilled before serving, about 15 minutes.

Makes 6 to 8 servings.

Orange Cream Dressing

3 egg yolks

½ cup sugar

½ cup strained orange juice

5 tablespoons strained lemon juice

Dash of salt

½ cup heavy cream

In the top of a double boiler, beat the egg yolks and sugar together until light; add the orange and lemon juice and the salt (just a few grains). Cook, stirring frequently until the mixture thickens; let cool to room temperature (refrigerate if made well ahead). Just before using, whip the cream and fold it into the cooled egg yolk mixture.

Makes about 1½ cups.

MA'S CHRISTMAS FUDGE BALLS

Jack Riley always thought these rich, fudgy, mouth-watering nut-coated cookies were better than candy. Tom, Jack's youngest, takes two at a time and says, "Yum, Dad!"

1½ cups sifted all-purpose flour

1 cup sugar

½ teaspoon salt

¾ cup butter or margarine, softened

2 ounces unsweetened baking chocolate, melted

¼ cup cold coffee

1½ cups rolled oats (quick-cooking preferred)

1½ cups finely chopped walnuts, more if needed

Preheat oven to 350°F. Into a large bowl, sift together the flour, sugar, and salt. Add the butter, chocolate, and coffee, beating well until smooth, about 2 minutes. Fold in the rolled oats. Roll mixture into balls, using about a tablespoon of dough for each ball (the ball should be about the size of a walnut); roll in the walnuts and place on an ungreased cookie sheet about 1½ to 2 inches apart. Bake until cookies set, about 10 to 12 minutes.

Makes 3 dozen cookies.

In the jolly winters
  Of the long-ago,
It was not so cold as now—
  O! No! No!
Then, as I remember.
  Snowballs to eat
Were as good as apples now.
  And every bit as sweet!

—James Whitcomb Riley

JANE WATSON HOPPING

Memories of Home

Our friend Johanna came to this country about 1918 or 1919, a war-bride from Germany who settled deep in midwestern farm country and who devoted a lifetime to farming with a well-loved husband, to a houseful of children, and to the Lutheran church.

Only at Christmastime was she filled with memories of her home across the sea and the holidays of her childhood. Among the many stories she told about her old-time family Christmases, our favorite was about the *Christkind*—a child dressed in a white robe, wearing a golden crown and having big golden wings, who came to earth at Christmastime as a messenger bringing gifts. Johanna remembers placing a candle in the window when she was a little girl to light him on his way.

As Christmas Eve crept upon us, Johanna gaily recalled the stores, markets, and bazaars of her childhood where one could buy colorful glass balls and all sorts of stars—metal, gold, silver foil, and those made of straw. There were also fairy-tale figures for sale that were carved out of wood and little men made of dried fruit and walnuts.

Johanna would tell us all about the beautiful handmade sweaters, stockings, hats, and scarves her mother and grandmother made for each member of their family, and about the Christmas tree, trimmed with lighted candles, ornaments of glass, polished apples, and gilded nuts.

JOHANNA'S CHRISTMAS STOLLEN (FRUIT LOAF)

On Christmas Eve, Johanna's family gathered about five in the afternoon to eat the *Christstollen*, after which they attended church and came home to open their gifts and share a late supper.

When we visited at Christmastime, we were served wine and *stollen*, which Johanna told us was traditionally kept in German homes for serving to guests over the holidays.

¾ cup milk
½ cup sugar
½ teaspoon salt
1 package dry or granulated yeast
¼ cup warm water (105°F to 115°F)
5 cups all-purpose flour
1 cup golden raisins
1 tablespoon finely grated lemon peel
8 ounces candied cherries, half of them coarsely chopped for cake batter, the remainder left whole for decorating stollen
¼ cup candied orange peel, coarsely chopped
¼ cup candied lemon peel, coarsely chopped

¾ cup candied citron, ½ cup coarsely chopped for cake batter, the remainder slivered for decorating stollen
¾ cup almonds ½ cup finely chopped for cake batter, the remainder cut in half for decorating stollen
1 cup butter or margarine, softened
½ teaspoon ground mace (freshly grated nutmeg may be substituted)
2 eggs, lightly beaten
¼ cup butter or margarine, melted
Easy Powdered Sugar Glaze (recipe follows)

In a small saucepan, heat the milk just until it forms bubbles around the edge of the pan. Remove from heat and add the sugar and salt; stir until dissolved. Cool to lukewarm (until a drop on the wrist feels neither hot nor cold).

Meanwhile, rinse a large bowl in hot water to warm. Pour into it the ¼ cup warm water; sprinkle the yeast over the top and let proof for 5 to 10 minutes. Then stir in the warm milk mixture and *2 cups* of the flour; beat until smooth, about 3 minutes (this develops gluten).

Cover bowl with a clean kitchen towel (without nap); let rise in a warm place until doubled in bulk, about 1 hour and 30 minutes. Meanwhile, grease 2 small cookie sheets; set aside.

To the bowl of risen dough, add the raisins, grated lemon peel, the coarsely chopped candied cherries, and the candied orange and lemon peel, candied citron, the ½ cup finely chopped almonds, the 1 cup softened butter, mace, eggs, and the *remaining 3 cups flour*; mix with a wooden spoon until blended. Turn onto lightly floured surface and knead until fruit and nuts are well distributed, about 5 to 6 minutes.

Divide the dough in half; shape each half into a ball. Roll or pat 1 of the portions into an oval, about 10 inches long and 6 inches wide at the widest part. Brush with *1 tablespoon* of the melted butter and fold dough in half lengthwise. Place on 1 of the prepared cookie sheets. Press down the folded edge of the dough lightly to crease it, then curve it into a crescent shape. Repeat with other portion of dough. Cover *stollens* with towels; let rise in a warm place until doubled in bulk, 1½ to 2 hours.

Preheat oven to 375°F. Bake until nicely browned, about 25 to 30 minutes. Remove from oven and brush top of each with the *remaining 2 tablespoons* melted butter. Transfer to a wire rack to cool. (If making ahead, see *Note* below.)

When thoroughly cooled, glaze with Easy Powdered Sugar Glaze, then while glaze is still soft, immediately decorate tops of *stollen* with flower patterns made of the 4 ounces candied cherries (leave whole or cut in half), strips of slivered citron, and the ¼ cup almond halves.

Makes 2 Stollen.

Note: Stollen may be made the week before Christmas: baked, thoroughly cooled, left unglazed and undecorated, packaged in freezer bags, and stored under refrigeration for at least 5 days. Then just before Christmas, remove from refrigeration, warm to room temperature, glaze and decorate.

Or, make *Stollen* 2 to 3 weeks in advance, package in freezer bags (double wrap) and freeze. When needed, remove from freezer, leave in bags until *Stollen* has warmed to room temperature, then remove from bag, glaze and decorate.

Easy Powdered Sugar Glaze

1 cup powdered sugar, sifted
1 tablespoon cold milk

¼ teaspoon vanilla extract or lemon extract

Place the sugar in a small bowl; add the milk and vanilla and blend until smooth. Use immediately (the glaze will harden as it cools).

Makes enough glaze for 2 Stollen.

DELICIOUS SUGAR PRETZELS

These sweet biscuits were a favorite with Johanna's children, who carried them outside by the handful to share with friends.

1 cup butter (no substitute), softened

⅔ cup sugar, plus ¼ cup for sprinkling on top of pretzels

2 eggs (1 whole, 1 separated)
1 teaspoon finely grated lemon peel
About 2 cups all-purpose flour,
sifted, plus ¼ cup for handling dough
¼ cup almonds, very finely chopped

Cream the butter until light. Gradually add the ⅔ cup sugar and continue beating until light. Mix in the whole egg and egg yolk. Add the lemon peel and beat well. Mix in just enough flour to make a soft dough, using at least 1¾ cups. Wrap the dough in waxed paper or aluminum foil and refrigerate for at least 3 hours. About 30 minutes before ready to shape the dough into pretzels, preheat oven to 375°F and grease a cookie sheet; set aside.

Turn the dough onto a floured surface; shape into long thin rolls and twist into pretzel shapes. Place on the prepared cookie sheet, about 2 inches apart. Beat the egg white into a froth and brush over tops of pretzels; sprinkle with the ¼ cup sugar and almonds. Immediately bake until set but not browned (lightly golden around the bottoms if you wish) about 10 to 12 minutes. Remove from oven and carefully transfer to a wire rack or an opened brown grocery bag to cool. When thoroughly cool, store in airtight container until ready to serve.

Makes about 2 dozen 2-inch pretzels.

SPRINGERLE *(ANISE CAKES)*

The flavor of anise sets these well-known German Christmas cakes apart from all others. Johanna's anise cakes were stamped with wooden molds —which had been passed down to her by her mother—into old-fashioned looking figures and designs. I use her recipe to make these anise cakes, cutting them into 2x1-inch bars, *Springerle* boards (stamps) or rolling pins used to press the design into the center of the cakes are available at gourmet shops.

4 eggs
2 cups sifted sugar
2 teaspoons finely grated lemon peel
About 4 cups all-purpose flour
1 teaspoon baking powder
½ teaspoon salt
1 tablespoon anise seed

In a large bowl, beat the eggs until light and lemon colored. Gradually add the sugar, about ⅓ cup at a time, beating well after each addition until creamy. Add lemon rind, stir a few strokes to blend. Then slowly add *1 cup* flour sifted with baking powder and salt; stirring to blend.

Then add *2½ cups* of the flour, beating just to blend. Turn the dough onto a lightly floured board and knead in enough of the remaining flour to stiffen dough. Refrigerate until well chilled, about 3 hours. Preheat oven to 325°F. Sprinkle a greased cookie sheet with the anise seeds; set aside.

Roll out the chilled dough to about ¼ inch thick, shaping it into a square or rectangle as you roll it. Using a 1-foot ruler to measure and a sharp knife, cut dough into 1x2-inch cookies. Place the cookies on the prepared cookie sheet, about 1½ inches apart. Bake until bottoms are golden but now brown, about 15 minutes. Remove from oven and let cool about 1 minute on the cookie sheet, then transfer to a wire rack or an opened brown paper bag to cool. Mellow for a few days or for a few weeks in an airtight container if you wish.   *Makes about 5 dozen cookies.*

When snow is here, and the trees look weird,
  And the knuckled twigs are gloved with
    frost;
When the breath congeals in the drover's beard,
  And the old pathway to the barn is lost;
When the rooster's crow is sad to hear,
  And the stamp of the stabled horse is vain,
And the tone of the cow-bell grieves the ear—
  O then is the time for a brave refrain!

When the gears hang stiff on the harness-peg,
  And the tallow gleams in frozen streaks;
And the old hen stands on a lonesome leg,
  And the pump sounds hoarse and the handle
    squeaks;
When the wood-pile lies in a shrouded heap,
  And the frost is scratched from the window-pane
And anxious eyes from the inside peep—
  O then is the time for a brave refrain!

—James Whitcomb Riley

🌿 A Christmas Blizzard

"You can never really get ready for a blizzard," our uncle Joseph Lawton used to say.

"You can sort of feel her though. She follows a bit of warm winter weather and comes in from way up North down over eastern Canada, blowin' in an icy-cold wind and lots of snow. The wind just sort o' goes clear through ya till you can't stand against it no more. I seen men blinded by the blowin' snow and bits of ice, till they lost their way and froze to death. Cattle or sheep move on ahead of the wind and pile up in fence rows and freeze.

"Sometimes there aint nothin' you can do, just don't go out in her any more than you have to. Ya gotta tie a rope to the barn so you don't go off in the wrong direction and freeze yerself. Seems like yer lucky if you can just keep the milk cow and the pigs and hens from freezin' up. I remember many a time we just sort 'o set her out and then counted our losses when it was over.

"One year, when Bud was about ten, we had this blizzard come in on Christmas Eve and hang around all the next day 'fore she let up any. We jest stayed in where it was warm and waited her out. The women went on with the cookin' and us men and boys played a little cards."

AUNT CLARY'S PORK CHOPS WITH WHOLE-WHEAT SAGE DRESSING

While this recipe serves only four to six, I can remember when Aunt Clary dished up enough chops to please seven men, five women, and an assortment of children.

4 to 6 pork chops, cut 1 inch thick
1 teaspoon salt
¼ teaspoon black pepper

Whole-Wheat Sage Dressing (recipe follows)

Preheat oven to 350°F. Grease an 11x7x1½-inch baking pan. Cut off all the extra fat from the chops and cube it. In a heavy frying pan render the cubes of fat without burning them. Remove any fat that does not liquefy and use the rendered fat for frying the chops as follows: Make 2 or 3 gashes along the fat edge of each chop so the meat doesn't curl during cooking. Arrange the chops in the frying pan with the hot fat and turn the heat down to medium; season chops on both sides with the salt and pepper and brown on both sides without cooking through. Transfer to a plate and cover to keep warm. Now prepare the dressing with about 3 tablespoons of the pan drippings.

When the dressing is ready, place it in a lightly greased 7¾x3⅝x2¼-inch baking pan and arrange the chops on top. Bake until meat is done, about 35 minutes. Serve with a zesty salad made with whatever leafy vegetables are available in winter—such as cabbage, swiss chard, and tender bits of kale—and dress with vinaigrette. *Makes 4 to 6 servings.*

Whole-Wheat Sage Dressing

About 3 tablespoons reserved pan
 drippings
½ medium-size onion, chopped
¾ cup chopped celery
2 cups Homemade Chicken Broth
 (page 201) or hot water
2 tablespoons chopped fresh parsley

½ teaspoon ground sage
½ teaspoon dried sweet marjoram
 leaves, pulverized
⅛ teaspoon celery seed
4 cups whole-wheat bread, cut into
 cubes (leave crust on)

In the drippings cook the onion and celery until clear but not browned.
Add the stock, parsley, sage, marjoram, and celery seed, then the cubed
bread. Remove from heat and stir to blend.   *Makes about 4–6 cups.*

SWEET AND SOUR
RED CABBAGE WITH APPLES

Grandma Meekins was Pennsylvania Dutch. We've always believed she
taught her Gaelic in-laws—including Aunt Clary—how to make this
"sweet and sour" cabbage.

Red cabbage is excellent when cooked with wine, vinegar, or lemon
juice; the acid not only enhances the flavor but sets the color.

1 (3-pound) head of red cabbage,
 shredded
¾ cup boiling water
3 large tart apples, pared, cored,
 and sliced
¼ cup vinegar

¼ cup, packed, light brown sugar
3 tablespoons butter, melted
2 teaspoons salt
1½ teaspoons all-purpose flour
Black pepper, to taste

Place the cabbage in the bottom of a large heavy skillet and add the
water; bring to a simmer and cook for 10 minutes. Arrange the apples
on top of the cabbage; combine the vinegar, sugar, butter, salt, flour,
and pepper in a small bowl and pour over the cabbage. Continue simmering until the apples are tender, about 10 minutes more. Cover while
the apples cook, if you wish.   *Makes about 6 servings.*

EXCELLENT PARKER HOUSE ROLLS

When I was a child, it seemed that no lady's holiday dinner was complete without a breadbasketful of hot Parker House rolls.

2 packages dry or granulated yeast
¼ cup warm water
2 cups milk
⅓ cup butter
4 tablespoons butter or margarine,
    melted (for brushing tops
    of rolls)

¼ cup plus 1 tablespoon sugar
2 teaspoons salt
About 6½ to 7 cups all-purpose
    flour

Soften the yeast with 1 tablespoon of the sugar in the warm water; set aside. Meanwhile, heat the milk so that it will be warm enough to melt the butter. Add the ⅓ cup butter, ¼ cup sugar and salt; stir until butter is melted and sugar dissolved. Set aside and cool to lukewarm. Test by dropping a little on the inside of the wrist; if it feels warm but not hot (105° to 115°F), add the yeast and 2 cups of the flour; beat thoroughly. Cover and let rise in a warm place until doubled in size, about 1 hour.

Then add enough of the remaining flour (this will take about 4 cups) to make a firm dough. Turn onto a smooth floured surface. Knead, using just enough remaining flour to coat the dough so that it does not stick to the hands. When the dough is elastic to the touch and has a satin sheen, place in a lightly greased bowl; cover and let rise again until doubled in bulk.

Knead again, then roll the dough ¼ inch thick and cut out with a large round cutter. Brush each round with some of the 4 tablespoons melted butter. Crease across the centers of each round with the back of a knife and fold round in half. Place rolls on a greased baking sheet about 1 inch apart. Cover and set in warm place to rise again until doubled in bulk before baking.

Bake in a preheated 400°F oven until light golden brown, 15 to 20 minutes.   *Makes about 2 dozen large rolls.*

UNCLE BUD'S CREAMY PUMPKIN PIE
WITH HONEY AND SPICE WHIPPED CREAM

From the time he was a boy, no one could eat as much pumpkin pie as Uncle Bud. In fact, we all knew to make an extra one when he was coming to supper. For him dessert time stretched clear into the evening, while everyone teased him about his tall, lanky fat-free frame and took a certain perverse pleasure in watching him savor one piece of pie with whipped cream after another.

Flaky Pastry Dough (recipe
  follows)
3 eggs
¾ cup, packed, light brown sugar
1½ cups cooked and strained
    pumpkin (canned pumpkin
    will do)
1 cup heavy cream
2 teaspoons ground cinnamon
½ teaspoon freshly grated nutmeg
½ teaspoon ground ginger
½ teaspoon salt
Honey and Spice Whipped Cream
  (recipe follows)

Preheat oven to 450°F. Prepare the pastry dough; cover and refrigerate while you prepare the filling.

In a large bowl, beat the eggs until thick and lemon-colored. Gradually add the sugar, beating until sugar dissolves. Stir in the cream, pumpkin, cinnamon, nutmeg, ginger, and salt. Set aside while you roll out the chilled dough.

Turn dough onto a floured surface and roll out and fit into a 9-inch pie pan; flute the edges.

Pull the oven rack about halfway out of the hot oven. Pour two thirds of the filling into the dough-lined pie pan; then set the pan in the center of the oven rack and pour in the remaining filling. Gently push the rack in place. Bake the pie at 450°F for 15 minutes; then reduce oven setting to 300°F and continue baking until a knife inserted in the center comes out clean, about 45 minutes more. Serve warm or cold with a dollop of Honey Spiced Whipped Cream. *Makes about 6 servings.*

Flaky Pastry Dough
1 cup all-purpose flour, plus flour
  for rolling out dough
½ teaspoon salt
½ cup cold butter
2 to 4 tablespoons cold water

Sift the flour and salt together into a large bowl. Cut the butter in, using a pastry blender or two dinner knives, or rub butter into the flour with your fingertips until all pieces of dough are the size of small peas. Gradually sprinkle just enough water to hold the pastry together, mixing lightly and quickly with a fork after each addition. (This leads to a flakier pie crust.) Turn dough onto a floured surface and form into a ball. Wrap in aluminum foil or waxed paper and refrigerate until needed.

Honey and Spice Whipped Cream
½ cup heavy cream
2 tablespoons honey, at room
  temperature
⅛ teaspoon ground cinnamon
Pinch of ground ginger
⅛ teaspoon ground nutmeg

Whip the cream until soft mounds form; add the honey, cinnamon, nutmeg, and ginger. Continue beating just until mounds of cream are firm enough to hold their shape. *Makes about 1 cup.*

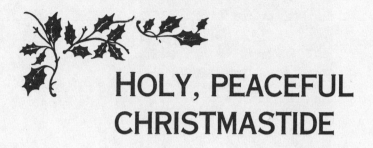

HOLY, PEACEFUL CHRISTMASTIDE

Perhaps the most beautiful piece of Christmas music performed all across the nation is George Frideric Handel's *Messiah*. Born in Halle, Germany, in 1685, Handel as a young boy was recognized for his musical genius. At twelve he played at the court of the king of Prussia. Later, despite the protests of Handel's father, who wanted him to become a lawyer, Handel played in the opera orchestra in Hamburg. Then, after years of study in Italy, he settled in England, where his musical career blossomed.

It was not until 1742 that his greatest oratorio, *Messiah*, was first performed—in Dublin, Ireland, with Handel himself conducting. He composed his masterpiece in less than twenty-five days, to be performed at a benefit program for the Dublin Foundling Hospital.

At the first performance in England the following year, King George II was so inspired by the beauty of the "Hallelujah Chorus" that he rose to his feet, as did the audience, and remained standing until the chorus ended, establishing a custom that is still followed today.

CHRISTMAS

When the days grow shorter
And the snow doth fall,
Children we hear singing,
"Christ he loveth all."

Then we hang our stockings
By the fireside,
And the children whisper,
"It is Christmas-tide."

—Katharine R. Welles
(age 10)

Earth's Hopes Awaken

At Christmastime around the turn of the century, when a young preacher (an educated man and not just a called-to-speak-the-word-of-God man) came to tend the flock, great effort was made to bring a choral group from the city to perform Handel's *Messiah* for the members of the little country church.

The farm folk, both excited about the special program the city preacher had arranged for them and also a bit pessimistic about the newfangled music, rushed about decking the church out in holly and evergreen wreaths; getting their chores done early; dressing in their

Sunday best; and finally hooking up the buggy and making sure everyone was in it.

The church was full, the women had seen to that. Children sat quietly, their mothers' hands on arms or shoulders. Fathers sat looking uncomfortable, black high-crowned hats gripped in work-twisted hands.

But with the first glorious sound of music, a hush quieter than lack of sound fell on the company. The folks, young and old, listened attentively as the singing dipped and swelled. Then, as the "Hallelujah Chorus" rang out, causing the rafters to tremble in adulation, well-worn hands went up in praise of God. Touched beyond belief, they recognized in the music the high praise to Him whom they loved.

Later, when the program was over, they spoke shyly to the chorus members and choral master and softly to each other, awed—not a little bit—by what they had just witnessed. Still wrapped in the music's beauty, unable to easily express themselves, and more or less unaware of the august origin of the music, they nibbled their cookies and drank their tea until they could slip off to more comfortable surroundings and talk and talk and talk about the fine Christmas program and the beautiful music.

CREAMY SOFT MOLASSES DROPS

The fragrance of these cookies always reminded Aunt Clary of home, of the crunch of snow beneath her feet as she went out to the barn to do chores, of the whisper of straw beneath the feet of the restless milk cow, eager to get back to a nuzzling calf. But most of all, the spicy aroma reminded her of family, of love and laughter, and cheerful greetings of friends.

3 cups all-purpose flour	¾ cup light cream
2 teaspoon baking soda	¾ tablespoon vinegar
2 teaspoons ground cinnamon	1 cup butter or margarine
1 teaspoon salt	1 cup sugar
1 teaspoon ground ginger	1 egg, well beaten
½ teaspoon ground cloves	½ cup molasses
½ teaspoon freshly grated nutmeg	

Preheat oven to 375°F. Into a medium-size bowl, sift together the flour, baking soda, cinnamon, salt, ginger, cloves, and nutmeg; sift again and set aside. Combine the cream and vinegar; set aside until vinegar begins to thicken the cream, about 5 minutes.

Meanwhile, in a large bowl cream together the butter and sugar until light. Beat in the egg and molasses. Alternately add the cream-vinegar mixture and flour-spice mixture to the butter-sugar mixture, stirring until well blended. Drop the batter by teaspoonfuls onto a greased cookie sheet, about 2 to 3 inches apart. Bake until golden brown and firm to the touch, about 10 minutes. Transfer to a wire rack or to an opened brown grocery bag to cool thoroughly, then store in an airtight container until ready to serve. *Makes about 6½ dozen cookies.*

ADA'S GRAHAM WAFERS

This old-time recipe was popular at the turn of the century. As a child, Ada copied it from her grandmother's cookbook. Ada often baked these cookies to take to church affairs.

½ cup butter or margarine	2 tablespoons warm water
½ cup, packed, light brown sugar	½ cup milk
1 egg, lightly beaten	1 teaspoon vanilla extract
1 teaspoon baking soda	2½ cups whole-wheat flour

Preheat oven to 350°F. Lightly grease a cookie sheet. In a large bowl, cream the butter and sugar together until light. Add the egg, stirring to blend. In a small bowl, dissolve the baking soda in the warm water; stir in the milk and vanilla and add to the butter-sugar mixture, stirring until thoroughly blended. Gradually add the flour, mixing well. Turn dough onto a smooth floured surface; shape into a ball, then pat out to flatten. Roll out to ⅛ inch thick and cut into 3x2-inch bars; place on the prepared cookie sheet. Bake until golden, about 15 minutes. Remove from oven and transfer to a wire rack to cool thoroughly. Store in airtight container until ready to serve. *Makes about 4 dozen cookies.*

LEMON CRISP COOKIES

Mother always made these crispy lemon cookies at Christmastime. I can still remember peeking out the back door, watching for Daddy and Grandpa to come in so we could surprise them. The cookies were so light and crispy that they were more suited to a ladies' tea or a special church or school doin's than to the cold, rough hands of country men who ate them by the handfuls and washed them down with hot coffee.

½ cup butter or margarine, softened	2 teaspoons finely grated lemon peel
1 cup sugar	1 egg, well beaten
1 teaspoon lemon juice	2 cups sifted all-purpose flour

1 teaspoon baking powder
⅛ teaspoon salt
1 egg white, whipped until foamy

Preheat oven to 375°F. Cream the butter and sugar in a medium-size bowl. Stir in the lemon juice and lemon peel. Add the whole egg, beating well. Into a large bowl sift together the flour, baking powder, and salt. Gradually add the dry ingredients to the butter-sugar mixture, beating until a smooth dough is formed. Cover and chill for about 30 minutes. Remove from the refrigerator and shape into a log about 1¾ inches in diameter. Cover and chill overnight. (It's important to chill the dough thoroughly so the butter stays in it when baked.)

The next day, slice the log of dough crosswise into ⅛-inch-thick cookies and place about 1 inch apart on an ungreased cookie sheet. Brush tops with the egg white for a smooth golden brown surface. Bake until lightly browned, about 10 minutes. Remove from oven and immediately transfer to an opened brown grocery bag to cool. Store in an airtight container until ready to serve.   *Makes about 1½ dozen cookies.*

THE CHRISTMAS LONG AGO

Come, sing a hale Heigh-ho
    For the Christmas long ago!—
When the old log-cabin homed us
    From the night of blinding snow,
    Where the rarest joy held reign,
    And the chimney roared amain,
With the firelight like a beacon
    Through the frosty window-pane.

Ah! the revel and the din
    From without and from within,
The blend of distant sleigh-bells
    With the plinking violin;
    The muffled shrieks asnd cries—
    Then the glowing cheeks and eyes—
The driving storm of greetings,
    Gusts of kisses and surprise.

JANE WATSON HOPPING

Sing—sweetest of all glees—
Of the taffy-makers, please,—
And, round the saucers in the snow,
　　The children thick as bees;

And sing each chubby cheek,
Chin and laughing lip astreak
With still a sweeter sweetness than
　　The tongue of Song can speak.

Sing in again the mirth
Of the circle round the hearth,
With the rustic Sinbad telling us
　　The strangest tales on earth!
And the Minstrel Bard we knew,
With his "Love-i-er so True,"
Likewise his "Young House-K-yarpen-ter,"
　　And "Loved Henry," too!

And, forgetting ne'er a thing,
Lift a gladder voice and sing
Of the dancers in the kitchen—
　　Clean from start to "pigeon-wing"!
Sing the glory and the glee
And the joy and jubilee,—
The twirling form—the quickened breath—
　　The sigh of ecstasy.—

The eyes that smile alone
Back into our happy own—
The leaping pulse—the laughing blood—
　　The trembling undertone!—
Ho! pair us off once more,
With our feet upon the floor
And our heads and hearts in heaven,
　　As they were in days of yore!

　　　　　　　　—James Whitcomb Riley

❧ WHEN THE OLD
LOG CABIN HOMED US

About 1900, Grandpa and Grandma Meekins loaded up their possessions and three small children—my Aunt Mable, Uncle Arch, and Uncle Ben—and moved into the wilderness, onto railroad land. Mother believes that there was some sort of lease on the land, but she also recalls that in those days there was a lot of open country everyplace. Towns were few.

Skilled at all the rural trades, among them farming and carpentry, Grandpa built a sturdy log cabin on the property for his family—the cabin in which Mother was born. By the time Mother was two or three years old, he had "proved up" the place, building a few outbuildings and a great swing for Grandma, one that she could swing high enough in to look out over the cabin into the woods beyond.

While Grandpa always talked fondly of those years in the wilderness, he longed to move to Rockville, where his parents lived. He was the youngest of their thirteen children, and his mother and father wanted him to bring his family and come home. His father and mother were getting older, the grandchildren were growing up unknown to them, and the hundred miles between them made them seem like they were a world away. So, when Mother was three and Aunt Hattie was a baby, they moved to Rockville, north and east along the Missouri Pacific Line (a railroad line) into farm country by the Osage River.

Mother barely remembers that first Christmas with her Grandparents. But Aunt Mable, who was several years older, remembers a handsome grandfather with graying red hair who held her on his knee and called her his little darling and some other word—maybe an Irish word whose meaning she never knew.

AUNT MAE'S BURNT SUGAR CAKE WITH BURNT SUGAR FROSTING

This recipe is an old one—very traditional and delicious.

3 tablespoons Burnt Sugar Syrup (recipe follows)	1¾ cups sugar
3 cups cake flour	1⅓ cups milk
1 tablespoon baking powder	1 scant tablespoon vanilla extract
½ teaspoon salt	4 egg whites, beaten into stiff peaks
¾ cup butter or margarine, softened	Burnt Sugar Frosting (recipe follows)

Preheat oven to 350°F. Line the bottoms of two 9-inch round cake pans with waxed paper, then grease the paper. Make the Burnt Sugar Syrup; set aside.

Sift together the flour, baking powder, and salt 3 times, ending with it in a medium-size bowl. Cream the butter; gradually add the sugar, beating until light and fluffy. In a small bowl, combine the milk, Burnt Sugar Syrup, and vanilla. Stir into the butter-sugar mixture sifted flour alternately with flavored milk. Lightly fold the egg whites into the batter, being careful not to decrease batter's volume. Gently spoon into the prepared pans. Bake until golden brown and firm to the touch, about 25 to 30 minutes. Remove cake layers to a wire rack. Once thoroughly cool, fill and frost the cake. *Makes one 2-layer cake.*

Burnt Sugar Syrup
½ cup granulated sugar
⅓ cup boiling water

Place ½ cup granulated sugar in a heavy-bottomed frying pan; cook over medium heat until sugar becomes a bubbly rich golden brown syrup. Remove from heat. Very carefully add ⅓ cup boiling water to the sugar (the water will make the syrup boil up). Set aside until needed.

Makes about 6 tablespoons.

Burnt Sugar Frosting
3 tablespoons Burnt Sugar Syrup   A few grains of salt
   (preceding recipe)   2 egg whites
1 cup sugar   1 teaspoon vanilla extract
1 teaspoon cream of tartar

In the top of a double boiler, combine the Burnt Sugar Syrup, sugar, cream of tartar, salt, and egg whites. Place over boiling water and beat with a rotary beater for 5 minutes. Add the vanilla and continue beating 2 minutes more. Remove from heat and use immediately.

Makes enough frosting for one 2-layer cake.

MARTIN'S PEANUT BUTTER CAKE

Some sixty-two years ago, when Martin was a little boy, he loved peanut butter. Far too often his mother would find him hidden in the pantry dipping it out of the jar with his fingers, getting at least three quarters of it into his mouth, the rest all over his hands, face, and clothes. Needless to say, the craving never left him, thus this rich sheet cake, which really needs little or no frosting.

3 cups sifted all-purpose flour
1 tablespoon baking powder
½ teaspoon salt
1 teaspoon vanilla extract
1 cup milk
2 eggs, lightly beaten
2 cups, packed, light brown sugar

1 cup peanut butter (crunchy preferred), at room temperature
½ cup butter or margarine, softened at room temperature
Simple Powdered Sugar Glaze (page 24) or Fudge Frosting (page 61), optional

Preheat oven to 350°F. Grease a 13x9x2-inch baking pan; set aside.

Into a medium-size bowl, sift together the flour, baking powder, and salt; set aside. Add the vanilla to the milk; stir in the eggs and set aside.

In a large bowl, combine the sugar, peanut butter, and butter, beating until light. Stir in the flavored milk alternately with the flour mixture, beating after each addition. Turn into the prepared pan. Bake until golden brown and firm to the touch, about 45 minutes.

Remove from oven and let cake cool in the pan set on a wire rack. Serve frosted or unfrosted with piping hot coffee.

Makes 1 large sheet cake.

EFFIE'S HONEY WHOLE-WHEAT ROLLS "PLUS"

When Effie brought rolls to the Christmas parties, we never knew quite what to expect, plain or "plus." The plain rolls were delicious, but Effie loved to stir things into the basic batter, like one or two tablespoons poppy, cardamom, caraway, anise, dill, or sesame seed, or a half-tablespoon*—more or less—of crumbled herbs. If she was really in a creative cooking mood, she might add a cup of shredded sharp cheese to the yeast-milk mixture and two tablespoons caraway seed as the dough was being finished.

Such honey whole-wheat rolls "plus" were always a favorite with the men and boys.

2 tablespoons dry or granulated yeast

2 cups lukewarm milk (105°F to 115°F)

⅓ cup honey, at room temperature
4 tablespoons butter, melted
2 eggs, lightly beaten
1 teaspoon salt

2½ cups unbleached all-purpose
flour
2 cups whole-wheat flour
1 tablespoon cardamom, caraway,
anise, or dill seed

Dissolve the yeast in the milk; let it sit until it has a frothy head before adding the honey, butter, eggs, and salt; stir together. Add the flours and beat with a large spoon until light (give it 250 strokes to develop the gluten). Scrape the batter from the sides of the bowl, cover bowl with a clean kitchen towel, and let rise in a warm place (about 80°F) until light and bubbly, about 30 minutes.

Meanwhile, preheat oven to 400°F and grease two 12-cup muffin pans. When the batter is well risen, stir down and beat again, using 10 to 15 strokes. Spoon into the prepared muffin cups. Bake until tops are golden brown and sound hollow when tapped lightly, about 25 to 30 minutes. Remove from oven and let rolls sit in the pans for about 8 minutes, then remove gently as they are quite light. Serve piping hot with butter that's been softened to room temperature and creamed. These rolls freeze well and reheat nicely for later use.

Makes 2 dozen rolls.

ALLSPICE TEA WITH HONEY

This richly flavored tea is ideal for use in winter because it warms you up. Mother sometimes made a cup or two at bedtime, but usually we sipped it while the family sat together at the table after a large Sunday or holiday meal.

To make the tea: Fill a teapot with freshly boiled water; allow it to stand in the pot until pot is well heated, then pour it out.

Measure allspice into the heated teapot, allowing ¼ *teaspoon ground allspice for each pint of boiling water* (don't use chemically treated water for tea). Measure and pour the boiling hot water over the allspice. Cover with the lid and a cozy (a small knitted or crocheted cover made for a teapot to keep it hot). Steep for 3 minutes. Sweeten with *honey* and serve piping hot.

A SONG FOR CHRISTMAS

Chant me a rhyme of Christmas
Sing me a jovial song—
And though it is filled with laughter,
Let it be pure and strong.

Let it be clear and ringing,
And though it mirthful be,
Let a low, sweet voice of pathos
Run through the melody.

Sing of the hearts brimmed over
  With the story of the day—
Of the echo of childish voices
  That will not die away.—

Of the blare of the tasseled bugle,
  And the timeless clatter and beat
Of the drum that throbs to muster
  Squadrons of scampering feet.

But O let your voice fall fainter,
  Till, blent with a minor tone,
You temper your song with the beauty
  Of the pity Christ hath shown:

—James Whitcomb Riley

Chant Me a Rhyme of Christmas

When we were growing up, our family loved to sing and dance. Most of us not only played instruments (banjos, guitars, fiddles, and mandolins), but could make them ourselves. The music was old—some of it so old no one knew who had written it—but the stories told were as new as yesterday, all about what people felt, and did, their transgressions and loves.

My grandfather played the mandolin and his voice was a clear, lovely tenor. When I was young, I would beg him to sing about star-crossed lovers, about camp meetings, and about one Christmas on Snowy Mountain when the creeks all flooded and young Alexander Dunbarton searched the mountains over, looking for his lost sweetheart, finally to find her in the woods, cold but alive. And how she had told him that an angel had stood guard over her the whole night through.

MAUD'S EXCELLENT
LEMON MINCEMEAT PIE
WITH FLAKY VINEGAR PASTRY

This favorite all-fruit Christmas mince pie is richly flavored and a delicious complement to a ham dinner. Maud often served a dinner of baked sweet potatoes, coleslaw, honey wheat rolls, home-canned string beans, and homemade pickles, and then, as a final treat, this pie.

Maud's Excellent Lemon Mincemeat
  (recipe follows)
Flaky Vinegar Pastry Dough (recipe
  follows)

Flour, for rolling out dough
2 recipes Sweetened Whipped Cream
  (page 60), optional

Prepare the mincemeat; let stand to mellow overnight in a cool place (refrigerate if you wish). The following day, prepare the pastry dough and chill for at least 30 minutes, before assembling the pie and baking it.

To assemble and bake the pie: Preheat oven to 400°F. Remove the pastry dough from the refrigerator; cut into 4 equal portions. On a floured surface, roll out 2 portions and line two 9-inch pie pans with them. Spoon half the mincemeat into each pie shell. Roll out the top crusts; then moisten edges of bottom crusts with a little cold water and cover filling with top crusts. Crimp the edges with a wide-tined fork and cut away any extra pastry from edges.

Bake at 400° for 20 minutes; then reduce oven setting to 350° and continue baking until pie is nicely browned, about 25 minutes longer. Remove from oven. Serve warm or at room temperature with a dollop of Sweetened Whipped Cream, if you like.   *Makes two 9-inch pies.*

Maud's Excellent Lemon Mincemeat

2 large lemons
2 large apples, peeled and chopped
½ cup butter, softened
1¾ cups sugar
1 teaspoon salt
1 teaspoon ground cinnamon
1 teaspoon ground ginger
½ teaspoon freshly grated nutmeg

½ teaspoon ground allspice
¼ teaspoon ground cloves
1 pound golden raisins (preferred)
  or dark raisins
½ cup candied lemon peel
½ cup light currants (dark if you
  can't find light)
½ cup chopped or slivered almonds

Extract the juice from the lemons and remove seeds; set juice aside. Put the lemon rinds in a medium-size saucepan, cover with water, and boil (changing the water twice) until the rinds are quite tender; drain. Pound rind into a paste with a potato masher and place in a bowl. Add the apples, butter, and sugar, stirring to blend. Stir in the reserved lemon juice. Add the salt, cinnamon, ginger, nutmeg, allspice, and cloves; stir to blend. Stir in the raisins, candied lemon peel, currants, and almonds. Put in a jar with a tight cover.   *Makes 6 to 8 cups.*

Flaky Vinegar Pastry Dough

3 cups all-purpose flour
1 teaspoon salt
1½ cups cold butter or margarine

1 egg, well beaten
5 tablespoons cold water
1 teaspoon white vinegar

Place the flour and salt in a large bowl and stir to blend. With a pastry blender or 2 kitchen knives, cut the butter into the flour until mixture is reduced to grains about the size of peas. In a small bowl, combine the egg, cold water, and vinegar, stirring well. Gradually add the liquid ingredients, tablespoon by tablespoon, to the flour mixture; stir with a fork until all the dry ingredients are moistened and mixture begins to hold together. Turn dough onto a lightly floured surface and knead just 2 or 3 times, then shape into a ball. Refrigerate at least 30 minutes before rolling out.   *Makes enough dough for 2 double-crusted pies.*

OLF-FASHIONED DATE AND NUT SMASH

This traditional candy is delicious and always wins praises for the candymaker. Use roasted pecans if you have them; if not, walnuts will do nicely. (Mother always preferred pecans in a Christmas batch.)

2 cups sugar
½ cup milk
1 cup dates, finely chopped
½ cup finely chopped roasted
   pecans or walnuts, plus ½ cup
   very finely chopped roasted nuts
   in which to roll the candy
1 tablespoon butter (no substitutes)
1 tablespoon vanilla extract

Combine the sugar and milk in a small saucepan and cook until it forms a soft ball when dropped into cold water (ball will hold its shape in water but flatten when removed), or until temperature reads between 234°F and 240°F on a candy thermometer. Remove from heat and add the dates, the ½ cup finely chopped nuts, and the butter and vanilla; stir until candy becomes very thick, pour out onto a thin tightly woven cotton cloth that has been dampened with cold water. Roll candy in the cloth from side to side until it is formed into a 1½-inch log. Next, roll in the ½ cup very finely chopped nuts; set aside on a piece of waxed paper or aluminum foil to cool, then cut into ½ inch slices.
Makes about 1 pound of candy.

SYTHA JANE'S SUGARED WALNUT MEATS

When Mother was a little girl, costly oranges were tucked into Christmas stockings to the delight of farm boys and girls who rarely saw them.

Frugal women of the day would gather up all of the peelings for candying or grating. And as they dropped them into fruited cake batters, or used them in recipes like this, the essence of Christmas could be savored all year.

1 cup, packed, light brown sugar	1 teaspoon vanilla extract
6 tablespoons heavy cream	3 cups walnut halves
1 teaspoon finely grated orange peel	Ground cinnamon
Pinch of salt	

Lay out a sheet of waxed paper. In a large saucepan, combine the sugar, cream, orange peel, and salt; stir until sugar dissolves. Cook to a soft-ball stage (234°F to 240°F). Remove from heat, add the vanilla and walnuts, and stir until the syrup is sugary; then immediately turn onto the waxed paper, quickly separate the nuts with a spoon before candy hardens, and sprinkle lightly with cinnamon.   *Makes about 3 cups.*

A CHILD'S CHRISTMAS CAROL

Christ used to be like you and me,
When just a lad in Galilee,—
So when we pray, on Christmas Day,
He favors first the prayers we say:
Then waste no tear, but pray with cheer,
This gladdest day of all the year:

O Brother mine of birth Divine,
Upon this natal day of Thine
Bear with our stress of happiness
Nor count our reverence the less
Because with glee and jubilee
Our hearts go singing up to Thee.

—James Whitcomb Riley

Our friend Ella Leone Ryland when she was twelve

🌿 WHERE OUR CHILDHOOD MEMORIES DWELL

As an unknown poet wrote:

> *All is well, we're home for Christmas*
> *Where our childhood memories dwell.*

For most of us, there is nothing like being home again for Christmas with the family gathered all about us. Dad enthroned in his old chair, festooned with children, Mother in the kitchen finishing preparations for Christmas dinner, unused to so much help. From room to room the faces have grown older, children taller, babies have been born. Even so, family bonds seem to grow stronger each year as we seem to collectively mature and as old jealousies, hurt feelings, and disappointments fade.

Glances fly from adult to adult and smiles break through as they share the joy in hearing the children's laughter and watching as the little ones scurry here and there, eyes beaming, eager to help, trying to be "little angels" for a day which delightfully reflects the warmth of the season.

Then, when the last part of the work is done, there is a pleasant kind of laughter among the women, a glow as one looks about. The tree is the best ever with its star shining on top, and there are presents from everyone to everyone piled clear out onto the floor. At the last moment daughters flurry about putting things back in place for Mother. The turkey roasting in the oven sends out promises of feasting to come, the sideboard is loaded, salads are chilling ready to be dressed, and Mother's rolls, tucked into pans and rising in a warm spot, will soon be ready for last-minute baking.

AUNT EL'S VINEGAR COOKIES

When Auntie dropped these cookies by teaspoonfuls onto the cookie sheet, she called them "mock lemon drops." If she rolled them into small balls and pressed them down into flat cookies she called them "vinegar cookies." We could never tell the difference, but thought her cookies were "melt-in-your-mouth special."

3 cups butter or margarine
3 cups sugar
3 eggs, well beaten
6 tablespoons cider vinegar
1 teaspoon vanilla extract

1 teaspoon lemon extract
7½ cups sifted all-purpose flour, placed in a large bowl
1 tablespoon salt
1½ teaspoons baking soda

Preheat oven to 350°F. In a large bowl, cream the butter and sugar. Add the eggs, vinegar, vanilla extract and lemon extract; stir to blend. To the flour add the salt and baking soda; stir thoroughly to blend, then sift mixture into the butter-sugar mixture and stir into a firm dough. Roll into walnut-size balls. Bake on an ungreased cookie sheet until set and very lightly colored, about 8 to 10 minutes. (Note: These cookies are almost white, even the bottom should be only very lightly browned.) Remove from oven and immediately transfer to a wire rack or to an opened brown grocery bag to cool. Once cool, store in an airtight container until ready to serve. *Makes 6 to 7 dozen cookies.*

OLD-FASHIONED
APPLESAUCE FRUITCAKES

Our family preferred these easy-to-make applesauce fruitcakes to the real thing. Mother's recipe makes three generous loaf cakes. Aunt Mable and Ada glazed the cakes lightly with a simple powdered sugar glaze. Aunt Clary left the cakes plain, unglazed, but decorated them by dipping the bottoms of nuts and candied fruit into a bit of glaze (two or three tablespoons powdered sugar thinned with a few drops of water) and sticking them on the top of the cake, leaving the sides undecorated.

¾ cup butter
2 cups, packed, light brown sugar
3 eggs
1½ cups unsweetened applesauce
3 cups all-purpose flour
1 teaspoon salt
1 tablespoon baking powder
1½ teaspoons baking soda
3 tablespoons ground cinnamon
1 teaspoon freshly grated nutmeg
¼ teaspoon ground ginger
¼ teaspoon ground cloves

6 cups coarsely chopped mixed
    candied fruits (such as citron,
    cherries, lemon and orange
    peel, dates, and figs)
2 cups dark raisins
2 cups light raisins
1½ cups nuts (use your favorite
    kind), chopped
Simple Powdered Sugar Glaze (page
    185) optional
Nuts and candied fruits for
    decoration, optional

Preheat oven to 325°F. Grease and flour three 9x5x2¾-inch loaf pans; set aside.

In a large bowl, cream together the butter and sugar until light. Add the eggs, one at a time, beating after each addition. Stir in the applesauce; set aside. In a medium-size bowl, sift together the flour, salt, baking powder, baking soda, cinnamon, nutmeg, ginger, and cloves. In a second large bowl, combine the candied fruits, raisins, and nuts. Scoop out about half a cup of the flour mixture and dust the fruit and nuts with it. Gradually stir the rest of the flour into the butter-sugar mixture. Pour the batter over the fruits and fold together. Divide the batter into 3 parts and pour it into the prepared pans; make sure it is well settled. Bake until a toothpick inserted into the center comes out clean, about 1 hour and 45 minutes. Remove from oven, let sit for about 10 minutes, then turn out of the pans onto a wire rack and let cool thoroughly. Wrap in aluminum foil for storage and keep refrigerated.   *Makes 3 loaf cakes.*

LOVELY CHOCOLATE LEAVES

Aunt Irene made fancy things. Among them were these lovely chocolate leaves, which appeared now and again on top of special-occasion cakes. Mother thought they would also be beautiful if served as candy on a pale pink glass plate or used for garnishing other desserts in addition to cakes.

About 3 dozen substantial leaves
from camellia bushes, lemon trees,
English laurel

1 pound dipping chocolate
½-inch artist's brush (like those used
for oil paints)

Note: When gathering the leaves, select ones with at least short stems and with attractive vein patterns on the undersides. Gather and wash a few extras since it's difficult to gauge exactly how many leaves one pound of chocolate will coat.

Wash and drain the leaves; let them dry completely.

Melt the chocolate in the top of a double boiler but don't wait until it is all melted; when it is soft and yet still holds its form, take it from the heat and stir into a smooth paste. Using the artist's brush, coat the underside of each leaf with a layer of chocolate about ⅛ inch thick; paint to the edge of the leaf, but don't overlap chocolate onto the top side. Let the chocolate dry, then chill in the refrigerator until thoroughly set. To remove the chocolate leaf from the real leaf, gently pull the real leaf away from the chocolate, starting at the stem end, while lightly holding the point of the chocolate leaf with the other hand; handle the chocolate quickly and as little as possible so as not to leave fingerprints on it. *Makes about 3 dozen.*

🌿 THE BIRDS OF CHRISTMAS

In all of Scandinavia, nature is glorified at the Christmas season.

When Grandpa was a little boy, he went with his father to the farm home of a family of immigrant Danes. He recalls drinking rich cold milk and eating Danish pastry while his father drank strong steaming coffee and talked about Danish Christmas customs and the price of hogs. After about forty minutes on the hard wooden bench, he was allowed to go outside with the family's children.

The boys, Hans, Knud, and Bertel, showed him the bits of suet and bread hung in the trees and the best sheaves of grain put out in many locations around the farm and home grounds. Knud, the oldest, told him that when the birds came to eat in great numbers, a year of good crops was foretold. Hans took him into the barns and told him that on Christmas Eve the farm animals were given extra portions of food, sometimes even human Christmas treats like fruitcake and cookies, and they are blessed with good wishes and told, "Eat well, this is Christmas Eve."

KAFFEKAGE *(DANISH PASTRY)*

Ada's parents owned a dairy farm. Her father started building it in 1907. He was an immigrant from a small farm in Denmark. His hams, bacon, butter, and eggs were always a cut above anyone's in the neighborhood. And, along with all the other work he did, he grew large crops of beets, potatoes, oats, barley, wheat, and rye, most of which he used to feed his livestock.

¾ cup plus 2 tablespoons milk
1 package dry or granulated yeast
¼ cup warm water (105°F to
  115°F)
¾ cup sugar
1¼ cups cold butter
¼ teaspoon salt

3 to 3½ cups sifted all-purpose
  flour, plus about ½ cup for
  kneading dough
1 egg, well beaten
Simple Powdered Sugar Glaze
  (recipe follows)

Scald the milk. Meanwhile, dissolve the yeast in the warm water; let stand 5 to 10 minutes until it forms a bubbly head. Set aside.

Measure into a large bowl, ¼ cup of the sugar, ¼ cup of the butter, and the salt. While the scalded milk is still hot, pour it over ingredients in bowl, stirring to blend. When mixture is lukewarm, blend in 1 cup flour, beating until very smooth; then beat in the egg. Stir in just enough additional flour to make a soft dough; you will need 2 to 2½ cups flour for this. Cover with waxed paper, then place a clean cloth on top. Let stand in a warm place (about 80°F) until double in bulk, about 45 minutes to 1 hour.

Cut ½ cup of the butter into pieces. Turn the dough onto a lightly floured surface and roll into an 18x12x2-inch rectangle. Pat one third of the butter pieces down the center one third of the dough. Then fold over one third of the dough (either the right or left third) to cover the butter. Next, fold over the other (right or left) third of the dough. With a rolling pin or with your hands, gently press down the open edges of the dough to seal. Carefully wrap the dough in waxed paper or aluminum foil and refrigerate for about 30 minutes.

Remove dough from the refrigerator and place on a floured surface with *butter section near the top*, one of the short ends toward you. Turn one-quarter way around to have pinched, open-under edge away from you. Roll dough out again into a 18x12x2-inch rectangle. Pat *half of the*

remaining butter pieces down center one third of dough and repeat folding, sealing, and chilling procedure. For a third time roll out dough into an 18x12x2-inch rectangle, dot with *remaining* butter pieces, and fold, seal, and chill as before.

After the final chilling, roll the dough into an 18x12x2-inch rectangle and cut into 3-inch squares. Stir together ½ *cup* butter and the *remaining* ½ *cup* sugar until well blended; spoon about 1½ teaspoons of the mixture into the center of each square. (*Note:* Fruit preserves may be substituted for butter-sugar filling.) Fold the opposite corners of the square up to meet in the center and press edges to seal. Place on ungreased cookie sheet; cover with waxed paper and a clean kitchen towel. Let rise in a warm place until nearly doubled in size. Bake until light golden brown, 8 to 10 minutes. Meanwhile, prepare the glaze if desired.

Once pastries are baked, cool on wire racks. Drizzle glaze over them while pastries are still warm.   *Makes 2 dozen pastries.*

Simple Powdered Sugar Glaze
2 cups powdered sugar
2 tablespoons milk
Drop of vanilla extract, optional

Blend the sugar and milk together until smooth. Add a drop of vanilla if you wish. Use immediately. *Makes enough to lightly glaze 2 dozen pastries.*

JULEKAKE
(NORWEGIAN CHRISTMAS BREAD)

When our old friend Edvard Amundsen was a boy, he lived with his grandfather, father, mother, four brothers, and one sister on a twenty-five acre farm in Norway. By the time he was fourteen, it was obvious that the ancestral acres would never produce enough to sustain the next generation. One of the boys would have to go to America to start a new life and it was decided by all, including Edvard, that he should be the one. The family then began to scrimp and save and Edvard took any off-farm work he could find, no matter how poorly it paid. By the time he was twenty-four, there was enough money for passage and a modest amount to buy land in North Dakota.

Frightened but full of hope, Edvard made his way to the "land of plenty" with the old language still on his tongue and only a few words of English. For eight years he cleared fields and planted them to wheat, barley, rye, and potatoes, put up barns and sheds, and raised a house. Then, at thirty-two years of age, he sent home for a good hard-working Norwegian girl to come and be his wife.

Once eighteen-year-old Inger arrived with her golden hair and skilled hands the butter tasted sweet, the meat cooked just right. The kitchen smelled of breads and cakes and strong coffee. There was much visiting, guests came, mostly homesick men who did not yet have a wife or family in the new land. And Christmas! It was like being in the old country, the laughing and singing and eating of Inger's *Julekake*, richly flavored with cardamom.

½ small orange
¾ cup golden raisins
1 cup boiling water
1 cup milk
1 package dry or granulated yeast
¼ cup warm water (105°F to 115°F)

½ cup butter
½ cup sugar
1 teaspoon salt
4 to 4½ cups all-purpose flour, plus about ½ cup for kneading
1 teaspoon ground cardamom
1 egg white, slightly beaten

Rinse the orange, cut into halves, remove any seeds, and force one half through a food grinder fitted with a medium blade into a small bowl; set aside. Place the raisins in a small saucepan and pour the 1 cup boiling water over them. Return water to a boil over high heat, then pour off water and drain raisins on paper towels; set aside.

Scald the milk. Meanwhile, dissolve the yeast in the ¼ cup warm water; stand 5 to 10 minutes until it forms a bubbly head. In a large bowl, combine the butter, sugar, and salt. Immediately pour the scalded and still-hot milk over them, stirring occasionally as the butter melts and the sugar and salt dissolve. When the mixture is lukewarm, gradually sift in *1 cup* of the flour and the cardamom, beating until smooth. Stir in the yeast, mixing well. Then add about *1½ cups* more flour and beat until very smooth. Beat in the ground orange, raisins, and enough of the remaining flour (about 1½ to 2 cups) to make a soft dough. Turn dough onto a lightly floured surface; cover and let rest 5 to 10 minutes.

Knead dough and form into a large ball, using just enough flour to prevent dough from sticking to hands. When it becomes elastic and has a sheen, place in a deep, greased bowl. Turn dough over so greased surface is on top. Cover with waxed paper and a clean kitchen towel and let stand in a warm place (about 80°F) until doubled in bulk, about 45 minutes.

Punch down the dough with your fist; then pull edges of dough into the center and turn dough completely over in bowl. Cover and let rise again until nearly doubled in size, about 30 to 40 minutes. Punch down and turn onto a lightly floured surface.

Preheat oven to 350°F. Lightly grease a 9x1½-inch round cake pan. Shape the dough into a ball, place in the greased pan, and flatten slightly. Cover and let rise until doubled in bulk, about 45 minutes.

Bake until light golden brown, about 45 minutes. Remove from oven momentarily and brush with the egg white, then return to oven and continue baking about 10 to 15 minutes longer.

Once finished baking, immediately remove bread from pan and place on a wire rack; let cool completely. Serve with hot coffee. Store wrapped in plastic wrap or aluminum foil.   *Makes one 9-inch loaf.*

SCANDINAVIAN STEEPED COFFEE

Throughout Scandinavia, good coffee is *steeped* coffee—water and coffee all heated together in the pot—and the result is strong flavored and boiling hot. To make such coffee, use an old-fashioned pot or any container in which you can boil water, and regular-grind coffee.

4 cups cold water plus ¼ cup to
   settle grounds
8 tablespoons ground coffee (regular
   grind)

1 egg, lightly beaten (for this recipe
   you will need 4 teaspoons of
   beaten egg)

Place the cold water and ground coffee in the pot. Bring very slowly to a boil, stirring occasionally. Immediately remove from heat and pour ¼ cup cold water into the pot to settle the grounds. To clarify the coffee, mix 1 teaspoon lightly beaten egg for each 2 tablespoons ground coffee used (the egg settles to the bottom of the pot and as it does it coagulates, trapping fine bits of ground coffee). Leave the pot on the stove and let the coffee steep for 3 to 5 minutes without heating. Then strain the coffee through a fine mesh strainer or an ordinary coffee filter into a server which has been preheated with boiling water. If necessary, reheat the coffee over low heat without letting it boil.

FROM THE SNOWSTORM

Announced by all the trumpets of the sky,
Arrives the snow, and, driving o'er the fields,
Seems nowhere to alight: the whited air
Hides hills and woods, the river, and the heaven,
And veils the farmhouse at the garden's end.
The sled and traveler stopped, the courier's feet
Delayed, all friends shut out, the housemates sit
Around the radiant fireplace, enclosed
In a tumultuous privacy of storm.

—Ralph Waldo Emerson

JANE WATSON HOPPING

🌿 SNOW CRYSTALS

When my sister and I were children, we used to try to catch snowflakes in our hands, and tried to look at them carefully before they melted, which amused our mother. Mother would tell us that "Nature is full of genius, full of divinity, so that not a snowflake escapes its fashioning hand," and she would also remind us that those words came from the pen of Henry David Thoreau.

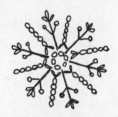

EFFIE'S SNOW PUDDING WITH ORANGE SAUCE

This light and airy pudding was always served on Christmas Eve after services that were attended by Effie's whole family and many of her friends.

½ cup cold water
2 tablespoons (2 packages)
    unflavored gelatin
2 cups hot water
1¼ cups sugar

⅓ to ½ cup strained lemon juice
6 egg whites, at room temperature
About 1 teaspoon vegetable oil (not
    olive oil)
Orange Sauce (recipe follows)

Lightly oil a 2½-quart decorative mold and turn upside down on paper towels to drain.

Pour the cold water into a small bowl and sprinkle the gelatin evenly over the top; let soften for about 5 minutes. Warm a medium-size bowl by holding it for a minute or so under hot water; then pour the hot water into it. Add the gelatin, stirring until dissolved. Stir in the sugar until dissolved, then add the lemon juice. Cool slightly, then chill in the refrigerator or set the bowl in a pan of ice and water until mixture is slightly thicker than the consistency of fresh, thick unbeaten egg whites (stale egg whites are thin). (*Note:* While refrigerated, stir occasionally. If chilled in ice water, stir frequently.)

When gelatin has thickened, beat the egg whites in a large bowl until stiff peaks form (the whites should stay in place when you partially invert the bowl.) Then beat the gelatin mixture until frothy. Gently fold the egg whites into the gelatin mixture. Turn into the prepared mold. Refrigerate until firm, about 1 hour. Serve unmolded onto a chilled serving plate with Orange Sauce on the side.

Makes 8 to 10 servings.

Orange Sauce

2 egg yolks, slightly beaten
⅓ cup sugar
¼ cup strained orange juice

1 tablespoon finely grated orange peel
½ cup heavy cream, whipped until soft peaks form

In the top of a double boiler, combine the egg yolks, sugar, and orange juice. Cook over simmering water, stirring constantly, until thickened. Set in a pan of ice water to chill quickly. Fold in the orange peel and whipped cream. Serve immediately or refrigerate if made ahead.

Makes about 1½ cups sauce.

THE LITTLEST LACE ANGEL

The women in our family have always saved bits of lace, ribbons, yarn left over from making a sweater or stockings, bits of crochet cotton, bits of embroidery floss, and fabric left over from our sewing, against the day when we would think of just the right thing to make out of our bright treasures.

Sheila's little lace angel was that kind of inspiration. The first one was made of cream lace left over from a friend's wedding gown. When she finished making the pattern for it and then made the angel, she set it on an upturned drinking glass in the middle of her dining-room table, where it sat through late fall and into the winter.

Then at Christmas she made an even fancier one, a fairy-light angel for the top of the Christmas tree. That year she taught several other women to make little lace angels and they tucked theirs in amongst the boughs of their decorated trees.

This year, Sheila has generously shared her angel pattern with us. She says, "My Christmas angels are easy to make, inexpensive, and fun."

MATERIALS

1 yard 4-inch-wide white or light-cream lace with 1 finished side
3 shades of embroidery floss: peach, apricot, and baby blue
1 ounce pillow stuffing
1 yard of ⅛-inch-wide satin ribbon
Sewing thread to match the lace
3 tiny silk flowers
Note: It is important to read all instructions before starting this project.

4 in. lace	SKIRT	ARM #1	ARM #2	BODY & HEAD 10 in.	
				WING #1 5 in.	WING #2 5 in.
20 in.		3 in.	3 in.		

Measure and *cut lace according to the pattern* into the following: 1 skirt, 2 sleeves, 2 wings, and 2 body-head pieces with the top of the head joined on a fold.

Using a pencil, *draw the face* on the front of the head and draw a line for the necklace. Embroider, using 4 strands of embroidery floss for all stitches. For the

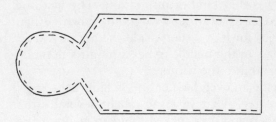

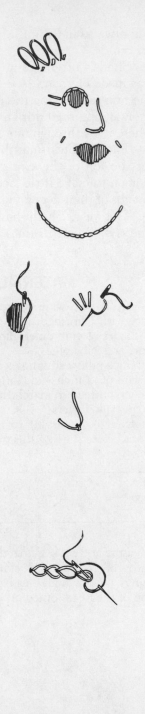

eyes work *a satin stitch back* and forth across each shape until it is filled. Then use a *straight stitch* to work the eyelashes and dimples (Exit at the desired starting point, and enter at the desired ending point.)

Use a *loop stitch* for the nose. Insert the needle at the back of the head and exit at the bridge of the nose. Enter again at the left nostril, exit at the tip of the nose. Hold loop with the thumb and return the needle back through the same holes, securing the loop as you do so. Exit through the back of the head. Clip off remaining floss.

For the necklace use a *chain stitch*. Bring the floss out at top of necklace line and hold loop with the thumb, insert the needle where it last emerged, bring the point out a short distance, and pull floss snug to the needle. Exit the rest of the way, keeping floss under the needle. Repeat for remaining chains of necklace.

Next stitch the head and body together with the sewing thread (⅛-inch seam allowance), leaving the bottom unstitched. Then stuff the body softly with pillow stuffing.

Using a *turkeywork embroidery stitch*, make the hair, using peach and apricot embroidery floss. Insert the needle at the back of the head, exiting at the hairline in the front. (Leave a tail of floss inside the head.) Make a loop and hold with the thumb while making an anchor stitch. Repeat to form all hair.

Next, fold each sleeve in half lengthwise at the shoulder. Stitch to the body with sewing thread. Gather skirt ⅛ inch from the raw edge with sewing thread and stitch by hand to the body at the angel's waist. Use the ⅛-inch satin ribbon as a waist sash; tie a bow in the front. Stitch the silk flowers to the sash at the bow.

Finally, gather the wings ⅛ inch from the raw edge. Stitch the wings together in the center of raw edges, then attach to back of body by handstitching.

WE WISH YOU
A MERRY CHRISTMAS

*From Our House
to Yours*

The holiday season inspires us all to thoughts of appreciation for those we care about. Enjoy these few lines from the warm and gentle poetry of Edgar A. Guest:

From *FIRST-NAME FRIENDS*

*The happiest men on earth are not the men
    of highest rank;
That joy belongs to George, and Jim, to
    Henry and to Frank;
With them the prejudice of race and creed
    and wealth depart,
And men are one in fellowship and always
    light of heart.
So I would live and laugh and love until my
    sun descends,
And share the joyous comradeship of honest
    first-name friends. . . .*

Merry Christmas! Arlene and Ralph, Mary and Con, Lee and Bob, Peggy and Earl, Reg, Gene, Margaret, Meg, Jane, Sally, Alison, Irene, Rene, Jim, and all the rest!

THROUGH THE WOODS

Grandmother, on a winter's day, milked the cows and fed them hay, slopped the hogs, saddled the mule, and got the children off to school; did the washing, mopped the floors, washed the windows, and did some chores; cooked a dish of home-dried fruit, pressed her husband's Sunday suit, swept the parlor, made the bed, baked a dozen loaves of bread, split some firewood and lugged in enough to fill the bin; cleaned the lamps and put in oil, stewed some apples she thought would spoil; churned the butter, baked a cake, then exclaimed "For heaven's sake, the calves have got out of the pen"—went out and chased them in again; gathered the eggs and locked the stable; back to the house and set the table, cooked a supper that was delicious, and afterward washed up all the dishes; fed the cat and sprinkled the clothes, mended a basketful of hose; then opened the organ and began to play, "When you come to the end of a perfect day."

—*Author Unknown*

MEG'S BROWN-BAG TURKEY WITH THREE-BREAD DRESSING AND CARAMEL-COLORED GRAVY

For many years we have loved this esay-to-prepare, quick-cooking braised turkey because the breast meat is always moist, the gravy richly flavored, and all of the meat—light and dark—well seasoned. At our house we carve the bird in the kitchen and serve it on a platter, sliced and garnished with sprigs of fresh parsley; sometimes we add huge black pitted olives to give a festive touch.

For family gatherings we arrange the sliced turkey meat in a flat casserole dish—one in which we intend to serve the turkey—and pour about one-quarter cup hot water flavored with a tablespoon of honey over the top; then we put on the cover (or cover the dish with a piece of foil) so the meat can be reheated to serving temperature (just before setting it on the table) without drying it out.

1 (12-pound) turkey	1 onion, peeled and quartered
¾ cup butter, softened	1 clove garlic, peeled or unpeeled,
Salt	as desired
Black pepper	Three-Bread Dressing (recipe
2 tablespoons dried sweet marjoram	follows)
leaves	Caramel-Colored Gravy (recipe
1 apple, quartered and cored,	follows)
unpeeled	
1 stalk celery, cut into several	
pieces	

Wash the turkey and remove any excess fat. Drain until surface is almost dry. Melt ¼ cup of the butter and pour over the outside of the turkey, rubbing it over all outer surfaces. Salt and pepper outside generously and sprinkle marjoram liberally over the breast, sides, and legs.

Tip the cavity up and sprinkle salt, pepper, and marjoram into it. Then fill the cavity to capacity with the apple, celery, onion, and garlic; set aside.

Generously butter the inside of a large brown grocery bag with the *remaining ½ cup* butter. (*Note:* The paper will become parchmentlike in the oven.) Then place the turkey, breast first, into the bag. Fasten bag shut with a wire twist. Place bagged turkey into a large ungreased roasting pan, breast side up. Refrigerate overnight.

The following day preheat oven to 375°F. Set the roasting pan containing the bag-wrapped turkey in the center of the oven. Bake (do not cover pan) until a meat thermometer inserted through the paper bag into the thigh-hip joint (close to but not touching the bone) reads 175°F, about 2½ to 3 hours. (*Note:* The dressing can be baked in the oven with the turkey during the last 45 minutes of roasting time.)

When turkey is done, carefully remove pan from oven. With a knife, puncture the bag near the bottom, being careful not to burn yourself as all of the juices trapped inside run free into the roasting pan. Remove paper from around turkey, then carefully lift turkey onto a serving platter; reserve pan juices for the gravy. Cover turkey loosely with aluminum foil and cover with a heavy kitchen towel to keep warm until ready to serve.   *Makes 8 to 10 servings with leftovers for sandwiches.*

Three-Bread Dressing

We make this dressing for almost any occasion and to serve with any roasted meat: Beef, pork, chicken, and especially with turkey.

1 (1-pound) loaf coarse-grained whole-wheat bread, torn into small pieces (leave crust on)

½ (1-pound) loaf well seasoned rye bread, torn into small pieces (leave crust on)

½ (1-pound) loaf golden egg bread, torn into small pieces (leave crust on)

1 pound pork sausage, crumbled into bits and fried (drain and reserve ¼ cup drippings)

1 large yellow onion, chopped

1½ cups chopped celery

1 pound mushrooms

1 clove garlic, peeled and minced

1 tablespoon dried oregano leaves (much preferred over any other seasonings for this dressing)

4 cups Homemade Chicken Broth (recipe follows)

About 1½ teaspoons salt

About ½ teaspoon black pepper

Combine the breads in a large bowl. Spoon the fried sausage over the bread but don't stir it in. Place the ¼ cup drippings from frying the sausage in a large frying pan; add the onion, celery, mushrooms and garlic. Saute until vegetables are clear. Remove garlic and discard, then add the chicken broth and oregano to the skillet. Bring to a boil. Pour over the breads, stirring to blend. Season to taste with salt and pepper. Add additional hot water as needed to make a moist dressing. (Make sure the dressing is moist; if it's dry when you put it in to bake, it will be more than dry when you serve it.) Spoon dressing into a greased 13x9x2-inch baking pan. Bake until puffed and brown, about 45 minutes.

Makes 8 generous servings.

Caramel-Colored Gravy

Let the *pan juices* cool in the roasting pan to lukewarm, then drop ice cubes into them which will quickly cool the fat. Stir cubes about so that the fat clings to the ice, then remove both before the ice melts. Dilute the pan juices to taste with water, then measure, noting how much there is. Place in a large saucepan. Adjust seasonings. Bring to a boil. Meanwhile, caramelize *1 tablespoon sugar* in a small cast-iron frying pan by heating it until it bubbles and turns rich dark brown, stirring constantly; do not let the sugar burn or it will have a bitter taste.

Pour the caramelized sugar into the boiling pan juices, spooning a little of the juices into the frying pan to wash all of the sugar out. Thicken the gravy by stirring in about *2 tablespoons cornstarch* dissolved in about *1 tablespoon cold water* for each cup of pan juices. Cook over medium heat until clear and thickened, about 5 minutes. Taste for seasoning. Add a pat or two of *butter* to enrich flavor, if you wish.

Makes 8 or more servings.

Homemade Chicken Broth

2 pounds chicken pieces (wings,
    drumsticks, and backs preferred)
    or use the neck of the turkey and
    only 1 pound of chicken parts
About 1 tablespoon butter
5 cups cold water
3 black peppercorns

Sprig of parsley
Sprig of sweet marjoram (or use
    about ½ teaspoon dried leaves)
1 rib celery
1 small onion, peeled
About 1 teaspoon salt

In a frying pan, brown about half of the chicken pieces in only about *1 tablespoon* butter. (This will improve the color and flavor of the broth.) Place the browned and unbrowned pieces in a large kettle or Dutch oven and pour the cold water over them. Let sit for about 30 minutes so the flavor can soak out into the water. Then add to the water the peppercorns, parsley, marjoram, celery, onion, and salt. Simmer until the chicken is tender and almost falling off the bone, about 1 hour. Remove from heat; strain the broth. (*Note:* The strained vegetables are usually discarded; the meat may be diced and put in the dressing or gravy, or saved for another use.) *Makes about 4 cups.*

PEACH HALVES
FILLED WITH FESTIVE COTTAGE CHEESE
ON RED-LEAVED LETTUCE

In winter, salad greens were either costly or nonexistent when I was a girl, so women grew a pot of parsley, chives, or a bit of herbs in kitchen windows. Mother used snippets of parsley to garnish this Christmas Day or pre-Christmas salad. I use red-leaved lettuce from the market.

8 large leaves of red-leaved lettuce,
    washed and dried
8 home-canned peach halves (store-
    bought will do)
1 pint cottage cheese, well drained
    (or use undrained ricotta or dry
    cottage cheese, which are more
    like homemade)

½ cup finely chopped roasted pecans
½ cup dried apricots, minced (well-
    colored and soft fruit preferred)
8 whole candied or maraschino
    cherries

Arrange the lettuce on 8 salad plates. Carefully (to keep them intact) drain the peach halves in a strainer.

In a medium-size bowl, blend the cottage cheese with the pecans and apricots. Arrange the peach halves on the lettuce, cut side up and spoon the cottage cheese filling on top. Garnish each serving with a cherry. Serve immediately.

Makes 8 servings.

HOME-CANNED PEAR RELISH

Mother made this holiday relish in the fall after the garden was stripped and when the hard Kiefer pears were in season. You will need five pint-size canning jars and brand-new self-sealing lids plus the metal rings for canning the relish.

2 quarts hard pears, washed,
    peeled, cored and ground in a
    food grinder
1 quart yellow winter onion,
    peeled and ground in a food
    grinder
1 quart green bell peppers,
    washed, stemmed and seeded,
    and ground in a food grinder
1 small fresh hot red pepper,
    washed, seeded, and very
    finely minced (wear gloves
    while handling the pepper and
    don't touch your eyes or
    mouth)
1 quart white vinegar
1¼ teaspoons salt

1½ tablespoons dry mustard
1 teaspoon ground turmeric
2½ teaspoons ground allspice
2 teaspoons ground cinnamon
1 teaspoon ground cloves
2 cups sugar

Combine all the relish ingredients in a large enamelware kettle or stainless steel soup pot. Bring to a boil, stirring occasionally to prevent sticking. Reduce heat and simmer for about 15 minutes. Meanwhile, put the brand-new canning lids in a pan and pour boiling water over them; *don't boil.* Set aside until ready to use.

When the relish is cooked, remove from heat and immediately pack into freshly scrubbed, sterilized, and still-hot canning jars to within ½ inch from the top. As each jar is filled, wipe the rims clean with a damp cloth; place a hot lid on top and screw on the metal ring fairly tightly. Process in a boiling water bath for 5 minutes. Remove and set in a draft-free spot until cool; test for an airtight seal. Label and date. Store upright in a cool dry place. (*Note:* To test for the seal, press down the center of the lid; if it is curved down and stays down, the jar is sealed.)

Makes about 5 pints.

PUMPKIN AND WALNUT CAKE
WITH CARAMEL FROSTING

By mid-December all of the giant and baby pie pumpkins have been in storage for nearly two months. Country women are using them in cookies, breads, pies, and puddings and for Christmas in this delicious old-style cake.

4 eggs, at room temperature and
    beaten to a froth
2 cups sugar
2 cups baked and strained pumpkin,
    (store-bought canned pumpkin
    will do)
1 cup butter, softened
2 teaspoons ground cinnamon
1 teaspoon baking soda

1 teaspoon vanilla extract
2 cups plus 1 teaspoon sifted all-
    purpose flour
¾ cup chopped walnuts, for cake
    batter
Caramel Frosting (recipe follows)
¾ cup very finely chopped walnuts
    for garnishing top of cake

Preheat oven to 350°F. Lightly grease and flour a 13x9x2-inch baking pan. In a large bowl, combine the eggs, sugar, pumpkin, butter, cinnamon, baking soda, and vanilla; gently beat until blended. Add 2 cups of the flour, stirring into a medium batter—one that is fairly stiff, yet not too thick to beat easily. Dust the chopped walnuts with the remaining 1 teaspoon flour and fold into the batter.

Pour the batter into the prepared pan. Bake until top is golden brown and firm to the touch, about 30 minutes. Remove from oven and cool in the pan. When completely cool, frost and generously sprinkle the very finely chopped walnuts over the top. Serve with piping hot coffee to holiday visitors. *Makes one large sheet cake.*

Caramel Frosting
If you prefer a thin layer of frosting, halve the recipe.

½ cup butter
1 cup, packed, light brown sugar
A few grains of salt (less than ⅛
    teaspoon)
¼ cup milk
2 cups powdered sugar

2 or 3 drops vanilla extract (not
    enough to overpower the caramel
    flavor)
Milk or cream, for thinning frosting
    if needed

Melt the butter in a medium-size saucepan; add the brown sugar and salt. Bring to a boil over medium heat; boil hard for exactly 2 minutes, stirring constantly. Immediately remove from heat and stir in the milk; then return to high heat and bring just to a full rolling boil. Remove from heat and cool until lukewarm. Stir in the powdered sugar, beating until smooth. If the frosting seems too thick, thin with a small amount of milk or cream. *Makes about 2 cups or enough for a large sheet cake.*

GRANDPA'S ELDERBERRY WINE

Elderberries are beautiful! They grow on a small tree or shrub and are a member of the honeysuckle family. The branches with finely cut leaves and clusters of small white flowers are lovely enough for bouquets. The berries are black, purple, and red (depending on the area in which they grow), and all are delicious made into jellies, wines, and pies.

Grandpa gathered elderberries in season, washed them gently, then put them in a large kettle with only enough water to keep them from burning and brought them to a boil. He held them at that temperature just long enough to scald them, then strained the juice through a cheesecloth into a crock. (*Note:* A wide-mouth gallon glass container may be used if you do not have a crock, but don't use a metal or plastic container.)

To each 10 cups of elderberry juice he gradually added 8 *cups of sugar.* The crock was then set away in a cool place to ferment and the wine was skimmed daily until clear. As the wine fermented, any small particles left in the juice settled to the bottom of the container. When bubbles ceased to rise to the surface of the liquid, a process that took about 2 weeks, the wine was ladled into scrubbed and sterilized bottles and sealed with new corks that had been scalded and laid aside to dry. To preserve the color and quality, Grandpa stored the elderberry wine in a cool, dark, dry place.

Makes 4 to 5 pints of elderberry wine for each 10 cups of elderberry juice and 8 cups of sugar.

AWAY IN A MANGER

Away in a manger,
  No crib for a bed,
The Little Lord Jesus
  Laid down His sweet head;
The stars in the sky
  Looked down where He lay,

The little Lord Jesus
  Asleep on the hay.

The cattle are lowing,
   The poor baby wakes,
But little Lord Jesus
   No crying He makes;
I love Thee, Lord Jesus!
   Look down from the sky,
And stay by my cradle
   Till morning is nigh.

Be near me, Lord Jesus,
   I ask Thee to stay
Close by me forever,
   And love me, I pray.
Bless all the dear children
   In Thy tender care,
And take me to heaven
   To live with Thee there.

—Anonymous

A CHILD'S CHRISTMAS CAROL

Mother's friend Lenora reminisces each year about her childhood home, the love she grew up with, and the simple holidays her family shared:

"The Christmases of my childhood have charmed me through all those passing years. Perhaps it was because childhood lasted and changed slowly and was one that was filled with love and family and the country life about us.

"I vividly recall one Christmas Eve and an old-fashioned church pageant. That was the year Mother made shepherd costumes for us out of burlap feed sacks and robes out of old velvet curtains on her treadle sewing machine. And Papa made a wooden cradle for the Christ child, which my baby brother Martin would lie in on that Holy night while Mother read from Luke. (We all had parts to play in the pageant.)

"The night of the pageant was filled with magic. The choir sang 'Hark! The Herald Angels Sing!' and we were told that Charles Wesley —who inspired the Methodist movement—wrote not only this carol (in 1739), but during his life wrote some six thousand hymns; among them is our favorite, 'Jesus, Lover of My Soul.' The congregation sang several old familiar carols, the children recited verses. And afterwards, we rode home in Papa's wagon. We counted the stars and marveled at the luminous moon which guided us home through the icy winter night. When

we could see the lamp in the window of our house, Papa, Mama, and I shouted with glee, because we knew that Grandpa had a warm fire waiting for us.

"There was nothing fancy and tinsel-wrapped then, but as Christmases come again and again, the memories of the homemade presents and decorations pull at my heartstrings. The lovely crooked tinfoil-wrapped cardboard star that topped our tree was perfect. The great tall tree that almost touched our twelve-foot ceilings was strung from top to bottom with popcorn and paper chains and was hung thick with polished apples. The whole house was festive: Santas made with red and white art-paper hung on walls and doors; the windows were filled with cookie stars and gingerbread men, which hung side by side on bits of string.

"Our gifts were simple, things that money couldn't buy: a red and green scarf, just finished in time by a loving grandmother; new boots to keep winter-cold feet dry; satin or velvet ribbons for our hair bought with Mother's summer pin money and kept hidden for months to surprise us.

JANE WATSON HOPPING

"Now, when my brother comes to visit at Christmas, he sings snatches of Christmas songs to my grandchildren and reminds us all that 'tis the season to be jolly.' Martin drags us all out to tramp through the woods while he tells the children about how, years ago, he chopped down the biggest tree our house could hold. And he tells them about the fragrance of pine and cedar that perfumed our rooms.

"When the children are in bed and he and I are alone, we remember Christmases that are long since gone, and we hold hands and take pleasure in the excitement once again in the air and my grandchildren's sparkling eyes, which bring back our own warm memories that grow dearer to us with each passing year."

A NOURISHING SOUP FOR CHILDREN

In cold December many a mother in the old-days put the soup pot on right after breakfast, so there would be a warm, nourishing meal ready for her large brood of children by lunchtime. Besides a large bowl of soup, the father and older boys might eat thick slabs of homemade bread and slices of cold roasted or boiled meat and drink from the never-empty pitcher of milk.

1 (about 3½-pound) chicken (thoroughly wash, and trim away all visible fat and much of the fatty skin)
3 quarts cold water
1 medium-size carrot, peeled and diced

1 small onion, peeled and chopped
2 stalks tender light-colored celery, chopped
1 tablespoon dried parsley
About 1½ to 2 teaspoons salt

Place the chicken in a large kettle and cover with the cold water. Add the carrot, onion, celery, parsley, and 1 teaspoon of the salt. Cover and simmer slowly until the meat is very tender and falls away from the bone, 2 hours or more. Adjust salt seasoning if needed. Remove from heat and, with a slotted spoon and a carving fork, transfer the chicken from the kettle to a platter; save for future use. (This lean, tender cooked chicken meat was often minced fine for the little children and put in their soup.)

Strain the broth and chill. Remove the congealed fat from the top of the broth, then strain broth again through a fine sieve or strainer, or through several layers of cheesecloth. If you wish, add a small portion of cooked rice or noodles to the broth or add any assortment of bland vegetables: peas, carrots, potatoes, and such.

Makes about 2 quarts of soup.

EFFIE'S ROSE-PETAL JELLY WITH GRAHAM MUFFINS

This lovely clear jelly, spread on wholesome muffins (or biscuits), was a favorite midmorning snack at Effie's house, particularly in the winter. She thought the rose essence reminded the children of playing about among the trees and flowers on warmer, sunny summer days. Start the jelly at least one day ahead.

1 quart fragrant red rose petals (see
    Note)
3 cups boiling water
6 cups sugar
Juice from 1 lemon, strained
2 (3-ounce) pouches of liquid pectin
2 teaspoons rose extract (found in
    specialty food shops)
Graham Muffins (recipe follows)

Note: Pick barely unfurled roses early in the morning before the heat and light destroy the roses' essential oils.

Pull the petals from the flowers and cut away the white base from each petal with scissors; then gently and quickly rinse petals in a bowl of cold water. Drain immediately.

Place the petals in a large ceramic or glass mixing bowl and pour boiling water over them. Set aside in a cool place for 24 hours or until the water leaches out the color and flavor.

After about 24 hours, strain the liquid into a large (8-quart) canning kettle; discard petals. Thoroughly scrub and sterilize 6 half-pint jars and metal rings. Keep jars hot. Put 6 brand-new lids in a saucepan and pour boiling water over them; *don't boil.*

Add the sugar to the rose-flavored liquid, stirring until dissolved. Stir in the lemon juice and bring to a boil over high heat. Immediately add the pectin and continue cooking and stirring until jelly comes to a rolling boil that cannot be stirred down. Boil exactly 1 minute (or according to directions on packages of pectin). Remove from heat.

Let the jelly stand for 1 or 2 minutes. Then with a metal spoon, carefully skim the foam from the top of the jelly, placing foam in a clean pint jar (the foam may be spread on bread or used to top ice cream). Quickly stir the rose extract into the jelly and, while still hot, ladle jelly into the very hot canning jars, filling 1 jar at a time and leaving ¼ inch headroom. (*Note:* Work quickly but carefully as hot jelly spilled on the skin sticks and produces a nasty burn.) Wipe jar rim with a clean damp cloth; put the hot lid in place and screw on the metal ring fairly tightly. Let sit in a draft-free place until cool, then label and date. Store in a cool, dark, and dry place. *Makes 6 half-pint jars.*

Graham Muffins

1½ cups graham (or whole-wheat)
   flour
1 cup all-purpose flour
3 tablespoons light brown sugar
1 teaspoon baking soda
1 teaspoon baking powder

½ teaspoon salt
2 eggs, beaten to a froth
1½ cups blinky (sour) milk or
   buttermilk
3 tablespoons butter, melted

Preheat oven to 400°F. Thoroughly grease the cups of two 12-cup muffin pans; set aside.

In a large bowl, combine the flours, sugar, baking soda, baking powder, and salt; mix thoroughly, then make a well in the center of these dry ingredients. In a small bowl, combine the eggs, milk, and butter. Pour into the well made in the dry ingredients and stir only until dry ingredients are moistened; *don't overmix.* Spoon the batter into the prepared muffin cups, filling them about two-thirds full. Bake until well risen and rich golden brown, 20 to 25 minutes. Serve piping hot spread with butter and rose petal jelly. *Makes 2 dozen muffins.*

CHILDREN'S RENNET CUSTARD

On farms all across the country, for everyday use and for special occasions, rennet custards have been a favorite with children and grownups alike. Sometimes we added an ounce of melted chocolate to the warming milk, or two beaten egg yolks for richness, but most often this simple version was preferred. Mothers like it because it's very quick and easy to make, and children like it because it tastes like vanilla pudding.

1 rennet tablet (an extract used for
   making cheese or to thicken
   sweetened flavored milk into
   curd)

1 tablespoon cold water
2 cups milk (skim or whole)

3 tablespoons sugar
1 teaspoon vanilla extract
A few grains of salt, to taste

Note: Available in grocery and health food stores.

Scald and dry four or five ½-cup-capacity glass dessert dishes; keep warm. Dissolve the rennet tablet in the cold water; set aside.

In a medium-size saucepan, heat together the milk, sugar, and vanilla over medium heat, stirring constantly, just until lukewarm (115°F to 120°F); when ready, the milk should feel only comfortably warm when you place a droplet of it on the inside of your wrist. Add the salt and dissolved rennet, stirring quickly just to barely blend in the rennet thoroughly. Immediately pour into the warm serving dishes and let sit until custard thickens, at least 10 to 15 minutes. When cooled, refrigerate until well chilled before serving. Garnish, if you wish, with any cake or pudding sauce or topping.   *Makes 4 servings.*

AN ORDER FOR A SONG

Make me a song of all good things,
And fill it full of murmurings,
Of merry voices, such as we
Remember in our infancy;
But make it tender, for the sake
Of hearts that brood and tears that break,
And tune it with the harmony,
   The sighs of sorrow make.

Make me a song of summer-time,
And pour such music down the rhyme
As ripples over gleaming sands
And grassy brinks of meadow-lands;
But make it very sweet and low,
For need of them that sorrow so,
Because they reap with empty hands
   The dreams of long ago.

Make me a song of such a tone,
That when we croon it all alone,
The tears of longing as they drip,
Will break in laughter on the lip;
And make it, oh, so pure and clear
And jubilant that every ear
Shall drink its rapture sip by sip,
   And Heaven lean to hear.

—James Whitcomb Riley

🌿 THE SWEDE'S CHRISTMAS

My father's friend "The Swede" loved to tell about Christmas in the old country.

"In Scandinavia," he would begin, "Christmas lasts a whole month, beginning on Saint Lucia Day, December 13, and ending on Saint Knut's Day, January 13. In the old days, everyone believed that the Christmas spirit was kept in the house by offering each visitor a bite to eat. So the women took great pride in their Christmas cooking, stretching the budget as far as it would go, making breads and puddings from secret or special inherited recipes. When I was a boy, most men still farmed and every family had its Christmas pig. Besides fresh pork like this roast, sausages and a great ham were set out on the holiday table."

FLASKKARRE (ROAST LOIN OF PORK WITH PRUNES AND APPLES)

1 (3- to 4-pound) boneless pork
   loin roast, trimmed (leave only
   ¼ inch or a little less of fat)
1 teaspoon salt
¼ teaspoon black pepper
2 cups water

2 cups dried prunes (pitted or
   unpitted)
3 large baking apples, pared, cored,
   and quartered (Winesap or
   another tart apple preferred)

Preheat oven to 325°F. Wipe the roast with a clean damp cloth. Combine the salt and pepper and rub on the meat (use more salt and pepper if you wish). Place in a roasting pan fitted with a rack. Insert a meat thermometer into the top center of the roast, taking care that the tip end of the probe rests in the center of the meat, not in fat. Roast uncovered until internal temperature reads about 185°F, about 1 hour and 30 minutes. (Allow about 40 minutes cooking time per pound.)

Meanwhile, place the water in a large saucepan. Add the prunes and simmer until partially tender, about 25 minutes; drain. Remove and discard pits if prunes were unpitted. About 30 minutes before the roast is done, arrange the prunes and apples around the pork and continue roasting.

When the roast is done, transfer to a serving platter. Serve whole to be sliced at the table, or if you wish, slice the meat, arrange on a platter. Garnish with the prunes and apples.   *Makes about 8 to 10 servings.*

DELICIOUS STUFFED EGGS

Flavored stuffed eggs have everywhere been a dish that young girls could make for family festivities. Mother encouraged us to be imaginative in preparing the filling.

6 hard-cooked eggs (see Note)
¾ teaspoon dry mustard
½ teaspoon salt
¼ teaspoon black pepper
1 tablespoon very finely chopped
   sweet onion
1 tablespoon strained lemon juice

3 tablespoons dairy sour cream
Mayonnaise, for adjusting texture of
   filling (Easy-to-Make Mayonnaise,
   page 116, preferred)
Dash of paprika
About 6 sprigs of parsley, for
   garnishing serving

Note: For a tender yolk, cook the eggs as follows: Place the eggs in a large saucepan; cover completely with cold or warm water. Cover pan and bring water just to boiling; immediately remove from heat and let eggs stand covered for about 20 minutes. Then plunge eggs into cold water to cool. To peel each egg, rub it between your palms to crack and loosen the shell, then start peeling at the large end.

Set out a medium-size serving platter. Peel the eggs and cut each in half lengthwise. Remove the yolks and put them in a medium-size bowl. Set egg whites cut side up on the platter. Mash the yolks with a fork. Stir in the mustard, salt, and pepper, then blend in the onion, lemon juice, and sour cream. Add enough mayonnaise to make the filling creamy and light.

Spoon the filling into the whites. Dust the stuffed eggs with paprika and garnish platter with parsley. (*Note:* You may also arrange pitted olives, radishes, or filled mushroom cups around the edge of the platter, if you wish.) *Makes 1 dozen stuffed eggs.*

THE SWEDE'S HOT POTATO SALAD

Made of simple farm ingredients, this salad is both delicious and a bit different from those usually seen. Serve it with meat, poultry, or fish.

6 medium-size potatoes, peeled and
   cut in half
2 tablespoons butter, softened
4 egg yolks, lightly beaten
¼ cup light cream
4 teaspoons cider vinegar
1 tablespoon salt

2 teaspoons sugar
1 teaspoon black pepper
¼ cup chopped fresh parsley
¼ cup chopped onions
Garnishes: Sprigs of parsley, pickled
   beets cut into thin strips, and/or
   lemon slices, as you wish

Place the potatoes in a large saucepan; cover with boiling water and cook until tender when pierced with a fork, about 20 minutes. Drain liquid off, then shake the potatoes in the pan over low heat to dry. Mash the potatoes until smooth; cover and set in a warm place to keep hot.

Meanwhile, cream the butter; blend in the egg yolks, cream, and vinegar. In a small bowl, combine the salt, sugar, and pepper and add to the egg yolk mixture; then stir in the parsley and onions. Add to the hot mashed potatoes, stirring to blend well. Turn immediately into a heated serving dish and garnish as desired with parsley, beets, and/or lemon slices. Serve immediately. *Makes about 4 to 6 servings.*

SWEDISH BROWN BEANS

My father brought this recipe home with him one day after a long wintertime visit and several good games of cribbage with his friend The Swede. The rugged old bachelor sent it to Mother, saying that in the old country brown beans were a favorite dish, prized for their interesting flavor.

1½ quarts water	1 cup dark corn syrup
2½ cups brown beans (preferred) or kidney beans (about 1 pound)	¼ cup cider vinegar
	1 tablespoon salt

Bring the water to a boil in a large saucepan that has a tight-fitting lid.

Meanwhile, wash and sort the beans. Gradually add the beans to the boiling water; do this slowly so the boiling doesn't stop. Reduce heat, cover pan, and simmer for 3 minutes. Remove from heat and let beans cool in the pan, uncovered, about 1 hour.

Then re-cover pan and simmer beans until tender, about 1 hour and 30 minutes to 2 hours, stirring once or twice; if necessary, add hot water to keep the beans covered with liquid. When the beans are tender, stir in the corn syrup, vinegar, and salt; continue cooking and stirring until sauce has thickened, about 45 minutes more.   *Makes 6 or more servings.*

SWEET SWEDISH RYE BREAD

This lovely bread is delicious served cold with fresh butter that's been softened to room temperature.

1 package dry or granulated yeast	1 tablespoon salt
¼ cup lukewarm water (105°F to 115°F)	1 tablespoon grated orange peel
	1 teaspoon caraway seed
½ cup, packed, dark brown sugar	½ teaspoon anise seed
⅓ cup molasses	1½ cups very hot water
2 tablespoons butter or margarine, softened	4 to 4½ cups all-purpose flour
	2 cups rye flour

In a small bowl, sprinkle the yeast over the surface of the warm water and let stand 5 to 10 minutes to proof.

Meanwhile, in a large bowl combine the sugar, molasses, 1 *tablespoon* of the butter, salt, orange peel, caraway seed, and anise seed. Pour the very hot (almost boiling) water over the sugar-molasses mixture and let cool until lukewarm. Meanwhile, grease a large deep bowl; set aside.

Once the mixture is lukewarm, sift 1 *cup* of the all-purpose flour over it, beating until smooth. Add the yeast, blending thoroughly. Add the rye flour and beat until smooth. Then, beat in enough of remaining all-purpose flour to make a soft dough. Turn onto a lightly floured surface. Let dough rest 5 to 10 minutes, then knead for about 5 to 10 minutes. (*Note:* Even if the dough seems a little sticky, don't knead in an excess amount of flour as that will make a heavy textured loaf.) Shape dough into a large ball and place in the prepared bowl. Cover with waxed paper and a clean kitchen towel. Let stand in a warm spot until doubled in bulk, about 45 minutes to 1 hour.

Punch down the risen dough with your fist; pull edges to the center and turn dough completely over in the bowl. Cover and let rise again until nearly doubled in size, about 35 to 40 minutes. Punch down the risen dough again and turn onto a lightly floured surface. Divide dough in half and shape into 2 balls. Place on a greased baking sheet, cover, and let rise until doubled in bulk, about 30 to 40 minutes. Meanwhile, preheat oven to 375°F.

Bake until lightly browned, about 25 to 30 minutes. Remove from oven; let sit about 10 minutes, then turn out of the pan and lightly butter tops of loaves with the *remaining 1 tablespoon* butter.

Makes 2 round loaves.

THE SWEDE'S GLÖGG

Now that our father is gone, none of us can seem to remember the name of the vibrant Swede, a hermitlike man who, during the hardest years of the Depression, lived in a cabin on a hillside near us. We do vividly remember his giving us crackers and offering us strong-smelling sardines while he played card games on rainy days with our father. We loved the old dog that lay at The Swede's feet, and the ceremonious way in which the huge rough man would toast our father at Christmas, almost shouting "*Skål!*" with each sip of Glögg.

1 cup blanched, sliced almonds	6 pieces candied lemon peel
1 cup dark raisins	1 bottle (25-ounce) claret
12 whole cloves	1 bottle (25-ounce) aquavit
10 cardamom seeds, peeled	1 cup sugar
6 (2½-inch) cinnamon sticks	

About a week before Christmas, The Swede slowly heated together almonds, raisins, cloves, cardamom seeds, cinnamon sticks, and candied lemon peel in a saucepan with just enough claret to cover, bringing the wine just to the boiling point, reducing the heat and simmering for about 8 minutes. He then removed the saucepan from the heat and let the contents cool; then he poured the spiced wine into a Mason canning jar, sealed it tightly, and set it aside in a cool place to steep and blend. (*Note:* The jar did not need to be sealed in the usual sense, only tightly closed.)

Several days later and just before serving, he emptied the spiced wine into a large saucepan, added the claret that remained in the bottle and the aquavit and heated all just to the boiling point, but did not let them boil.

Meanwhile, he placed a sieve over a second saucepan, put the sugar in the sieve and, using a ladle, poured some of the hot mixture from the saucepan over the sugar, then ignited the sugar with a match. He continued to pour the liquid over the sugar until the sugar was completely melted. (The liquid flamed until it was extinguished by placing a cover over the saucepan.)

When all the sugar had melted through the sieve, the *Glögg* was ready. The Swede served his in mugs, spooning a few of the almonds and raisins into each portion. He stored any leftover *Glögg* in corked bottles for future use.   *Makes 10 to 15 servings.*

GOD BLESS US EVERY ONE

"God bless us every one!" prayed Tiny Tim,
Crippled and dwarfed of body, yet so tall
Of soul, we tiptoe earth to look on him.
High towering over all.

He loved the loveless world, nor dreamed indeed
That it at best could give to him, the while,
But pitying glances, when his only need
Was but a cheery smile.

And thus he prayed, "God bless us every one!"—
Enfolding all the creeds within the span
Of his child-heart; and so, despising none,
Was nearer saint than man.

I like to fancy God, in Paradise,
Lifting a finger o'er the rhythmic swing
Of chiming harp and song, with eager eyes
Turned earthward, listening—

JANE WATSON HOPPING

The Anthem stilled—the Angels leaning there
Above the golden walls—the morning sun
Of Christmas bursting flower-like with the prayer,
"God bless us every one!"

—James Whitcomb Riley

"GOD BLESS US EVERY ONE!"

Kneeling beside a plump, cozy featherbed in warm flannel sleepwear, with Mother or Father nearby, children of the past said their prayers every night. At Christmas many soft children's lips mumbled or sang this final verse from Phillips Brooks's lovely carol "O Little Town of Bethlehem," just before all of the "God Blesses":

> O holy Child of Bethlehem!
> Descend to us, we pray;
> Cast out our sin, and enter in,
> Be born in us today.
> We hear the Christmas Angels
> The great glad tidings tell;
> Oh, come to us, abide with us;
> Our Lord Emmanuel!

AN ANGEL'S LIGHT KISSES

These light kisses are just right for little boys and girls, particularly for the two little maids we love: Rachel, a flaxen-haired sweetheart, and Naomi Rose, whose name means pleasant and whose baby rose-bud mouth is too small yet for cookies.

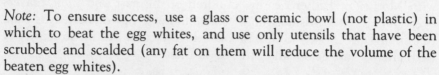

> 3 egg whites, at room temperature
> 1 teaspoon vanilla extract
> ½ teaspoon cream of tartar
> ¼ teaspoon salt
> ¾ cup sugar

Note: To ensure success, use a glass or ceramic bowl (not plastic) in which to beat the egg whites, and use only utensils that have been scrubbed and scalded (any fat on them will reduce the volume of the beaten egg whites).

Preheat oven to 300°F. Line 2 cookie sheets with aluminum foil or opened brown grocer bags, cut to fit the pans.

In a large very clean nonplastic bowl, combine the egg whites, vanilla, cream of tartar, and salt. Beat into soft peaks, then gradually add the sugar, beating until the whites stand in stiff peaks. Drop by teaspoonfuls about 1 inch apart on the cookie sheets; each mound should be about 1½ inches across. Bake about 20 minutes, then turn off the oven, open the oven door slightly, and let the kisses dry out in the hot oven for about 30 minutes. Remove pan from oven; peel kisses off the foil or brown bag and cool on a wire rack. When completely cool, store in an airtight container until ready to serve.   *Makes about 4 dozen kisses.*

GRANDMA HOPPING'S TURKISH DELIGHT

This old-time jellied candy was made in orange, lemon, pineapple, lime, peppermint, and cinnamon flavors. Grandma and women like her made theirs with fruit purees.

> 3 tablespoons unflavored gelatin
> ½ cup orange or pineapple juice, or
>   diluted lemon or lime juice (see
>   Note)
> Finely grated rind of orange, lemon,
>   or lime (optional)
>
> 2 cups sugar, plus sugar for coating
>   candy
> ½ cup light corn syrup
> ½ cup hot water
> Food coloring, optional

Note: If making peppermint or cinnamon-flavored candy, soften the gelatin in cold water instead of fruit juice, flavor with oil of peppermint or cinnamon after cooking the syrup to a soft ball stage, and omit the grated fruit rind.

In a small bowl, soften the gelatin in the fruit juice; let stand for about 5 minutes to soften. Meanwhile, in a large saucepan combine the 2 cups sugar with the corn syrup and hot water, stirring long enough to dissolve the sugar. Bring to a boil over medium-high heat and cook to the soft-ball stage (234°F to 240°F). Add the softened gelatin (food coloring if desired and the grated rind, if using); stir to dissolve gelatin. Rinse an 8x8-inch cake pan under cool running water and pour the candy into it. Set aside to cool at room temperature, then refrigerate overnight.

The next day, turn the candy onto a smooth surface that has been liberally sprinkled with sugar. Cut the candy into strips and roll in the sugar; lay out to dry. When the candy strips are dry to the touch, they may be wrapped individually in plastic wrap and stored in an airtight container. *Makes about 4 dozen pieces.*

AUNT IRENE'S ANGEL TORTE WITH LIGHT CREAM-CHEESE FROSTING

While this light and lovely torte is a favorite Christmas Eve cake, Aunty could be persuaded to bake it earlier in December. Filled and topped with a light cream-cheese frosting and sprinkled with sliced almonds, it not only looks good but brings praises from men and women alike.

3 cups sifted cake flour	1¼ cups milk
1 tablespoon baking powder	4 egg whites, at room temperature
½ teaspoon salt	Light Cream-Cheese Frosting (recipe
½ cup butter or margarine	follows)
1½ cups sugar	⅓ cup sliced almonds
1 teaspoon vanilla extract	A few red candied cherries, optional

Preheat oven to 375°F. Grease and flour two 9-inch round cake pans. Sift together the flour, baking powder, and salt; sift mixture twice more. In a large bowl, cream the butter until smooth; gradually add the sugar and vanilla, creaming until light and fluffy. Alternately add the dry ingredients and milk to the sugar-butter mixture, beating after each addition. In a separate bowl, whip the egg whites until stiff but still moist. Add about one third of the egg whites to the batter, gently stirring them in, then gently (so as not to lose volume) fold in the remaining egg whites, about one third at a time; don't overwork the batter.

Divide the batter between the prepared pans. Bake until light golden brown or until a toothpick inserted into the centers of the layers comes out clean, 25 to 30 minutes. Let cool in the pans for about 10 minutes, then turn the layers onto a wire rack to cool completely.

When the cake is completely cool, cut each layer in half horizontally, creating 4 thin layers. Place one layer, cut side up, on a cake plate; with a spatula, spread slightly more than 1/3 cup frosting over the top (but not sides). Put another layer on top, spread with frosting, and cover with the next layer. Continue adding frosting and layers until tops of all layers are frosted, then sprinkle with almonds, and, if desired, stud the top with red candied cherries. (*Note:* If you wish, increase the frosting recipe by half and frost the entire cake.)   *Makes one 4-layer cake.*

Light Cream-Cheese Frosting

1 envelope (1 tablespoon) unflavored gelatin	1/2 cup sugar
1/4 cup cold water	1 tablespoon vanilla extract
1 cup light cream	1 (8-ounce) package cream cheese, softened

Soften the gelatin in the cold water for 5 minutes.

Heat the cream and sugar together in a small saucepan, stirring occasionally (the mixture should not boil). Add the gelatin and continue stirring until dissolved. Remove from heat; let cool completely, then stir in the vanilla. In a small bowl, whip the cream cheese until light. Slowly add the gelatin mixture, stirring to blend. Cover and refrigerate until thickened and spreadable.

Makes about 3 cups or enough to fill and frost the top of one 4-layer cake.

> O Christmas tree, O Christmas tree,
> How lovely are your branches.
> In summer sun, in winter snow,
> A dress of green you always show.
> O Christmas tree, O Christmas tree,
> How lovely are your branches.

Oh Christmas tree, O Christmas tree,
With happiness we greet you.
When decked with candles once a year,
You fill our hearts with yuletide cheer.
O Christmas tree, O Christmas tree,
With happiness we greet you.

While the carol "O Tannenbaum" ("O Christmas Tree") has never become as popular in the United States as it has always been in Germany, the traditional English version has a hauntingly beautiful quality about it that speaks of deep forests and early-day Christianity. Without being told, one senses its origins, shrouded in obscurity and its rich feel of the Middle Ages.

A FAVORITE CHRISTMAS LEGEND

Our favorite Christmas legend is about the miraculous revelation of the first Christmas tree on Christmas Eve some twelve hundred years ago. It came about because a young Englishman of noble Anglo-Saxon birth was called by God to become a monk. Even though in the monastery young Winfirth distinguished himself as a scholar and preacher, he chose to follow the example of other Saxon monks and set out as a missionary to Frisia, where he hoped to convert pagan Germanic tribesmen. The venture failed because of war and political hostility. So young Winfirth went to Rome, where he was commissioned by the Pope to evangelize Germany and to counteract the influence of the Irish monks there.

While laboring among the pagan tribes, winning over chieftains, and converting and baptizing great numbers of heathens, Winfirth came upon a group of worshippers gathered at the Oak of Geismar about to sacrifice little Prince Asulf to the god Thor. With the aid of the Almighty, Winfirth halted the sacrifice, rescued the little prince, and cut

down the "blood" oak. As it fell, a young fir appeared, and the ardent young missionary declared that the fir was the "tree of life," a symbol of Christ. Standing beside it, Winfirth once again preached his message of Jesus' birth to the Germanic tribesmen.

OUR FAMILY'S FAVORITE HONEY OAT CRUNCH

Baked by the younger set and eaten by handfuls by all, this easy-to-make recipe is a favorite for teaching young cooks to bake. Since the ingredients are always on hand, and the recipe small enough so that, should a tiny cook misunderstand her mother's directions and put more salt than sugar in the dough or too much ground ginger, Mama with unruffled calm could tell her to throw out the ruined batch and try again.

¼ cup butter or margarine	1 cup all-purpose flour
⅓ cup, packed, light or dark brown sugar	2 teaspoons ground ginger
1 generous tablespoon honey	1 teaspoon baking powder
1½ cups quick-cooking rolled oats	¼ teaspoon salt

Preheat oven to 350°F. Grease a large (about 15x12x1½-inch) cookie sheet or 2 smaller ones. Heat the butter, sugar, and honey together just until smooth. In a large bowl, combine the oats, flour, ginger, baking powder, and salt and add to the butter mixture; stir well until mixture becomes a firm dough. Roll the dough by teaspoonfuls into balls in the palm of your hands. Place on the cookie sheet(s) about 2 inches apart; flatten slightly. Bake until golden brown, about 5 minutes. Remove from oven; leave on cookie sheet(s) for 5 minutes, then transfer to a wire rack or an opened brown grocery bag and cool. Store in an airtight container until ready to serve. *Makes about 2 dozen cookies.*

AUNT EL'S HUMBLE PIE

Aunty loved to make humble pie at Christmas since she thought the flavor and attitude were perfect for the season. Little did she know that traditionally such pies, made of the inner and less choice parts (humbles) of deer, were given to servants at hunting feasts and that the attitude she so admired spoke of a low station in life. Blessed by innocence, she made and served the most delicious "humble pies" in the county.

Crisp Lard Pie Pastry Dough (recipe follows)

2½ cups Pan-Dripping or Stock Gravy (recipe follows)

2 cups roasted or boiled venison
shoulder meat, cut into bite-
size pieces

2 cups pared and thinly sliced
potatoes

½ cup chopped onions

½ cup pared and thinly sliced
carrots

½ cup canned peas, optional

Prepare the dough; refrigerate. Next, make the gravy; let sit at room temperature until cool.

When the dough is chilled, roll out ¼ inch thick. Combine the cooled gravy with the venison, potatoes, onions, carrots, and, if using, the peas; place mixture in a 2-quart casserole dish. Fit the dough over the top loosely, trimming off the excess. Cut generous slits in the top to let steam out while baking. Flute the edges of the dough with your thumb and forefinger to make a pretty border around the pie. Bake until crust is well browned, about 45 to 50 minutes.   *Makes 4 or 5 servings.*

Crisp Lard Pie Pastry Dough

1 cup all-purpose flour, plus ¼ to
½ cup flour for rolling out
dough

¼ teaspoon salt

⅓ cup chilled pork lard

4 to 6 tablespoons cold water

Sift the flour and salt together. Cut in the lard with 2 dinner knives or a pastry cutter. (*Note:* Do not use your fingertips to blend in the lard; it has a lower melting point than harder fats like butter, margarine, or shortening and, if warmed, will soak into the flour, making the crust less flaky.) Add just enough of the cold water, 2 tablespoons at a time, until mixture will hold together; blend it in with a fork. Handling the dough quickly and as little as possible, roll it into a ball. Refrigerate until chilled thoroughly before rolling it out.   *Makes enough dough for 1 humble pie.*

Pan-Dripping or Stock Gravy

2 cups thin pan drippings from
roasting the venison (skim fat off
top and enough water if needed
to make 2 cups) or 2 cups
skimmed venison, beef, or
chicken stock

3 tablespoons cornstarch
½ cup water
Salt and black pepper

Heat the pan drippings or stock in a medium-size saucepan to a rolling boil. Meanwhile, dissolve the cornstarch in the water, stirring to blend. Stir the cornstarch into the boiling drippings and cook just until the gravy becomes clear, about 3 to 5 minutes, stirring occasionally. Season to taste with salt and pepper. Set aside to cool.   *Makes about 2½ cups.*

A YOUNG COOK'S
CABBAGE AND CARROT SALAD
WITH HOMEMADE HONEY MAYONNAISE

In the old days, girls as young as ten or twelve contributed a dish to holiday feasts and, while compliments tended to be left-handed, boys "made a fuss" over their cooking. This easy-to-make salad was a favorite with mothers and daughters alike, especially since indoor and outdoor storage areas were bulging with winter vegetables such as cabbages (red, white, green, and crinkled Savoy) and carrots, even three-foot-long carrots for stock. While this recipe was quite commonplace, women and girls had their "secret" ingredients which lifted it out of the ordinary.

2 cups shredded cabbage
1 cup peeled and shredded carrots
1 medium-size apple (Golden
    Delicious preferred), peeled and
    finely chopped
½ cup golden raisins

½ cup chilled Homemade Honey
    Mayonnaise (recipe follows)
Salt and black pepper
A sprinkling of freshly grated nutmeg
    (a secret ingredient)

In a medium-size bowl, combine the cabbage, carrots, apple, and raisins. Add just enough mayonnaise to moisten the salad. Salt and pepper lightly, then sprinkle with nutmeg and gently fold to blend. Serve the remaining mayonnaise on the side.   *Makes 6 to 8 servings.*

Homemade Honey Mayonnaise
¼ cup light honey
Juice from 1 lemon (about 2
    tablespoons)

½ cup farm sour cream whipped
    (once whipped, it should yield ⅔
    to 1 cup of whipped sour cream)
    or use 1 cup dairy sour cream
    (unwhipped)

Stir the honey and lemon juice together until the honey is thinned. Add the sour cream.   *Makes about 1 cup mayonnaise.*

OLD-FASHIONED BUTTERED KALE

Granny, a tall raw-boned woman with a kindly face who had come as a girl from Scotland to the Midwest, loved kale. This hardy non-heading cabbage pokes its tender young head out of the snow early in spring and unfurls its loose-spreading curled leaves. Ready for fresh greens at the end of winter, Granny would gather a generous panful, as many as she could find, and fix them for her wintertime supper.

| 4 pounds kale | Black pepper |
| Salt | 1/3 to 1/2 cup butter, melted |

Wash the kale and trim away all heavy stems. Cook uncovered in a large saucepan of boiling water until tender, about 25 minutes. Drain and chop. Season to taste with salt and pepper. Spoon melted butter over each serving and pass the potatoes! *Makes 6 to 8 servings or about 3 cups.*

EXCEEDING ALL

Long life's a lovely thing to know,
With lovely health and wealth, forsooth,
And lovely name and fame—But O
The loveliness of Youth!

—James Whitcomb Riley

THE LOVELINESS OF YOUTH

Growing up on the farm in Missouri, and, like all country children, being allowed to run free, imbibing the spirit of the earth at a time when it was more pristine than now, Mother at an early age learned how long it took for ducklings to hatch, where the wild mint grew, and about clouds that brought rain and wind that preceded a thunderstorm. She learned, without being taught, about procreation and about the creative and destructive power of nature.

As she grew older, she came to realize that at the heart of all man's wit and wisdom, creativity, and understanding of the human condition, there is a universal body of knowledge, free for the taking. And sadly she learned that nothing is forever.

Now at eighty-four, she talks gently to us—those of us who will be her survivors—about leaves that fall in God's own time to prepare the earth for spring.

MOTHER

Soft and gentle
With fragile grace
Lovely to behold
Her aged face.

Bright youth gone,
The hands are slow
Yet from her now,
Strength and wisdom flow.

To her loved ones,
She bequeaths
Tenderness, mercy
And fallen leaves.

—J.W.H.

SNOWFLAKE WAFERS

This crisp wafer-thin cookie is as delicate and fragile as a snowflake. It's excellent for a lady's tea or a child's delight.

1 cup butter, softened   *cup for rolling cookies*
⅓ cup heavy cream   *About ½ cup sugar*
2 cups all-purpose flour, plus ½

In a large bowl, thoroughly blend the butter and cream together. Add the 2 cups flour and stir mixture into a soft dough. Cover bowl and refrigerate about 30 minutes to 1 hour.

Meanwhile, preheat oven to 375°F. Remove the chilled dough from the refrigerator and divide it into 3 portions. On a lightly floured surface, roll each portion of dough ⅛ inch thick; cut into 1½-inch rounds with a cookie cutter.

Pour the sugar on a piece of waxed paper and coat both sides of each round with it. Place rounds on an ungreased cookie sheet and prick each with a fork 2 or 3 times.

Bake until set but not brown, about 7 or 8 minutes. Let cookies sit on the cookie sheet for 5 minutes, then transfer to a wire rack to cool. Delightful when freshly baked, these cookies begin to lose their delicacy when stored for more than a few hours.   *Makes 5 dozen cookies.*

ARCHIE'S CHRISTMAS GUMDROP JUMBLES

These cookies are nice for a children's party. The color and flavor make them perfect for serving with cold milk or vanilla ice cream.

2¾ cups sifted all-purpose flour
 1 teaspoon salt
 ½ teaspoon soda
 1 cup dairy sour cream
 ¼ cup butter or margarine,
    softened

2 eggs, beaten to a froth
 1 teaspoon vanilla extract
 1½ cups, packed, light brown sugar
 3 cups gumdrops, cut into bits
 1 cup finely chopped walnuts,
    optional

Into a medium-size bowl, sift together the flour, salt, and baking soda. In a large bowl, combine the sour cream and butter, blending well. Add the eggs and vanilla, stirring to blend them in. Stir in the sugar, taking care to work out lumps. Add the flour-mixture to the sour cream mixture and stir into a soft dough. Fold in the gumdrops (and walnuts, if using). Refrigerate the dough until the oven is hot.

Preheat oven to 375°F. Drop the dough by rounded teaspoonfuls, about 2 inches apart, onto an ungreased cookie sheet. Bake until firm to the touch, about 10 minutes. Remove from oven and immediately transfer to a wire rack or onto an opened brown grocery bag to cool. When completely cooled, store in an airtight container until ready to serve.

Makes about 5 to 6 dozen cookies.

ROLY-POLY SNOWMEN WITH LEMON ICING

When the weather was too bad outside, Mother would help us make these sweet, puffy little snowmen. Now that we are grown, each year as Christmas comes around both my sister Sheila and I still recall the fragrance of the baking snowmen and the unexpected zest of the lemon icing.

2 packages dry or granulated yeast
½ cup warm water
½ cup lukewarm milk (105°F to 115°F)
½ cup sugar
1 teaspoon salt
2 eggs, beaten to a froth
½ cup butter or margarine, softened

4½ to 5 cups all-purpose flour
Lemon icing (recipe follows)
12 golden or dark raisins, cut in half (for snowmen's eyes)
3 candied cherries, cut into quarters (for snowmen's mouths)

In a large bowl, combine the yeast, water, milk, sugar, and salt; stir to blend. Let sit 10 minutes until yeast is dissolved and has formed a frothy head. Stir in the eggs, then the butter. Add 2½ cups of the flour and beat into a smooth batter. Cover and let rise in a warm place until doubled in bulk, about 45 minutes. Stir down and add enough of the remaining flour to make a smooth elastic dough that can easily be handled. Turn onto a smooth lightly floured surface and knead for about 5 minutes. Divide the dough into 12 equal portions. On a large greased cookie sheet (or 2 small ones) make each portion of dough into a snowman as follows: Make a large round bun for the body and a smaller ball for the head and press together; then roll some of the dough into ½ inch arms and 2-inch legs; pinch arms and legs on the body, taking care to have a smooth connection. Let rise until nicely puffed, about 30 minutes. Bake until light golden brown, about 20 minutes. Remove from oven and let snowmen sit on the cookie sheet until partially cooled, then with a long spatula transfer them onto a piece of kraft paper (an opened brown grocery bag will do nicely).

Once completely cool, spread with lemon icing, and while icing is still soft, put the snowmen's eyes and mouths in place. Serve to children (and adults) on demand. *Makes 12 snowmen.*

Lemon Icing

3 cups powdered sugar
2 tablespoons heavy cream, more if needed to make icing spread smoothly

1 tablespoon lemon juice
½ teaspoon finely grated lemon peel

In a medium-size bowl, combine the sugar and 2 tablespoons cream, beating until a thick icing is formed. Add the lemon juice and lemon peel; stir to blend. Then add just enough additional cream, if needed, to thin the icing so that it will spread thinly and smoothly over the snowmen. Use immediately. (*Note:* When icing is made with heavy cream, it sets up faster and is firmer than a butter icing; therefore, quickly spread it over the snowmen, then promptly stick the eyes and mouths in place.) *Makes enough to ice 12 snowmen.*

BETTY'S CHOCOLATE MOUNDS

It seems little girls who become great cooks, like Aunt Clary's great-niece Betty, show an early interest in fixing good things to eat. This easy-to-make chocolate-mound recipe is a little girl's recipe, one that is not too original, but one that brings praise and compliments from the whole family—especially younger and older brothers.

½ pound milk chocolate
1 ounce unsweetened baking
  chocolate

½ teaspoon vanilla extract
3 cups crisp cornflakes

Lay a piece of waxed paper out on a flat cookie sheet. Then cut both kinds of chocolate into bite-size pieces. In a heavy-bottomed saucepan, combine both chocolates and melt over very low heat. Remove from heat; stir in the vanilla and cornflakes, mixing thoroughly. Immediately drop by teaspoonfuls onto the waxed paper; if needed, use your fingertips to shape into mounds. Let stand 3 to 4 hours at cool room temperature to harden slowly; do not refrigerate. No complicated storage method is needed as these chocolate mounds will be eaten quickly by an eager family.   *Makes about 2 dozen small mounds.*

PEACE ON EARTH

At our house we love to wake up a few mornings before Christmas to find that the mountains surrounding us are white with snow. Better yet, it's lovely to wake in the night and become aware of silence, and to hop out of bed onto the cold floor of our unheated upstairs bedrooms and wake everyone to come peek out of the window at soft giant snowflakes drifting down past us to land on the roof just below, on the winter-bare cherry tree, and on the ground two stories away. And then to dash back to bed and cuddle down among the warm comforters and quilts.

When the children were small, they would immediately begin to make plans to build a snowman with friends or take the inner tubes and sleds out into the front pasture.

Morning found all the children in the neighborhood up on the farm to play. The boys and older girls disappeared into the fields. But to my delight, Colleen—long brown braids flying—and Tracy, her best friend, would play in the yard and about the farm buildings, holding their arms wide, dropping full length to the ground to make little angels everywhere in the snow.

THE FAMILY JEWELS

When Aunt Clary was very old, the great chestnut knot of hair of her youth had diminished to white wisps; the glorious singing voice had

grown thin and trembled as she spoke. But those of us who loved her realized that she, more than any other relative, was our link with the past, that every story she told, every remembrance, was a living part of our family heritage—one might call them the "family jewels"—to be protected and hoarded for children to come.

Some of us children (grandchildren and great-grandchildren, nieces and nephews, a whole flock of little ones) loved to visit with her. Rocking very gently back and forth, Aunt Clary basked in the attention and would recall her childhood, which seemed to be the most vivid of all memories to her. Often, no matter what the season of the year, she would tell about Christmas in the log cabin in the woods, about her home there and her family, about snow and snowbirds, about mice in the barn that stole the grain, about a simple Christmas dinner and Old Todd, a single man who lived about five miles from them through the woods, who was always invited.

When she tired of the commotion and grew weary, she would make tea, knowing full well that once we had had a spot of tea with her and a

JANE WATSON HOPPING

piece of her fruited gingerbread we would consider ourselves dismissed—
until the next time.

AUNT CLARY'S OLD-FASHIONED
FRUITED GINGERBREAD

Old-time women made this cake with lard and sometimes did not have
the luxury of candied fruits, so they chopped a bit of their dried fruit to
add to the cake.

½ cup dark raisins
½ cup chopped walnuts
¼ cup chopped mixed candied fruit
    peel, or use half candied lemon
    peel and half candied orange
    peel
2⅔ cups all-purpose flour, plus 2
    tablespoons for dusting raisins,
    walnuts, and candied fruit peel
1 tablespoon ground cinnamon
1 tablespoon ground ginger

Scant 1 tablespoon baking powder
1 teaspoon ground cloves
1 teaspoon salt
½ cup butter or margarine
½ cup, packed, light brown sugar
2 eggs, lightly beaten
1 cup boiling water
1 cup dark molasses
1 teaspoon baking soda
Sweetened Whipped Cream (page
60)

Preheat oven to 350°F. Dust the raisins, walnuts, and candied fruit peel
with the 2 tablespoons flour; set aside. Grease a 13x9x2-inch baking
pan. Set aside. Into a medium-size bowl, sift the 2⅔ cups flour, cinnamon, ginger, baking powder, cloves, and salt; set aside.

In a large bowl, cream together the butter and sugar; add the eggs
and beat until light. In a small bowl, combine the boiling water and
molasses together; add the baking soda, stirring until dissolved, then add
to the batter. Gradually add the flour, stirring well. Fold in the raisin
mixture. Pour the batter into prepared pan. Bake until the cake springs
back when lightly pressed with your fingertips in the center, about 30
to 35 minutes. Cool cake in the pan. Serve while still warm or at
room temperature, cut into 3-inch squares and topped with Sweetened
Whipped Cream.   *Makes a large sheet cake or about 12 servings.*

TRILBY CREAM

This light, lovely dessert is perfect for topping off heavy holiday meals or for serving with coffee to carolers, evening visitors, or ladies in the afternoon.

1 cup heavy cream
1 egg white, beaten until stiff peaks form
1 cup tiny marshmallows
½ cup slivered almonds

½ cup orange pulp, membranes and seeds removed (or, if you wish, use well-drained canned mandarine oranges)
1 tablespoon powdered sugar
About 6 candied cherries

Whip the cream until soft peaks form; fold in the egg white; add the marshmallows, almonds, orange pulp, and powdered sugar, stirring only enough to blend. Serve immediately in chilled sherbet cups with a candied cherry on top. *Makes about 6 servings.*

EASY-TO-MAKE GOLDEN FRITTERS

Ada's family ate these fritters hot, sprinkled with cinnamon sugar or with fruit syrup drizzled over them. We like ours quite plain, with just a little powdered sugar dusted over them.

2 cups hot water
⅓ cup butter or margarine
2 cups all-purpose flour

6 eggs
Vegetable oil, for frying
Sifted powdered sugar, optional

In a large saucepan, boil the water; add the butter and return to a boil. Stir in the flour. Remove from heat and when mixture is nearly cool, beat in the eggs, one at a time, beating well after each addition. Drop this stiff dough by teaspoonfuls into 1½ to 3 inches of hot (375°F) vegetable oil and fry until golden brown on both sides, about 3 to 4 minutes in all. Lift out of the hot oil with a slotted spoon; drain on absorbent paper. Sprinkle with powdered sugar, if desired. Serve immediately. *Makes about 4 dozen.*

AN OLD-TIME RECIPE FOR A WELL-MADE DAY

This bit of homey wisdom circulated through our family until I think almost every woman had a copy in her cookbook, then it was passed around the neighborhood.

> Take a little dash of water, cold,
>   and a little leaven of prayer,
> And a little bit of morning gold,
>   dissolved in the morning air.
> Add to your meal some merriment
>   and a lot of kith and kin;
> And then, as a prime ingredient,
>   plenty of work thrown in.
> But spice it all with the essence of love
>   and a whiff of play
> Let the wise Old Book and a glance above
>   complete the well-made day.

> Makes more than one happy life.

> Margaret Harries

🌿 SWEET FRAGRANCES

Aunt Clary used to tell us how when she was a girl there was always something about Christmas baking that made it different from all the baking done throughout the rest of the year.

"We youngin's" she would say, thinking about younger brothers and sisters, "begged to beat the eggs and stir in the sugar and stick our fingers into the creamy batter to test it for flavor.

"Mother always put in the spices herself. We just sat around and whiffed in the smell of them and guessed from what far-off land they'd come. The boys were *so helpful:* They'd run out to get more wood for Mother's fire, hoping to be rewarded with a cookie or two. We girls cracked out jars full of nutmeats and threw the shells into the fire, where they burned hot as the oil in them caught fire.

"When Papa came in from doing chores at supper time, he'd sniff and sniff until finally to our delight he'd say, 'Smells like Christmas in here.' And after we'd eaten our supper, Mama would let each of us sample a little, choosing our favorite treat from all we'd made that day. If any of us asked her if there would be enough left for Christmas, she'd laugh and say, 'Well if there isn't, I expect we could just bake up some more.' "

CHRISTMAS FRAGRANCE

It's Christmas time at our house,
Anyone could tell,
Even if you couldn't see
You'd know it by the smell.

There's fragrant air adrifting
That's loaded with good sniffs
Of gingerbread and popcorn
And baking cookie whiffs.

The kitchen's full of odors
Of pudding, steam and cake
And lots of other goodies
My mother likes to make.

There's an aroma from the greens too,
That mingles with the rest,
But if the truth were really told
I like food fragrance best.

For I think the Christmas bouquet
Is a treat that's hard to beat
With its tantalizing promise
Of the things we're going to eat.

—Solveig Paulson Russell

AUNT CLARY'S
OLD-FASHIONED RAISIN BUNS
WITH RUM BUTTER FROSTING

Effie, who loved Aunt Clary like a mother, served these buns with hot coffee and a lot of conversation. She would show you a new crocheting pattern and tell you all about the newest baby in town. She had an opinion about everything, and as the men complained, she was almost always right.

2 tablespoons dry or granulated yeast
¼ cup lukewarm water (105°F to 115°F)
1 cup milk
¼ cup butter or margarine
⅔ cup sugar
1 teaspoon salt

1 tablespoon ground cinnamon
1 teaspoon vanilla extract
½ teaspoon freshly grated nutmeg
2 eggs, beaten
5 cups sifted all-purpose flour, placed in a medium-size bowl
1 cup golden raisins
Rum Butter Frosting (recipe follows)

Place the yeast in a small bowl and pour the lukewarm water over it; stir to blend. Set aside until a frothy head has formed, about 10 minutes. Meanwhile, scald the milk in a small saucepan. Remove from heat and add the butter, sugar, and salt; set aside to cool until lukewarm.

When butter mixture is lukewarm, stir well, then add the cinnamon, vanilla, nutmeg, yeast, and eggs. Pour mixture into a large bowl and add 3 *cups* of the flour, stirring into a thick batter; beat well to develop gluten. Add the raisins and enough of the *remaining* flour to make a soft dough. Turn dough onto a floured surface and knead until elastic and satiny. Wash the bowl in hot soapy water, scald, and dry. Grease the bowl and place dough back in it; cover and let rise until doubled in bulk, about 45 minutes. Meanwhile, grease two 13x9x2-inch baking pans.

Gently punch down dough and form buns by pinching off small balls of dough about the size of a large egg; roll gently between the palms of your hands and tuck them close together in the greased pans. Let rise until doubled in bulk, about 35 minutes or more; the dough should look puffy and feel quite light to the touch when you press it gently with your fingertips.

While the dough is rising, preheat oven to 375°F. When well risen, bake both panfuls at the same time until golden brown, about 20 to 25 minutes. Remove from oven and let cool for about 10 minutes in the pans; then turn onto a wire rack. When lukewarm, spread Rum Butter Frosting over the tops with a knife or spatula. Serve warm or at room temperature. *Makes about 4 dozen rolls.*

Rum Butter Frosting

4 tablespoons butter, softened
2 cups powdered sugar
About 2 tablespoons milk

About 2 tablespoons rum (or brandy
if you wish)

In a small bowl, stir together the butter and sugar. Add 1 *tablespoon* of the milk and 1 *tablespoon* of the rum; stir. Then add as much of the *remaining* milk and rum as needed, beating to make a light, smooth, spreadable consistency. Use immediately. *Makes ⅔ cup or slightly more.*

AUNT MAE'S CHRISTMAS
CREAM CAKE WITH LEMON BUTTER GLAZE

Old-fashioned cooks had a steady supply of cream, summer and winter: Cows were—and still are—bred to calve at two different times during the year, so that their lactation periods overlapped, producing milk throughout the entire year. A summer cow has her calf about February or March, and a winter cow has her calf about October or November. The cow whose calf is born in February produces milk from spring to fall, and her cream is a rich, deep golden color because of the chlorophyll in the grass she eats. A winter cow eats hay and grain; and even alfalfa hay, which is green, stored during the summer months for winter use, will not keep the color of her cream bright. The cream produced by a winter cow is equally rich but almost white; on old-time farms it was a godsend for wintertime use. The winter cream we used in this recipe kept the color of the cake nice and light. If you don't have a cow, store-bought cream is fine.

4 eggs, well beaten
2 cups sugar
3 cups all-purpose flour
1 tablespoon plus 1 teaspoon baking powder
½ teaspoon salt

2 cups heavy cream
1 tablespoon strained lemon juice
1 teaspoon grated lemon peel
1 teaspoon vanilla extract
Lemon Butter Glaze (page 70)

Preheat oven to 350°F. Grease and flour a 10-inch tube pan; set aside. Pour the eggs into a large bowl. Add the sugar and beat until blended. Into a medium-size bowl, sift together the flour, baking powder, and salt. In another bowl, combine the cream, lemon juice, lemon peel, and vanilla. Alternately add the flour mixture and cream mixture to the egg-sugar mixture. Pour into the prepared pan. Bake until light golden and a toothpick inserted into the center comes out clean, 45 to 50 minutes. Remove from oven and let sit in pan for about 10 minutes, then loosen cake from pan with a spatula and turn out on a large serving plate to cool. When the cake is lukewarm, spoon the glaze over the top and let it run down the sides. Cool completely before serving.

Makes 1 tube cake.

GREAT-GRANDMA MEEKINS'S SNICKERDOODLES

When great-grandma baked, she *baked*. Years of cooking for a large household of children (she had thirteen boys and girls) had taught her that it took just as much time to clean up after a small recipe as a large one and that anything that made a dozen or two would barely go around.

1½ cups butter, softened
1½ cups sugar
2 eggs, beaten into a froth

2¾ cups all-purpose flour
2 teaspoons cream of tartar
1 teaspoon baking soda

1/4 teaspoon salt
Cinnamon Sugar Coating (recipe
  follows)

Preheat oven to 400°F. In a large bowl, thoroughly mix the butter, sugar, and eggs. Stir in the flour, cream of tartar, baking soda, and salt, blending to make an easily handled dough. Form rounded teaspoonfuls into balls, using your fingertips. Roll each ball in cinnamon sugar coating and place 2-inches apart on an ungreased cookie sheet. Bake until set, about 8 to 10 minutes. Immediately remove from cookie sheet to a wire rack or opened brown grocery bag to cool. When thoroughly cool, store in airtight containers until ready to serve.   *Makes about 6 dozen cookies.*

Cinnamon Sugar Coating
In a small bowl, combine 2 *tablespoons sugar* and 2 *tablespoons ground cinnamon*, mixing thoroughly. Use to coat balls of cookie dough.
Makes 1/4 cup.

CHRISTMAS
RED-PLUM PUFF PUDDING

Mother made puff pudding all through the year out of fresh fruits as they came in season and with home-canned fruits in winter. During the holiday season, most of us loved this red plum puff for family gatherings. However, some folks bemoaned the fact that women were not making a "golden puff pudding" with canned peaches. And there were those who didn't care a fig for color and thought "apple puff pudding" with plenty of cinnamon couldn't be beat.

2 cups home-canned or store-
  bought pitted, red-fleshed
  plums, drained, plus 1/2 cup
  reserved juice
2 1/2 tablespoons quick-cooking
  tapioca

2/3 cup sugar
1/8 teaspoon salt
1/2 cup heavy cream or 8 scoops of
  ice cream (vanilla preferred),
  optional
Plum Puff Batter (recipe follows)

Preheat oven to 325°F. Grease a 13x11x2-inch baking pan or a 2-quart deep baking pan; set aside. In a medium-size saucepan, bring the plums and juice to boil over medium-high heat. Meanwhile, combine the tapioca, sugar and salt. When plums are boiling, gradually add the tapioca-sugar mixture to the fruit; boil briskly for 1 minute. Then pour into the greased baking pan and set over the heating oven to keep hot while making the plum puff batter.

When the batter is made, stir fruit gently, then pour batter over it. Bake until pudding is light golden brown, about 50 minutes. (Test with a toothpick.) Serve warm with a little heavy cream spooned over it or with ice cream.   *Makes 8 servings.*

Plum Puff Batter

¼ cup plus 2 tablespoons sugar
 2 eggs, separated and at room
   temperature

⅛ teaspoon salt
¼ teaspoon cream of tartar
½ cup sifted cake flour

In a large bowl, combine the sugar and egg yolks, beating until light. With a wire whisk or an electric mixer, beat the egg whites with the salt until foamy. Add the cream of tartar and beat until stiff enough to stand in moist peaks; do not overbeat. Fold the egg yolk mixture into the egg whites, then fold in the flour, a small amount at a time.

Make enough batter for 1 red plum puff pudding.

CRADLE HYMN

Hush, my dear, lie still and slumber;
  Holy angels guard thy bed;
Heavenly blessings without number
  Gently falling on thy head.

Sleep, my babe, thy food and raiment,
  House and home, thy friends provide;
All without thy care, or payment,
  All thy wants are well supplied.

How much better thou'rt attended
  Than the Son of God could be,
When from heaven He descended,
  And became a child like thee!

Soft and easy is thy cradle;
  Coarse and hard thy Saviour lay,
When His birthplace was a stable,
  And His softest bed was hay.

See the kindly shepherds round Him,
  Telling wonders from the sky!
When they sought Him, there they found Him,
  With His Virgin-Mother by.

See the lovely babe a-dressing;
   Lovely infant, how He smiled!
When He wept, the mother's blessing
   Soothed and hushed the holy child.

Lo, He slumbers in His manger,
   Where the honest oxen fed;
Peace, my darling! here's no danger!
   Here's no ox a-near thy bed!

Mayst thou live to know and fear Him,
   Trust and love Him all thy days;
Then go dwell forever near Him,
   See His face, and sing His praise!

I could give thee thousand kisses,
   Hoping what I most desire;
Not a mother's fondest wishes
   Can to greater joys aspire.

—Isaac Watts

A Babe of Long Ago

Mothers of long ago sat in small "nursing rockers" to breast feed their babies and then held them close while they gently rocked and sang lullabies to them until the eyelids fluttered over sleep-dimmed eyes. Such a woman likened her baby's softly opened mouth to a rosebud; the pale sleeping face, the soft fine hair to that of an angel straight from God. She sang lines like "sleep my little one, sleep my pretty one, sleep." Or perhaps she sang a lullaby like this ancient one:

> Sleep baby sleep, thy father watches the sheep
> Thy mother shakes the dreamland tree
> And down come pleasant dreams for thee,
> Sleep baby sleep.

And when the song was sung and the final line repeated softly over and over until the child was completely relaxed—"in a state of repose" she might say—then she would carefully stand up and put the baby in the cradle for his or her life-sustaining nap.

A SWANSDOWN LOAF
WITH ORANGE MIST FROSTING

This light, delicious cake has always been a favorite with the children in the family. Older folks thought it was a Christmas cake, but the little ones wanted their mothers to make it for birthdays and other special occasions all year 'round.

3 egg whites, at room temperature	¾ cup milk
1¼ cups sugar	1 teaspoon vanilla extract
2 cups sifted cake flour	Orange Mist Frosting (recipe
2½ teaspoons baking powder	follows)
¾ teaspoon salt	
½ cup butter or margarine, softened	

Preheat oven to 375°F. Line the bottom of a 10x10x2-inch baking pan with waxed paper, then grease the paper; set aside. For the meringue, beat the egg whites with a rotary beater until foamy; gradually add ½ *cup* of the sugar, beating only until meringue stands in soft peaks. Set aside.

Into a medium-size bowl, sift together the flour, baking powder, and salt. In a large bowl, cream the butter until soft; add the *remaining 1 cup* sugar and stir until light. In a cup, combine the milk and vanilla. Alternately add the flour mixture and flavored milk to the butter-sugar mixture. When well blended, gently fold in the reserved meringue until thoroughly combined.

Turn into the prepared pan. Bake until light golden brown and firm to the touch, about 30 minutes. Remove from oven and cool in pan or immediately transfer to a cake plate. When cake is thoroughly cooled, top with orange mist frosting.

Makes 1 small sheet cake or about fourteen 2½-inch-square servings.

Orange Mist Frosting

1 egg white
¾ cup sugar
2 tablespoons plus one teaspoon
  strained orange juice

2 teaspoons strained lemon juice
½ teaspoon grated orange peel
A few grains salt

Combine the egg white, sugar, orange juice, lemon juice, orange peel, and salt in the top of a double boiler; mix thoroughly. Cook over rapidly boiling water, beating constantly with a rotary beater, until frosting will stand up in peaks, about 4 minutes. Remove top of double boiler from over boiling water and continue beating until thick enough to spread.

Makes enough to frost 1 small sheet cake.

AUNT CLARY'S BRAMBLE CAKES

Each year Aunt Clary put on her old torn straw hat and went into the fields and along the streams to pick wild blackberries. Then when the weather cooled down and Thanksgiving and Christmas was at hand, she made her yummy bramble cakes.

½ teaspoon baking powder
⅛ teaspoon salt
2 eggs, at room temperature
½ cup sugar
1½ cups sifted cake flour
½ teaspoon vanilla extract
½ to ⅔ cup blackberry jam or jelly
Seven-Minute Frosting (recipe
  follows)
Shredded coconut

Preheat oven to 400°F. Prepare pan by lining the bottom of a 15x10x1½-inch pan with waxed paper, then grease paper and sides of pan.

Combine the baking powder, salt, and eggs, beating until the mixture is completely foamy. Add the sugar, a small amount at a time and beat until the spongy mixture piles up thick in the bowl. Gently fold in the flour, then the vanilla.

Pour this fluffy batter into the prepared pan and spread with a spatula evenly over the bottom, taking care to fill the corners. Bake just until light-colored and done, about 10 minutes. Remove from oven and use a small pointed knife to loosen cake from pan by cutting around the edges and lifting the corners. Invert pan onto a clean kitchen towel (without nap) that has been liberally dusted with powdered sugar, and coax the cake out with the spatula.

Remove the paper and cut off all crisp edges. Cool on a wire rack, then cut cake in half horizontally. Put together as layers, spreading jam or jelly in-between. Cut into 18 servings. Spread the frosting over the tops and sides of each small cake and immediately sprinkle with shredded coconut. Serve on cake plates with forks. *Makes 18 cakes or 18 servings.*

Seven-Minute Frosting

  2 egg whites, unbeaten   *Pinch salt*
1½ cups sugar   *1 tablespoon white corn syrup*
  ⅓ cup water   *1 teaspoon vanilla extract*

In base of double boiler bring 2 or more inches of hot water to a full boil (water should not touch the bottom of the top pan). In the top combine egg whites, sugar, water, salt, and corn syrup. Beat with whisk or electric beater until well blended, about 1 minute. Then set top in place over rapidly boiling water. Constantly beat egg mixture at full speed while cooking and scrape frosting from bottom and sides of the pan frequently, using a spatula. Cook until frosting hangs in stiff peaks when the beater is removed, barely 7 minutes. Remove double boiler top from base. Add vanilla and beat until thick enough to spread, 1 or 2 minutes. At this point don't scrape bottom or sides of pan too closely, or you may cause the frosting to become granular. *Makes enough to frost 18 bramble cakes.*

BABY TEA PUFFS

These little tea puffs are bite sized and are a treat that even small children can enjoy.

½ cup butter   *2 cups sifted all-purpose flour*
  1 cup boiling water   *4 eggs*

Creamy Vanilla Filling (recipe   ½ cup powdered sugar, more as
  follows)   needed for dusting puffs

Preheat oven to 450°F. In a saucepan, melt the butter in the water over
high heat. Sift the flour into the boiling mixture. Cook, stirring constantly, until the mixture leaves sides of pan in a smooth cohesive mass.
Remove from heat.

Add the eggs, one at a time, to the flour mixture; beat thoroughly
after each addition, then beat steadily until mixture looks satiny or
breaks off when spoon is raised.

Drop the batter by teaspoonfuls onto an ungreased baking sheet.
Bake in the 450° oven 15 minutes; then reduce oven setting to 350° and
continue baking for 10 minutes more. Remove from oven and transfer
to a wire rack or an opened brown paper bag to cool.

Meanwhile, prepare the filling and set it aside to cool. When the
puffs and filling are cool, make a slit in one side of each puff with a sharp
knife and fill with the filling; once a number of the puffs are filled, sift a
fine coating of powdered sugar over the tops. Continue filling puffs and
dusting with powdered sugar until all are finished. Serve immediately.
(Note: Because the filling contains eggs, leftover puffs must be
refrigerated.)   Makes about 4 dozen.

Creamy Vanilla Filling
 2 cups milk   2 tablespoons butter or margarine
 ¼ cup cornstarch   1 tablespoon vanilla extract
 ½ cup sugar   ½ recipe Sweetened Whipped Cream
 ⅛ teaspoon salt   (page 60) optional
 2 eggs, lightly beaten

In base of a double boiler put about 2 inches of hot water; set top in
place (water in the base should not touch the bottom of the top pan).

Pour 1½ cups of the milk into the top pan and heat until tiny bubbles
appear around the edge of the pan. Meanwhile, in a medium bowl
thoroughly combine cornstarch, ¼ cup of the sugar and salt. Add the
remaining ½ cup milk and stir into a smooth paste. Slowly add the scalded
milk from the top of the double boiler to the paste, stirring constantly
to keep lumps from forming. Immediately return the mixture to the top
pan and cook, stirring frequently, over boiling water until smooth and
thick enough to mound slightly, about 15 minutes.

Next, stirring constantly, slowly pour about ⅓ of the cooked filling into the lightly beaten eggs; blend well and return this mixture to the double boiler; stir constantly. Cook 5 minutes more over rapid boiling water (continue to stir). Remove from heat; add butter; pour into a bowl. Cool, then add vanilla. For a richer filling fold in ½ recipe of Sweetened Whipped Cream. Cover and refrigerate to chill.

GOLDEN APRICOT NUGGETS

One Christmas Effie filled a lovely carved wooden chest with these candies and gave it to one of the little boys who for one night was a Magi. After the pageant the Kings from the East shared a few nuggets, but kept all the rest of the wealth for themselves.

1 pound dried apricots (select well-colored slightly soft fruits)

⅛ pound candied orange peel, tender and moist (preferred)

⅛ pound candied lemon peel, tender and moist (preferred)

Sugar

Grind the apricots, orange peel, and lemon peel twice in a meat or food grinder, using the finest blade. Knead mixture together a few times to form a cohesive mass. Shape into ½-inch balls and roll in sugar; set aside on waxed paper to dry for about 30 minutes, then store in an airtight container until ready to serve.

Makes a little more than a pound of nuggets.

THE OLD-FASHIONED BIBLE

How dear to my heart are the scenes of my childhood
That now but in mem'ry I sadly review;
The old meeting-house at the edge of the wildwood,
The rail fence and horses all tethered thereto;
The low, sloping roof, and the bell in the steeple,
The doves that came fluttering out overhead
As it solemnly gathered the God-fearing people
To hear the old Bible my grandfather read.
The old-fashioned Bible—
The dust-covered Bible—
The leather-bound Bible my grandfather read.

—James Whitcomb Riley

THE OLD MEETING-HOUSE AT THE EDGE OF THE WILDWOOD

In the old days fancy churches were rare in farm country and out west. For the most part the men of the community built a small building that was sometimes called a meeting house or a chapel. Often there was no bona fide minister, pastor, or preacher. Instead, members of the congregation read texts from the Bible.

AUNTIE'S EGGNOG
FOR GROWING CHILDREN

On Uncle Jake's farm, milk right out of the jug appeared on the table at every meal. But if you were ill, or for special occasions like Christmas Eve, Auntie would whip up milk drinks (eggnogs). Invariably hers were nonalcoholic, since she belonged to the WCTU—Women's Christian Temperance Union. But she might dress them up by making them with thin cream instead of milk, or top one made of milk with whipped cream, then dust it with freshly grated nutmeg.

4 eggs
4 cups milk
¼ cup sugar
1 teaspoon vanilla extract
¼ teaspoon salt

1 recipe Sweetened Whipped Cream
  (page 60)
Dusting of freshly grated nutmeg,
  optional

Beat the eggs until light and frothy. Add the milk and sugar and continue beating until well blended. Add the vanilla and salt and beat a few more whips. Pour immediately into tall glasses, leaving room for the whipped cream (¼ cup or more). Add the whipped cream and dust with nutmeg, if desired.   *Makes 3 large glasses or 4 small ones.*

AUNT EL'S
OLD-FASHIONED BLACK WALNUT AND
SWEET POTATO PIE

When Aunt El made this spicy, buttery pie (testing it ahead of time for Christmas), her kitchen was full of mittened and scarved relatives who had come in from the snow—young and old alike—sniffing the aroma and recalling other times they had savored thick wedges of such pie while clustered about that same stove gossiping, until their bodies relaxed and their clothes were dried.

Plain Double-Crust Pie Pastry
  Dough (recipe follows)
½ cup butter, softened
1 cup, packed, light brown sugar
2 cups cooked and well mashed
  sweet potato pulp

6 eggs, lightly beaten
⅔ cup dark corn syrup
⅔ cup milk
1 teaspoon salt
1 teaspoon vanilla extract
2 cups black walnuts, minced

Prepare the pastry dough; refrigerate until very cold before rolling out. Preheat oven to 400°F. In a large bowl, cream together the butter and sugar. Add the potatoes and eggs; stir to blend. Add the syrup, milk, salt, vanilla, and black walnuts; blend together well.

Remove the pastry dough from the refrigerator, and divide it in half. Roll out each half on a lightly floured surface and line two 9-inch pie pans with it; cut off extra dough from edges, leaving about 1 inch draped over rims. Evenly fold the dough under to form a double edge and flute with your thumbs and forefingers or with a wide-tined fork.

Pour the filling into the pastry shells, filling shells about two thirds full before placing in the oven, then add the remaining filling to the shells (this prevents spilling). Bake in the 400° oven for about 10 minutes; then reduce oven setting to 325° and continue baking until crust is golden and a knife blade inserted into the center of the custard comes out clean, about 35 minutes longer. Remove from oven and let cool to lukewarm or cooler before serving.   *Makes two 9-inch pies.*

Plain Single-Crust Pie Pastry Dough
2 cups all-purpose flour   ⅔ cup chilled pork lard
1 teaspoon salt   4 or 5 tablespoons cold water

Combine the flour and salt in a medium-size bowl; stir to blend. Cut the lard into the flour using a pastry cutter or two forks until the mixture becomes granular. (*Note:* Do not blend this fat into the flour with your hands as it has a lower melting point than shortening, butter, or margarine.) Moisten the mixture with just enough cold water, sprinkling in 1 tablespoon at a time, to form a cohesive mass. Turn onto a lightly floured surface and shape into a ball; wrap in aluminum foil or waxed paper and refrigerate until very cold before rolling out.

                    Makes enough dough for 2 single-crusted pies.

MOTHER'S DUNKIN' DOUGHNUTS

On cold winter evenings just before Christmas, Mother would tell us about our Pennsylvania Dutch great-grandmother and would make

doughnuts that she thought were a family legacy from her. Whether they were or were not, we all thought they were delicious.

1 package dry or granulated yeast
¼ cup lukewarm water (105°F to 115°F)
2 cups milk, heated to lukewarm
½ cup sugar
1½ teaspoons salt
4 tablespoons butter or margarine, melted
2 eggs, well beaten
1 tablespoon lemon juice

2 teaspoons finely grated lemon peel
6 cups all-purpose flour
Vegetable oil or pork lard, for frying doughnuts
Sugar, (see recipe for Lemon Butter Glaze, page 70, or Chocolate Glaze, page 72, for coating doughnuts)

In a small bowl, soften the yeast in warm water. Set aside for 10 minutes until a frothy head has formed. In a large bowl, pour the warm milk over the sugar and salt, stirring to dissolve. Add the butter and stir to blend. Add the eggs, lemon juice, lemon peel, and about 4 cups of the flour; beat until mixture is a smooth dough. Cover with a clean kitchen towel and set in a warm place until double in bulk, about 45 minutes. Then stir down, beat for about 5 minutes, cover and let rise again.

Add the remaining 2 cups flour to the dough. Turn onto a floured surface. Knead the soft dough for a minute or two. Roll out dough about ½ inch thick and cut out with a doughnut cutter. Place on a lightly floured cookie sheet and let rise until doubled in bulk, about 45 minutes to 1 hour.

When the doughnuts are puffed and almost doubled in bulk, heat the oil between 365°F and 375°F. (Note: The oil is hot enough to fry doughnuts when it will brown a crust of bread in 1 minute.)

When doubled in bulk, ease the doughnuts, raised side down, into the hot oil and fry until cooked through and brown on both sides, about 2 to 3 minutes. Drain on a folded, brown grocery bag or on paper towels. While still warm, sprinkle with sugar on both sides or brush tops while still warm with Lemon Butter Glaze or Chocolate Glaze.

Makes about 3 dozen doughnuts.

OLD ENGLISH GINGER NUTS

Great-aunt Alice immigrated with her brothers to these shores at the turn of the century. She spent the remaining years of her life keeping house for her unmarried younger brothers, who built a thriving dry goods business in Kansas. These were her favorite tea biscuits.

1 cup butter or margarine	1 teaspoon baking soda
1 cup sugar	3 tablespoons ground ginger
1 cup light molasses	4 cups all-purpose flour

Preheat oven to 375°F. In a large saucepan, heat the butter with the sugar and molasses until warm. Remove from heat. Add the baking soda and ginger. Then add the flour all at once and stir together (still in the pan). Let the dough cool, then roll it into small balls the size of walnuts. Place on a lightly greased cookie sheet, about 2 inches apart. Bake until lightly browned, 8 to 12 minutes. Remove from oven; let cool on the cookie sheet for 10 minutes, then carefully transfer to a wire rack or an opened brown grocery bag for thorough cooling; while still warm, the cookies will be buttery soft and must be handled with care. Do not stack; instead set each cookie out separately and don't handle it until cool. When kept in an airtight container, these spicy cookies will keep for several weeks. *Makes about 4 dozen cookies.*

From "GOD REST YOU MERRY, GENTLEMEN"

God rest you merry, Gentlemen,
Let nothing you dismay,
For Jesus Christ our Saviour
Was born on Christmas Day;

To save us all from Satan's pow'r,
When we were gone astray:
O tidings of comfort and joy.

Now to the Lord sing praises,
All you within this place,
And with true love and brotherhood

Each other now embrace;
This holy tide of Christmas
All others doth efface:
O tidings of comfort and joy.

—E. F. Rimbault

OF CAROLS AND CAROLERS

When I was a girl, we considered caroling one of the highlights of the Christmas season. We, a mixed crowd of varying ability who all loved to sing, gathered at the little old church. First we checked to see who had come out, how many alto and tenor voices were present, if one of the men had come to sing bass, and if there were enough sopranos.

Then, when we are all ready, heavily booted with warm coats and scarves on, the night around us crisp, starry and very still, we strolled through the tiny town of Rocklin singing for those who had especially asked us to come and for those who opened their windows and doors and called out to us. We sang the ancient carols: *"Hark! The Herald Angels Sing!," "Joy to the World," "O Come, O Come Emmanuel," "Silent Night, Holy Night!," "It Came Upon a Midnight Clear,"* and *"There's a Song in the Air,"* among others. Afterwards we would all gather at the little Rocklin church. It was an old-fashioned white building with simple wood benches, and it held about fifty people if it was packed. In the children's Sunday school room, which was very plainly furnished with a few tables and chairs, we would feast on hot chocolate, tea, and coffee, and maybe some sponge cake and Christmas cookies, which had been baked by the women of the church.

THERE'S A SONG IN THE AIR

There's a song in the air!
There's a star in the sky!
There's a mother's deep prayer,
And a baby's low cry!
And the star rains its fire while the beautiful sing,
For the manger of Bethlehem cradles a King!

There's a tumult of joy
O'er the wonderful birth,
For the Virgin's sweet boy

Is the Lord of the earth.
Ay! the star rains its fire while the beautiful sing,
For the manger of Bethlehem cradles a King!

In the light of that star
Lie the ages impearled;
And that song from afar
Has swept over the world.
Every hearth is aflame, and the beautiful sing
In the homes of the nations that Jesus is King!

We rejoice in the light,
And we echo the song
That comes down through the night
From the heavenly throng.
Ay! we shout to the lovely evangel they bring,
And we greet in His cradle our Saviour and King!

—Josiah Gilbert Holland, 1872

EFFIE'S GRANDMOTHER'S WINE JELLY

Effie recalls that pre-Christmas dinner guests at her grandmother's house were served dessert and coffee later in the evening, after the men had lit their pipes or cigars and the women of the family had done the dishes and come back into the parlor to sit and visit for a while.

This wine jelly was one of her grandmother's special desserts. She would break up the jelly with a fork and serve it in dessert dishes with a spoon full of heavy cream.

1 envelope unflavored gelatin	⅓ cup sugar
¼ cup cold water	½ cup strained orange juice
½ cup hot water	Juice from 1 lemon, strained
¾ cup sherry	

Sprinkle the gelatin over the cold water; set aside for about 5 minutes to soften. In the top of a double boiler, combine the hot water, sherry, and sugar; heat until sugar dissolves, stirring occasionally. Add the gelatin, stirring until dissolved. Stir in the orange and lemon juices. Pour into an attractive serving bowl; cool to room temperature, then refrigerate until set. *Makes 4 dessert servings.*

OUR FAMILY'S FAVORITE EGGNOG SPONGE CAKE

I like to serve this delicious cake, spiced with mace, with hot tea or coffee in the afternoon, or for carolers who have just come in out of the cold.

1 cup sifted cake flour	2 tablespoons butter or margarine,
1 teaspoon baking powder	softened
¼ teaspoon salt	½ cup hot milk
¼ teaspoon ground mace	¼ teaspoon finely grated lemon peel
3 eggs	Eggnog Filling (recipe follows)
⅔ cup sugar	Freshly grated nutmeg, optional

Preheat oven to 375°F. Line a 10-inch square baking pan with waxed paper; do *not* grease.

Sift together the flour, baking powder, salt, and mace 3 times; set aside. In a large bowl, beat the eggs with a rotary beater until foamy. Gradually add the sugar, beating constantly until very thick and light.

Add the butter to hot milk and heat until melted; add to the egg-sugar mixture, mixing quickly. Add the lemon peel and the flour mixture; beat with the rotary beater just until smooth.

Turn the batter into the prepared pan. Bake until firm to the touch and golden, about 15 minutes. Meanwhile, make the filling; refrigerate until ready to use.

Cool the baked cake in the pan until thoroughly cooled, then remove from pan and cut horizontally into 2 layers. Spread 1 layer with the chilled eggnog filling and cover with the other layer. Top with ½ cup heavy cream that's been whipped and flavored with sugar to taste and a drop or two of vanilla extract. Dust top lightly with nutmeg, if desired.

Makes about sixteen 2½-inch square pieces.

Eggnog Filling

2 egg yolks
4 tablespoons sugar
A few grains salt
1 cup milk, scalded
½ cup sherry wine or 1 tablespoon
    sherry flavoring

A very light dusting of freshly grated
    nutmeg (a light hand is needed
    here)

In the top of a double boiler, mix together the egg yolks, sugar, and salt. Add the milk, stirring constantly. Cook over medium heat until the mixture begins to steam and thickens enough to coat a spoon. Remove from heat and add the sherry or sherry flavoring and the nutmeg; stir to blend. Chill before using.

Makes about 1½ cups.

AUNT CLARY'S
CHOCOLATE FRUIT DROPS

Aunt Clary was usually a frugal woman, "a bit on the tight side" the family would say, but at Christmas she dug into her sugar bin, took out hidden cocoa, raisins, dates, and various kinds of nuts she had laid by in season or had bought with "pin money" (a small amount women earned from selling extras eggs from their flocks of hens or from buttermaking). Out would come her old family recipes and she would bake up a storm, making cakes, breads, and delicious cookies like these old-fashioned chocolate fruit drops.

½ cup butter or margarine, plus 2 tablespoons for greasing cookie sheets

⅔ cup, packed, dark brown sugar

2 eggs, well beaten

1 tablespoon milk or light cream

1½ cups all-purpose flour, plus 2 tablespoons for dusting walnuts and dates

¼ cup unsweetened cocoa powder

2 teaspoons baking powder

1 teaspoon ground cinnamon

½ teaspoon baking soda

½ teaspoon salt

½ cup chopped walnuts

½ cup chopped dates or dark raisins

Preheat oven to 350°F. Grease a 15x12x1-inch cookie sheet with *1 tablespoon* of the butter.

In a large mixing bowl, cream the ½ cup butter and sugar together. In a separate bowl, combine the eggs and milk. In a third bowl, sift together the 1½ cups flour, cocoa, baking powder, cinnamon, baking soda, and salt; add to the butter-sugar mixture alternately with the egg-milk mixture. In a small bowl, dust the walnuts and dates with the 2 tablespoons flour, then add to the cookie dough. Drop batter by tea-spoonfuls onto the cookie sheet, about 2 inches apart. Bake until cookies are firm to the touch, about 12 to 15 minutes. Remove from oven and immediately let cookies cool on a wire rack or a piece of kraft paper (an opened brown grocery bag will do nicely). Regrease cookie sheet with the *remaining 1 tablespoon* butter before baking the second batch of cookies. When thoroughly cool, store in an airtight container in a cool, dry place until ready to serve.   *Makes about 3 dozen cookies.*

ADA'S CRISP SUGAR COOKIES

Thin, crisp, and of excellent flavor, these cookies appeared annually on Ada's gold-rimmed cookie plate. Served with fragrant hot coffee to the ladies' sewing circle, the cookies brought many compliments and a reminder from some women that they would look forward to sharing them again next holiday season. And Ada, always a thoughtful woman, sent cookies home with each lady for her children.

½ cup butter

½ cup pork lard

1½ cups sugar

2 eggs, well beaten

¼ teaspoon almond extract

¼ teaspoon finely grated lemon peel

½ teaspoon baking soda

3 tablespoons dairy sour cream

3 cups all-purpose flour

½ teaspoon salt

Colored sugar, chopped nuts, or candied fruits (for decoration), optional

In a large bowl, cream the butter and lard together. Add the sugar and beat until light. Add the eggs, almond extract, and lemon peel, stirring until light. In a cup, dissolve the baking soda in the sour cream. Add the baking soda-sour cream mixture to the butter-sugar mixture, blending well. Add the flour and salt, stirring until a medium dough (one that gives some resistance when kneading and does not stick to the hands) has been formed. Wrap in waxed paper or aluminum foil and chill until very cold.

Preheat oven to 350°F. On a lightly floured surface, roll the chilled dough out as thin as a dime (like pie crust). Cut into Christmas shapes with holiday cookie cutters. Decorate with colored sugar, chopped nuts, or candied fruit, if you wish. Bake until light golden brown, about 8 minutes. Remove from oven and immediately transfer to a wire rack or an opened brown grocery bag to cool. While these cookies are usually made for immediate serving, they may be kept for about a week in an airtight container. *Makes about 4 dozen cookies.*

A GIFT OF LITERACY

The years of the Depression are said to have left an invisible scar on all of us who are old enough to remember it. But for some of us there are also warm and tender memories of those difficult times. Our good friend Margaret Hall, fifty-eight now, recalls a childhood Christmas in 1937 or 1938:

"Each year, on the last Saturday before Christmas, we all gathered at Auntie's home for a feast and gift exchange. As a child, those occasions always meant a good time with relatives, but when I was eight or nine, I learned that the endless clan-gatherings had a more serious purpose, spoken or unspoken: They were a time for sharing.

"That year I had told everyone who asked that I wanted a book for Christmas: I had visions of having books of my own, not just those from the library, which had to be returned. When the appointed night came and we went to Auntie's, I couldn't wait to take off my coat and surreptitiously pass around the tree, looking for a rectangular package that might contain a book.

"By the time we sat down to dinner, I was certain that there were no books under the tree and that I would get a scarf, bath salts, or some frilly thing. And while the others ate, did dishes, laughed, and kidded Uncle Bud about a big box in the corner behind the tree, I sat apart. Even as the presents were passed out, I didn't really pay too much attention to the trinkets that piled up in my lap.

"Then Uncle Bud, the great bear who loved to tease, pulled the large

box out of the corner, picked it up, groaned and complained about how heavy it was, and staggered about with it, while everyone laughed. That is, until he plunked it down right in front of me; then it was my turn to be pestered about the contents of the box and urged to pull off the paper so everyone could finally find out what was inside.

"With a little tugging, we could readily see the lovely homemade wooden bookcase filled with every treasure a child's heart could desire: *Tom Sawyer, Robin Hood, Little Women,* Dicken's *A Christmas Carol, Ivanhoe,* and more."

OLD-FASHIONED HAM
WITH RAISIN SAUCE

From those warm family holidays and the sharing of plenty comes this recipe for an old-fashioned ham and the raisin sauce that went with it.

Wash a fully-cured and smoked ham and put it in a large pot; cover with boiling water 2 inches above the top of the meat. Simmer, partially covered, until the internal temperature of a meat thermometer reads 160°F, or for 25 or 30 minutes per pound. Once cooked, set the ham in a cold place overnight (refrigerate it if you can), and let it cool in the broth in which it was cooked.

When ready to prepare the ham for serving, first remove the caked fat from the surface of the broth; discard the fat or save it for seasoning other dishes like beans. Transfer the ham from the broth to a roasting pan; peel off the rind and all except about ¼ inch of the fat. Discard the broth (we think it is too salty for cooking).

Score the ham and glaze with a mixture of ½ *cup honey, 1 tablespoon butter,* and *1 tablespoon water* that's been heated together. Meanwhile, preheat oven to 350°F. Bake the ham, uncovered until the meat is heated through and the glaze sets and takes on a rich color, about 30 to 40 minutes. Serve hot for Christmas dinner, or hot or cold for a holiday buffet, with *Raisin Sauce* (recipe follows).

Allow 2 to 3 servings per pound of uncooked bone-in ham.

Raisin Sauce

1 *cup dark or light raisins*	¼ *cup cold water, for dissolving*
2 *cups apple cider or apple juice*	*cornstarch*
3 *tablespoons cornstarch*	2 *tablespoons butter*

In a medium-size saucepan, soak the raisins in the cider about 30 minutes to reconstitute; then bring to a boil and boil 1 minute. Remove from heat. Dissolve the cornstarch in the cold water and stir into the raisin-cider mixture. Continue cooking over high heat until the sauce is thick, about 3 to 5 minutes, stirring almost constantly. Stir in the butter. Serve warm with hot ham (or hot smoked beef tongue) and cold with cold ham (or cold smoked beef tongue).   *Makes about 2½ cups.*

ADA'S BAKED SWEET POTATOES WITH HONEY APPLE-BUTTER SAUCE

In spring on the farm in Missouri, Grandpa grew plants for his sweet potato patch by burying last season's potatoes in rich loamy soil in hotbeds. The plants, which developed from the eyes of the potatoes, were later set out in the fields. By fall there was a bountiful harvest, most of which was put in storage for winter.

Since sweet potatoes did not keep as well as the Irish potatoes, Grandma and her daughters began using them immediately and continued throughout the fall into December, making pies, puddings, breads, and other delicious dishes—besides baking or boiling them. Even so, before and after Christmas a great platterful of plain baked sweet potatoes was served with Ada's honey apple-butter sauce to everyone's satisfaction.

Honey Apple-Butter Sauce:
    6 tablespoons spiced apple butter
    ¼ cup light-colored honey
    4 tablespoons butter
    2 tablespoons water
    Dash of freshly grated nutmeg

6 whole unpeeled sweet potatoes
    (select ones large enough to make
    2 servings each)
Butter or margarine, for preparing
    sweet potatoes for baking

Place all the ingredients for the sauce in a small saucepan; set aside. Wash the sweet potatoes; dry and generously rub skins with butter or margarine. Place on a baking sheet; set aside.

About 40 to 45 minutes before dinner, bake the sweet potatoes in a 350°F oven (along with rolls or dressing if you wish) until tender (they should feel a little soft if pinched between your thumb and forefinger); baking time may vary a little but allow at least 40 to 45 minutes. While the potatoes cook, heat the sauce without letting it boil; add more butter if desired. When the potatoes are done, split each one in half lengthwise; arrange on a hot platter cut side up and spoon 1 tablespoon or more sauce over each half. Serve while piping hot, with the remaining sauce on the side.   *Makes 12 servings.*

EASY-TO-MAKE
CARROT AND APPLE SALAD

Beginning before Christmas and for quite a long while after, the late ripening Arkansas Black apples that were stored in the pantry perfumed our whole house. These crisp-fleshed apples turn a simple old-time carrot and apple salad into something entirely new.

2 cups, well packed, grated carrots
1 large fragrant and flavorful apple
    (Arkansas Black preferred),
    cored and chopped, with or
    without peel
½ cup dark or light raisins
½ cup finely chopped celery,
    optional
½ cup finely chopped walnuts,
    optional

½ cup Easy-to-Make Mayonnaise
    (page 116) or Homemade
    Honey Mayonnaise (page 224)
2 tablespoons cider vinegar (lemon
    juice may be substituted)
1 tablespoon sugar (omit if apple is
    very sweet)
Salt and black pepper, to taste

In a medium-size bowl, combine the carrots, apple, and raisins. (If using celery and walnuts, put them in now.) In a small bowl, combine the mayonnaise, vinegar, and sugar and stir to blend; pour over the carrot mixture, folding together. Salt and pepper to taste. Chill before serving.   *Makes 4 to 6 servings.*

AUNT MABLE'S PEPPERMINT-STICK-CANDY SHEET CAKE WITH SEVEN-MINUTE FROSTING

Aunt Mable Porter's notion of cake tended to be large and a bit flashy. For this one she would buy a box of small peppermint stick candies wholesale through her tiny restaurant. We children, growing up in the Depression, were awe inspired to see such riches. And wonder of wonders, even after she had taken enough candy for her cake, she would give the rest to us to divide among ourselves.

1 cup butter or margarine	1 tablespoon plus 1 teaspoon baking
3 cups sugar	powder
2 cups milk	6 egg whites, stiffly beaten
1 teaspoon vanilla extract	1 cup coarsely ground peppermint
5 cups cake flour	stick candy
¼ teaspoon salt	Seven-Minute Frosting (recipe
	follows)

Preheat oven to 350°F. Grease a 15x11x2-inch sheet-cake pan. In a large bowl, cream together the butter and sugar until light and fluffy. Combine the milk and vanilla and add alternately with *4 cups* of the cake flour to the butter-sugar mixture; stir to blend, then beat lightly. Sift the *remaining 1 cup* flour with the baking powder and salt and add to the butter mixture. Fold in the egg whites. Turn into the prepared pan. Bake until light brown and springy to the touch, about 40 minutes. Remove from oven; transfer cake to a wire rack to cool in the pan. Frost when cake is thoroughly cool and, while frosting is still moist, sprinkle the coarsely ground peppermint stick candy over the top.

Makes 1 sheet cake or about 30 to 35 servings.

Seven-Minute Frosting
   2 egg whites
1¾ cups sugar
   6 tablespoons cool water
   1 teaspoon vanilla extract
Red food coloring

In the top of a double boiler, combine the egg whites, sugar, and cold water. Place over boiling water and cook for 7 minutes, using a rotary beater to beat constantly. Remove top of double boiler from over boiling water. Add the vanilla and continue beating until a frosting consistency. Add just enough food coloring to turn frosting light pink. Use immediately.   *Makes enough to ice a 15x11x2-inch sheet cake.*

AUNT MARY'S OATMEAL MACAROONS

These delicious macaroons, brought traditionally to the Christmas feast by Aunt Mary, could turn grownups into mischievous children. The huge plateful, covered with a light kitchen towel, was always carried in and protected by Uncle Charlie. Even so, the macaroons rarely survived the trip from his car to the Christmas sideboard. Young Cris or another innocent giggling child, encouraged by Aunt Katie or Aunt Nan, usually snitched a few off the plate, which brought about a loud cheer by other rowdy family members who then immediately laid siege on the plate and wiped it clean.

2 eggs, separated and at room
   temperature
1 cup, packed, light brown sugar
1 tablespoon butter or margarine,
   melted
2 teaspoon baking powder

1 teaspoon vanilla extract
¾ teaspoon salt
½ teaspoon freshly grated nutmeg
2½ cups rolled oats (quick-cooking
   preferred)

Preheat oven to 350°F. Lightly grease a cookie sheet; set aside. Beat the egg whites until stiff peaks form. In a large bowl, blend together the sugar and butter. Add the egg yolks, baking powder, vanilla, salt, and nutmeg, stirring to blend; then add the oats, mixing thoroughly. Lightly fold in egg whites; do this gently so they don't lose their volume. Drop by ½ teaspoonfuls onto the prepared cookie sheet, about 2 inches apart. Bake until well risen and lightly browned, about 10 minutes. Remove from oven and immediately transfer to a wire rack or to an opened brown grocery bag to cool. When cool, serve to all comers, as these are special when very fresh. Store if you must in an airtight container, or put in a plastic bag and freeze, taking them out as needed; leave the rest for another time.   *Makes about 5 dozen macaroons.*

BRING A TORCH, JEANNETTE, ISABELLA

Bring a torch, Jeannette, Isabella!
Bring a torch, to the cradle run!
It is Jesus, good folk of the village;
Christ is born and Mary's calling:
Ah! ah! beautiful is the Mother!
Ah! ah! beautiful is the Son!

Softly to the little stable,
Softly for a moment come;
Look and see how charming is Jesus,
How He is white, His cheeks are rosy!
Hush! hush! see how the Child is sleeping;
Hush! hush! see how He smiles in dreams.

This lovely seventeenth-century carol came from Provence, the southeastern region of France. The English version, a close translation, is by British composer and organist Edward Cuthbert Nunn.

THE HOLY HOURS
OF CHRISTMAS

Although Christ's birth, foretold in the Bible, and the events that accompanied it were dramatic (the shepherds watching their flocks, the angel, the heavenly host praising God, saying "Glory to God in the highest, and on earth peace, good will toward men"), it would have been easy to disbelieve that this small baby, wrapped in swaddling clothes and lying in a manger, was the Son of God, come to earth to save mankind.

Who could have guessed that this one life would influence mankind more than any other, and that his message would be primarily one of love—one that taught love of God; respect for parents; responsible behavior; kindness and respect for strangers, neighbors, and friends; sharing; self control; compassion; and much more.

How could simple shepherds or even wise men have guessed that multitudes of lives would be changed throughout the centuries because people of all ages and walks of life would be so touched by Jesus' humble birth and his teachings: the parables, the Sermon on the Mount, the Beatitudes, the passionate message of the coming Kingdom of God. Who among them could have imagined his tragic death on a cross. What cynic among them could have envisioned all of the atrocities perpetrated in his name.

Even so, on that holy night, new hope was born, and is born again every year, that men might one day lay down their weapons; that they might change enough so that they could become conservers of life and not destroyers; that they might see the earth as one of God's greatest gifts and turn their hands to protecting it for time to come; that they might look beyond the pigmentation of any man's skin and see that the likenesses inside are much greater than the differences without and thus become brothers of mankind.

JEWELED CRANBERRY APPLE JELLY SALAD

In the old days, women made the jelly salad by cooking cranberries and apples together and then straining them through their cloth jelly bags to get a clear juice. Today we prefer to use a good-grade commercial cranberry-apple juice. Serve this salad alongside meat.

1½ tablespoons unflavored gelatin
¼ cup cold water

2½ cups strained cranberry-apple juice

½ cup drained maraschino cherry
    juice (add water if necessary to
    make ½ cup liquid)
1 cup drained maraschino cherries

8 large lettuce leaves
8 ounces sour cream, optional
8 ounces cream cheese, optional

Sprinkle the gelatin over the cold water; let soften about 5 minutes.
Meanwhile, combine the cranberry-apple juice and maraschino cherry
juice in a medium saucepan. Heat until hot, but do *not* let boil. Remove
from heat. Add the gelatin; stir until dissolved. Pour into eight ½-cup
molds, then spoon a few cherries into each cup. Refrigerate until set. To
serve, unmold onto salad plates lined with lettuce leaves. (*Note:* If you
wish, blend 8 ounces dairy sour cream with 8 ounces of cream cheese
until light and spoon a small dollop on top of each salad.)

Makes 8 servings.

LADY GOLDEN SPONGE CAKE

Light and tender, the texture of this excellent cake is surpassed by none.
Make sure all the ingredients are at room temperature before making the
cake.

4 eggs
1 tablespoon water
Finely grated rind from 1 lemon
1 tablespoon strained lemon juice
½ teaspoon vanilla extract
¼ teaspoon salt

1 cup sifted cake flour (transfer 3
    tablespoons of this sifted flour
    into a cup and set aside until
    called for in recipe)
1 cup sugar
1¼ teaspoons baking powder

Preheat oven to 350°F. In a large bowl, combine the eggs, water, lemon
rind, lemon juice, vanilla, and salt. Beat with a rotary or electric beater
for 5 minutes. Into a medium-size bowl, sift together the flour (minus
the 3 tablespoonfuls) and sugar; sprinkle mixture evenly over the egg
mixture and beat for 1 minute. Add the baking powder to the 3 tablespoons flour in the cup, stirring to blend; add to the batter and beat 1
minute longer.

Pour into an ungreased 7½- or 8-inch tube pan. Bake until lightly browned and firm to the touch, about 35 to 40 minutes. Remove from oven and let cake cool upside down in the pan. Once cool, loosen cake from sides of the pan with a thin spatula or knife; turn out onto a serving plate. Serve unfrosted or with Lemon Butter Glaze (page 70).

Makes 1 tube cake.

RUBIES IN THE SNOW

Ada's littlest grandson named these candies. Filled with Christmas spirit and with stories about a babe in a manger and Kings from the East following a star, Ned decided these candies looked just like rubies that one of the Magi had dropped in the snow as he passed by on his journey to Bethlehem.

Butter, for greasing platter
3 cups sugar
⅔ cup water
½ cup light corn syrup
3 egg whites, at room temperature

⅛ teaspoon salt
½ teaspoon vanilla extract
8 or more candied cherries,
  quartered or halved

Grease a large platter with butter. In a large saucepan, boil the sugar, water, and corn syrup together until a drop of this hot syrup will form a hard ball when dropped into ice water. (Note: If done, the syrup will separate into hard threads when it hits the water, but can thereafter be shaped into a hard ball with your fingers, one that will roll about on a chilled buttered salad plate; or let mixture reach 250°F to 268°F on a candy thermometer). Remove from heat.

Using a rotary or electric beater, whip the egg whites with the salt in a large bowl until stiff peaks form. Pour the syrup slowly into the egg whites, beating constantly until mixture passes the glossy stage and forms peaks when the beater is raised. Immediately pour onto the buttered platter and strew the candied cherries over the top. Cool; then cut into 1-inch pieces. *Makes about 1½ pounds candy.*

TOPAZ CIDER

Effie liked to serve this cider on Christmas Eve. Sometimes she would set out sticks of cinnamon bark to stir it with, and often she served it over ice.

4 cups apple cider, chilled
2 cups orange juice, chilled

2 cups weak tea, chilled
Juice from 1 lemon, strained

In a 2-quart punch bowl, combine the cider, orange juice, and tea. Add lemon juice to taste (I use a little less than 2 tablespoons). Serve in glasses filled with ice.   *Makes about 8 cups before adding ice.*

THE MEANING OF CHRISTMAS

When the hustle and bustle is over
And the last of the gifts has been wrapped,
And the cookies and cakes are all ready
For the big Christmas plans you have mapped;

When the children are quiet and dreaming
Of the presents Saint Nick will bestow,
And the fire on the hearth burns less brightly,
And the clock has struck twelve long ago;

You relax by the embers and ponder
On this happiest evening of all . . .
On the meaning of Christmas to mankind
By Christ's birth in the low cattle stall.

In the giving of gifts upon Christmas,
People pattern the Father above
Who, in giving His Son, gave His best gift . . .
So the meaning of Christmas is love.

—Delphia Cline Freeman

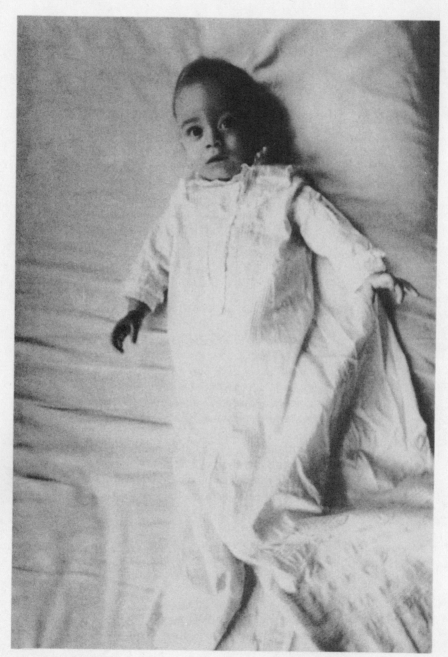

An angel child

WHAT CHILD IS THIS

On the day before Christmas, we could count on receiving a fruitcake and a holiday visit from Iris McFarland, a neighbor of twenty or more years. She loved to chat over coffee and reminisce about her "little birds," the children whom she had taught through her thirty-eight years in our local elementary school.

Born into poverty in the early thirties and greatly influenced by those times, Iris wholeheartedly believed that when a stable home and loved ones are the center of a child's life, the human spirit can rise above almost anything. When she talked about her children—"our hope for the future," she called them—the shoulders lifted and the pale blue eyes flashed or misted, depending on whether the tale she told was humorous or sad. It was always shocking to hear this soft-spoken primary teacher cry out against what she termed, "the shameful waste of budding creativity, intellectual development, and character," which she thought was eroding the nation.

From *WHAT CHILD IS THIS?*

What Child is this, Who, laid to rest,
On Mary's lap is sleeping?
Whom angels greet with anthems sweet,
While shepherds watch are keeping?

This, this is Christ the King
Whom shepherds guard and angels sing:
Haste, haste to bring Him laud,
The Babe, the Son of Mary.

— William Chatterton Dix

AN OLD-TIME SCHOOL PAGEANT

Many children of the past came to school with verbal skills acquired almost entirely through imitation at home and reading skills dependent on whether or not hard-working parents could spare time—or had the skills themselves—for such tutoring. But once there, good teachers and textbooks worked miracles even in poorly equipped country schools.

Old-time textbooks were creatively done, filled with etchings, poetry, fables, legends, and folk tales. They offered material whose purpose was to inspire the child to partake of the feast before him or her, to open up the story world, and through a budding love of reading give each one the power that reading brings.

First readers contained adventurous stories like "The Hen and the Bag of Flour," "The Sky Is Falling," "The Hungry Fox," all with a moral tucked in. Older pupils were taught that language is communication of thought and the use of language is an art. Penmanship and poetry and fables that contained moral lessons were part and parcel of learning to spell and punctuate.

Children of all ages memorized poetry, which they recited with appropriate gestures. Such "memory work" was thought to strengthen the ability to remember. (Older people today can often render those poems they learned by heart in an old-time school.)

Every occasion was used to enrich the child's life and develop character. The community was always involved. This was particularly true at Christmastime. All the children and many of the adults in the surrounding countryside took part in the school pageant and perhaps also in a church pageant.

Perhaps our favorite old-time school Christmas pageant story is about the time Freddie, the smallest child in Mother's family, had a long "piece" to say, all by himself on the stage.

At age seven, Freddie thought he needed all the help he could get to "do it right," and he got it from a loving family; Mother, Father, brothers and sisters, and even Great-grandpa listened to him recite his piece, over and over. When the night for his performance came, at least eighteen relatives went to school to enjoy the pageant and share in "the boy's triumph."

The moment came, the lights were turned down, a makeshift curtain was pulled back by many small, eager hands. Freddie, dressed like a shepherd, stepped forward, looked at the audience, and froze. From the front row his family watched tears gather in his eyes and, almost as one, they whispered:

> Why do bells for Christmas ring?
> Why do little children sing?

And Freddie's trembling voice took it up:

> Once a lovely, shining star,
> Seen by shepherds from afar,
> Gently moved until its light
> Made a manger-cradle bright.
>
> There a darling Baby lay
> Pillowed soft upon the hay.
> And his mother sang and smiled,
> "This is Christ, the Holy Child."
> So the bells for Christmas ring,
> So the little children sing.*

At which point the whole family misted up and had only barely recovered when refreshments were served by the Mother's Committee.

* "Christmas Song" by Lydia A. C. Ward

A SIMPLE FRUITCAKE

Made of everyday ingredients except the candied citron and candied orange peel, which we considered a special treat, this old-fashioned fruitcake rivaled the fancier cakes that were more heavily laden with nuts and candied fruits. This cake was and is an excellent one to serve to drop-in holiday company with coffee or tea.

½ cup butter or margarine,
  softened
1 cup, packed, light brown sugar
2½ cups all-purpose flour
1½ cups unsweetened and
  unflavored applesauce
1 pound dark or light raisins
¼ cup candied orange peel, minced
¼ cup candied citron, minced
¼ cup candied cherries, quartered,
  optional

2 teaspoons ground cinnamon
1 teaspoon freshly grated nutmeg
1 teaspoon ground cloves
½ teaspoon salt
2 teaspoons baking soda dissolved
  in 1 teaspoon vinegar
Simple Powdered Sugar Glaze (page
  24), optional

Preheat oven to 350°F. Cream the butter and sugar together until light. Add the flour, applesauce, raisins, candied orange peel, candied citron, candied cherries, cinnamon, nutmeg, cloves, salt, and dissolved baking soda. Mix thoroughly. Pour into a greased round 10-inch cake pan. Bake until firm to touch, about 1 hour and 30 minutes. Glaze, if you wish, with a Simple Powdered Sugar Glaze. *Makes one round holiday loaf cake.*

LIGHT-AS-A-SNOWFLAKE GINGERBREAD

When unexpected relatives came to visit and brought boxes of fudge, divinity, or any of a number of different kinds of cookies to put under the tree for Christmas day, the women often "stirred up" a little ginger-bread to serve with coffee while everyone chatted about holiday plans that were afoot.

½ cup butter, plus 1 tablespoon for
  greasing baking pan
2 cups sifted all-purpose flour
1½ teaspoons baking soda
1 teaspoon ground cinnamon
1 teaspoon ground ginger
½ teaspoon ground cloves

½ teaspoon salt
½ cup, packed, light brown sugar
2 eggs, beaten until almost as stiff
  as whipped cream
¾ cup light molasses
1 cup boiling water

Preheat oven to 350°F. Grease a 13x9x2-inch baking pan with the 1 tablespoon butter. In a medium-size bowl, sift together the flour, baking soda, cinnamon, ginger, cloves, and salt; set aside.

In a large bowl, cream the ½ cup butter until light and lemon-colored. Gradually add the sugar, beating until light and fluffy. Gradually add the eggs, stirring thoroughly. Add one fourth of the flour-spice mixture to the butter-egg mixture and blend well, then add the molasses, beat until smooth. Next, beat in the remaining flour-spice mixture, then the boiling water and stir until well blended. Pour into the prepared baking pan. Bake until firm to the touch, or until a toothpick inserted into the center of the gingerbread comes out clean, 40 to 45 minutes.

Remove from oven and place pan on a wire rack to cool for at least 10 minutes. Serve while still warm, without icing, right out of the pan. Serve any cold leftovers with whipped cream. *Makes one large sheet cake.*

AN OLD-FASHIONED LEMON PUDDING

When Mother was growing up, women baked bread on Saturday for the following week—sometimes more than a dozen loaves—and for the big dinner after church they made several pies and a cake or two. In those days, neighbors and friends often dropped in unannounced for a little Sunday afternoon visit and since large families often came by, plenty of treats were needed.

½ cup stale white bread with crust
   removed
2 cups milk
½ cup sugar
⅓ cup butter
3 eggs, separated and at room
   temperature

3 tablespoons lemon juice
Finely grated rind from 1 lemon
   (about 2 teaspoons)
½ cup golden raisins, optional
¼ cup heavy cream, optional

Preheat oven to 325°F. Grease a 1-quart baking dish. Put the bread in a small bowl, pour the milk over it, and let soak for about 10 minutes. Meanwhile, in a large bowl cream together the sugar and butter until light. In a small bowl, lightly beat the egg yolks and add them to the sugar-butter mixture, blending well.

Now add the lemon juice, lemon rind, and the raisins, if using, to the thoroughly soaked bread. Fold the bread and milk into the sugar-butter mixture to incorporate. Beat the egg whites until stiff but not dry and fold into the other ingredients until well blended. Place mixture in the greased baking dish. Bake until done and top is browned, about 45 minutes. To test doneness, insert a knife blade into the center of the pudding; if it comes out clean, the pudding is done. Remove from oven and let sit for 15 minutes or until lukewarm before dishing up, or serve cold with 1 tablespoon cream spooned over each serving.

Makes 4 servings.

LITTLE CHRISTMAS STARS

These crisp little cookies are delicious when served after dinner with coffee, or are a treat when tucked away in Christmas baskets, particularly for families with children. Great-aunt Nancy liked to thread some of them—using a heavy sewing needle and white cotton thread—and hang them on her Christmas tree.

1 cup butter or margarine,
    softened, plus about 1
    tablespoon for greasing cookie
    sheet(s)
½ cup sugar, plus sugar for rolling
    out dough
1 egg, lightly beaten

2 teaspoons vanilla extract
3 cups sifted all-purpose flour, plus
    about ½ cup for rolling out
    dough
½ teaspoon baking powder
⅛ teaspoon salt

In a large bowl cream the 1 cup butter until light. Gradually add the ½ cup sugar and beat until fluffy. Stir in the egg and vanilla, beating until well blended. Sift the flour with the baking powder and salt and add to the butter mixture, stirring to form a soft dough. Cover and refrigerate until thoroughly chilled, about 30 minutes to 1 hour.

    Preheat oven to 350°F. Lightly butter a 15x12x1½-inch cookie sheet or 2 smaller ones. Divide the chilled dough into thirds; roll out one portion at a time, keeping the other portions refrigerated. Generously cover a flat, smooth surface with sugar. Roll the dough to ⅛ inch thick. Cut into small star-shaped cookies, using about a 2-inch cookie cutter and as much sugar as needed to keep them from sticking. Place cookies about 2 inches apart on the buttered cookie sheet(s). Bake until edges are lightly browned, 8 to 10 minutes. Remove cookies from oven and cool on a wire rack or on an opened brown grocery bag. Once cooled, store in an airtight container.   *Makes 5 to 6 dozen cookies.*

THE CHILDREN'S FAVORITE CARAMEL CORN

This easy-to-make caramel corn has been a favorite snack in our family for years. It stays crispy when stored in an airtight container and is delicious eaten with a crisp apple and washed down with icy-cold milk.

2 cups, packed, dark brown sugar
½ cup white corn syrup
½ cup butter
½ cup margarine
½ teaspoon baking soda
⅙ teaspoon salt

⅛ teaspoon cream of tartar
8 quarts of freshly-popped popcorn (remove all hard or scorched pieces)
2 cups peanuts, optional

Preheat oven to 200°F. Set out a large roasting pan. In a heavy-bottomed saucepan, combine the sugar, corn syrup, butter, and margarine. Bring to a boil without stirring. Continue cooking until the syrup turns dark, 4½ to 5 minutes. Remove from heat and stir in the baking soda, salt, and cream of tartar. Pour over the warm popcorn; mix lightly but thoroughly. Place in the roasting pan and bake until crisp, about 1 hour. Pour out on waxed paper and separate kernels. Stir in the peanuts now if you wish.   *Makes 8 to 10 cups caramel corn.*

"SUGAR AND SPICE AND EVERYTHING NICE" WITH OATMEAL CRISP TOPPING

At our house these old-fashioned spicy cupcakes, flavored with just a hint of lemon and filled with walnuts and golden raisins, were delicious with or without their crispy topping. The topping, sometimes containing finely chopped nuts, was a special treat on a day when Mama had a few extra minutes to "fancy up" her for-after-supper baked goods.

2 cups all-purpose flour
1 cup, packed, light brown sugar
1 teaspoon ground cinnamon
1 teaspoon baking soda
½ teaspoon salt
½ teaspoon freshly grated nutmeg
¼ teaspoon ground cloves

2 eggs
1 cup light cream
½ cup butter, melted
1 teaspoon finely grated lemon peel
Juice from 1 lemon, strained
Oatmeal Crisp Topping (recipe follows)

Preheat oven to 375°F. Grease two 12-cup cupcake tins or line them with fluted paper baking cups.

In a medium-size bowl, sift together the flour, sugar, cinnamon, baking soda, salt, nutmeg, and cloves. In a large bowl, whip the eggs into the cream. Slowly add the flour mixture, stirring to blend, then stir in the butter, lemon peel, and lemon juice; beat well. Spoon about ⅓ cup of the batter into each cupcake cup and sprinkle with the oatmeal crisp topping, using it all. Bake until cupcakes are well puffed and a rich golden tan and the topping has lightly browned; the tops should also spring back when lightly pressed. Remove from oven and let cupcakes cool in the pan for about 5 minutes, then carefully transfer to a wire rack to finish cooling. (*Note:* don't turn the cupcakes upside down to remove from the pan or the topping might crack off.)   *Makes 24 cupcakes.*

Oatmeal Crisp Topping
½ cup quick-cooking rolled oats
½ cup all-purpose flour
⅓ cup butter or margarine, softened

¾ teaspoon ground cinnamon
¾ teaspoon ground nutmeg

Thoroughly combine all the topping ingredients, mixing until it has a mealy consistency.   *Makes enough topping for 24 cupcakes.*

SNOW IN THE AIR

Snow is in the air—
    Chill in blood and vein,—
Winter everywhere
    Save in heart and brain!
Ho! the happy year will be
    Mimic as we've found it,—
Head of it—and you, and me—
    With the holly round it!

Frost and sleet, alack!—
    Wind as bleak as wrath
Whips our faces back
    As we foot the path;—
But the year—from there to here—
    Copy as we've found it,—
Heart up—like the head, my dear,
    With the holly round it!

—James Whitcomb Riley

🎄 SNOWBOUND CHRISTMAS

Our friend George grew up in northern Minnesota. He recalls one special Christmas when one of the fiercest snowstorms that their part of the state had ever known came upon them:

"About three days before Christmas, me and Mama decided to take the wagon into town to get some candied citron and some other 'fancies' for her cooking. But we never had the chance; that night it come upon us. Next morning, we couldn't a got the wagon out of the barn if it was a life-and-death matter. Couldn't hardly see to get to the stables to tend the horses or the barn to milk the cow. Never did make it out to pick up the frozen eggs and Pa had to feed the chickens for us.

"That night it was so cold Mama brought up her flatirons, all hot and toasty and wrapped in a piece of flannel blanket, and put them in bed with me. For the first time in my life, she let me say my prayers laying flat on my back. Next morning not a shrub or small tree but was covered with snow. It was so quiet and cold it was sort of spooky. Mama said it would probably pass before Christmas Day, but the snow kept coming down and drifting. Finally Pa told me not to expect my grandma or grandpa—not the uncles, aunts, or cousins either.

"I started to cry but Mama told me to straighten up, that she needed some help with this make-do Christmas. She started pulling things out of the pantry and store house, and putting a Christmas dinner together for the three of us. I pouted and felt cheated, but we put up the tree and decorated it. She made cookies and cooked a big piece of ham. We toasted sweet potatoes until they were buttery soft. And we had an old-fashioned dried-apple fruitcake with my favorite cider glaze. It was a beautiful Christmas."

AN OLD-FASHIONED DRIED-APPLE FRUITCAKE WITH GEORGE'S FAVORITE CIDER GLAZE

To make this cake slightly richer, you can add one cup of raisins and half a cup of chopped nuts. Don't be too stingy with the glaze and sprinkle a few finely chopped nuts over the glazed top. Serve with hot coffee or icy-cold milk.

3 cups dried apples
Cold water, for soaking apples
2 cups light molasses or sorghum
1 cup butter, softened
1 cup brown sugar
1 teaspoon ground cinnamon
1 teaspoon freshly grated nutmeg
½ teaspoon ground cloves

4 cups all-purpose flour
1 teaspoon baking soda
½ teaspoon salt
3 eggs, well beaten
1½ cups sour milk
George's Favorite Cider Glaze
(recipe follows)

Reconstitute the apples by soaking them in cold water overnight.

The following day, drain and dry off the apples; then finely chop. Place apples in a medium-size saucepan; add the molasses and cook over medium heat until tender stirring once or twice, for about 15 minutes. Set aside to cool.

Meanwhile, preheat oven to 325°F. Grease and flour a 10-inch tube pan. Cream the butter with the sugar; stir in the cinnamon, nutmeg, and cloves. Sift the flour with the baking soda and salt into a medium-size bowl; set aside. Combine the eggs and butter-sugar mixture, mixing well; add the apple-molasses mixture and stir to blend. Next, alternately add flour and sour milk and beat well together. Turn batter into the prepared pan. Bake until cake springs back when lightly pressed, about 2 hours. Remove from oven and set pan upright on a wire rack to cool.

When cool, carefully remove cake from the pan and glaze with George's Favorite Cider Glaze. *Makes 1 tube cake.*

George's Favorite Cider Glaze
1 cup powdered sugar
½ teaspoon ground cinnamon
⅛ teaspoon freshly grated nutmeg

Pinch of salt
2 tablespoons butter or margarine
About ¼ cup apple cider

In a small bowl, combine the sugar, cinnamon, nutmeg, salt, butter, and just enough cider to make a soft spreadable glaze.

Makes about ¾ cup.

MOTHER'S CHRISTMAS STORY

Once, as we sat about the fire in our bathrobes on a cold December evening, Mother told us this touching Christmas story about the strength, beauty, and kindness of our grandmother, whom we had never known. While it was a somewhat tragic story about a scarlet-fever epidemic that swept through the countryside just before Christmas, the melding of past and present made our grandmother so real to us that visions of her linger still:

"The fever came without much warning late in 1908, when we (Grandma Meekins, Grandpa Peak, all of us children, Mother and Dad) lived in a two-room house on a rented farm in southwestern Missouri. Real quicklike the little children got sick (the fever is hardest on children under five). Some families would have several children down at the same time. None of us got very sick with it, but nevertheless our family was right in the middle of it all, because our mother was known to have healing hands. She just seems to know what to do to help the sick.

"So, when the fever came, folks would send a wagon for her—sometimes in the middle of the night—and she would settle us down, give endless instructions about our care to Dad and Grandma, and then go out again and again to help hard-pressed parents take care of their little ones.

"On one of the farms there was a family of new people who kept very much to themselves. There was a lot of speculation in the community about where they had come from and why, but we farm folks hadn't learned much about them. Mama thought the man had probably been a teacher or lawyer or something like that where he had come from. His wife was a fragile-looking woman with soft curly hair and gentle manners. Unlike most of the neighbors and us, they had only one child, a beautiful little girl about three years of age with golden-red curls.

"One night their wagon came to get Mother. We could all hear the father at the door, asking Mama to please come and stay with his wife until it was over, one way or another. We children—boys cuddled in one bed, girls in another—knew that what our mother was doing was important, but we all missed her and wished that she would stay home with us. None of us moved as we listened to her gather up her things, and none of us cried when we heard the door close behind her.

"This time while she was gone, we all worried about the little girl, and we children were fussy until even Dad, Grandpa Peak (Mama's father), and Grandma seemed edgy. Then much to our relief, Mama came home. The child was better; Mama knew that she would live. In a two-room house there's nothing private, so we heard Mama talking to Dad that night. Her voice low, she told him about the long vigilant hours, the worry, the unbearable sorrow of the child's parents as they tried to face the thought that their child might not live. And we all went to sleep listening while Dad murmured softly to her.

"As the first day of winter came, December began to wane, and so did the sickness; children began to regain their strength. Folks began slowly to pick up their lives where they had left off.

"Then, just before Christmas, Dad got a yellow letter from the postman in town, telling Dad that he had received a box from Sears and Roebuck. Dad hadn't ordered anything and didn't have any money to pay for it, so he refused to leave his work (which was in a shambles) and take the wagon fifteen miles to town—a day's ride, there and back. We all begged him to go. Mother and Grandma (his mother) thought he should at least see what was in it. Then, as he looked long at our mother and listened to her, we could see him changing his mind. And he agreed to go.

"The town folks thought there was quite a mystery about the large wooden crate that had come with his name and address on it, postage paid. When he saw how big it was, he didn't quite know what to do. Finally, after a bit of fussing with anyone he knew that was standing around watching, he agreed to take the box home with him, open it, and see what was inside. If it even looked like it might belong to someone else, he would bring it back.

"Meanwhile, at home we could hardly stand the suspense, so we cleaned and scrubbed the house. For the first time in weeks, Mama cooked—things our father liked. Then about dark, Dad drove into the yard. It took both him and Grandpa to wrestle the huge box into the house and open it.

"Inside there were children's dresses, shirts, underwear, shoes, boots, toys—not just single things, but whole outfits for each of us, all in the right sizes, everything chosen to please the one it was meant for. There were men's overalls and shirts, and pieces of fabric for women's dresses, with buttons and a little lace included. I can't remember it all, but I *do* remember there was a beautiful big pile of ribbons for our hair and store-bought candy.

"When he saw the treasures, the value of which would amount to half or more of the cash money that he could earn on the farm in a year's time, Dad balked. He was going to take it all back. It wasn't his! Grandpa Peak persuaded him that someone had probably done it for them as a gift to Mother. So, because Dad loved her and would not deliberately deny her anything he could give, he let us keep all of the things.

"Throughout the years, we all had our suspicions about where the box had come from: Some of us thought the neighbors had gone in together to do us a kindness in payment for Mother's healing during the epidemic, others thought it might have been the "new people" who were

so grateful for Mother's help with their child. But we never knew for sure, even though we asked various folks about it. No one, even if he knew, not even any of the children, let it out where that box came from."

Then, almost like an epilogue, Mother told us that the new people had built a small church on the corner of their property and that the man preached and the woman taught Sunday school. And that it was such a blessing to the whole community because, until then, families could only read to each other out of the Bible in their own homes and hardly ever went to church which was fifteen miles away—a hard day's ride there and back with old folks and small children.

GRANDMA'S BAKED RICE PUDDING

When all of the family was at home on the farm in Missouri, Grandma and Great-grandma did a lot of cooking to keep Grandma's family of ten fed. Sometimes in the evening one or the other of the women would put a baked rice pudding in the oven for bedtime snacking.

3 eggs	¼ teaspoon salt
3 cups milk	2 cups cooked rice
½ cup sugar	3 tablespoons butter
1 teaspoon vanilla extract	About ¼ teaspoon ground cinnamon

Preheat oven to 350°F. In a large bowl, beat the eggs until frothy. Add the milk, sugar, vanilla, and salt, beating until the sugar dissolves. Add the rice and stir to blend. Pour the mixture into a buttered 2-quart baking dish, dot with the 3 tablespoons butter and dust with cinnamon. Bake until a knife blade inserted in the center comes out clean, about 45 minutes. Serve hot or cold.   *Makes about 8 servings.*

GREAT-GRANDMA MEEKINS'S DUNKIN' DOUGHNUTS

Mother recalls fondly that when her mother was away from home, she and her brothers, especially her brother Ben, begged their grandmother to make dunkin' doughnuts. She and Ben would skim icy-cold milk and pour it into two large pitchers. Hattie, Mother's little sister, would set out the coffee mug, for who dunked in a glass?

About 4½ cups all-purpose flour	¾ cup plus 2 tablespoons milk
1 tablespoon plus 1½ teaspoons baking powder	Finely grated rind from 1 orange
1 teaspoon salt	2 tablespoons orange juice
½ teaspoon nutmeg	½ cup finely minced nuts (pecans preferred)
3 tablespoons butter or margarine, softened	Vegetable oil or pork lard, for frying doughnuts
1 cup sugar	Granulated or powdered sugar, for dusting doughnuts, optional
2 eggs, well beaten	

Into a medium-size bowl sift 3½ cups flour with the baking powder, salt, and nutmeg; set aside.

In a large bowl, cream together the butter and sugar until well blended; stir in the eggs. In a small bowl, combine the milk, orange rind, and orange juice. Alternately add the flour mixture and milk mix-

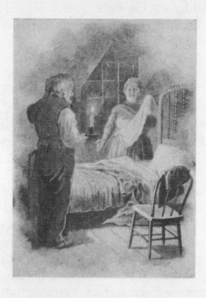

ture to the butter-sugar mixture, beginning and ending with flour. Add the nuts and just enough additional flour (this will take ½ *cup or less*) to make a soft easily-handled dough. Refrigerate for at least 1 hour.

Turn dough onto a lightly floured surface and roll out to ½ inch thick. Cut out doughnuts with a floured doughnut cutter. Shape all trimmings into a ball; roll out and cut into more doughnuts.

Heat 1½ inches of oil to between 365°F and 375°F. (*Note:* The oil is hot enough to fry doughnuts when it will brown a cube of bread in 1 minute.) Ease the doughnuts into the hot oil until golden brown and done, about 3 minutes, turning frequently; as soon as they rise to the surface, turn them with a long-handled fork, being careful not to pierce doughnuts or the oil will soak into them. Fry only as many doughnuts as will float easily on the fat. Carefully remove cooked doughnuts from the oil with the fork or a large slotted spoon, letting the excess oil drain off for a few seconds before draining on absorbent paper (a brown grocery bag will do nicely). Serve as is or dust with granulated or powdered sugar.   *Makes about 2 dozen doughnuts.*

COUSIN JOAN'S "SOMETHIN' SWEET WITH A LID ON IT" SPREAD ON WHOLE-WHEAT YEAST MUFFINS

When the Meekins family gathered for a potluck, each of the little cousins got to have their favorite goodies. Joan, a tall, thin child with pretty brown hair and lovely big eyes, always begged for sweets, which usually was something in a covered dish or canning jar, such as this wonderful orange marmalade.

1 dozen large navel oranges	*Grated rind from 1 lemon*
About 5 cups sugar	*2 tablespoons strained lemon juice*

Grate the rind from enough of the oranges to yield *1 cup* grated rind; set aside. Pare the 12 oranges, cutting deep enough to remove all membrane and separate into segments without membranes; the yield should be about 5 cups.

In a large saucepan, combine the (about) 5 cups orange segments and grated orange rind with the grated lemon rind and lemon juice. Add *1 cup* sugar for each cup of orange segments. Place this marmalade mixture over high heat and bring to a boil, stirring frequently. Boil vigorously until the liquid gets syrupy, about 15 minutes, stirring and skimming for the first 5 minutes of cooking; do *not* overcook. Then pour quickly into freshly scrubbed and sterilized pint or half-pint canning jars that are still very hot; fill jars to ½ inch from the rims. Immediately wipe jar rims with a clean damp cloth; cover with new lids prepared according to manufacturer's directions and screw on sterilized metal rings fairly tightly. Set aside on a folded towel until thoroughly cool; then check the lids to see that they have airtight seals. To test for a properly sealed jar, press down the center of the lid; if it is curved down and stays down, the jar is sealed. Label and date. Store in a cool, dark, and dry place.

This marmalade, since it's made without commercial pectin, has a delicate texture and is much like a preserve; it will not jell firm.

Makes about 6 half-pint jars.

Whole-Wheat Yeast Muffins

1 tablespoon dry or granulated yeast	*1½ teaspoons salt*
¼ cup lukewarm water (105°F to 115°F)	*1 egg, well beaten*
1 cup milk	*1 cup all-purpose flour*
2 tablespoons butter or margarine, melted	*1½ to 3 cups whole-wheat flour*
2 tablespoons honey	*Extra melted butter or margarine, for brushing on muffins once out of oven*

In a large bowl, dissolve the yeast in the warm water; let sit 5 to 10 minutes. Meanwhile scald the milk; remove from heat and add the 2 tablespoons butter, honey, and salt. Cool to lukewarm.

Add the milk mixture and egg to the yeast; stir to blend. Add the all-purpose flour and enough of the whole-wheat flour to make a thin

JANE WATSON HOPPING

pancake-like batter (sponge); stir until smooth; beat well to develop the gluten. Scrape the batter from the sides of the bowl; cover with a clean cloth and let rise in a warm place until doubled in bulk, about 30 minutes.

Stir down the batter by beating 15 to 20 strokes. Spoon into 12 to 16 greased muffin cups; cover and let rise again until light, about 25 or 30 minutes. Bake in a preheated 400°F oven until golden brown, about 25 minutes. Remove muffins from oven; let cool for about 5 minutes, then brush with melted butter and remove from pan. Serve while still piping hot. *Makes 12 to 16 muffins.*

IT IS COMING TONIGHT

The earth has grown old
with its burden of care,
But at Christmas it always is young.
The heart of the jewel
burns lustrous and fair,
And its soul full of music
breaks forth on the air,
When the song of the angels is sung.

It is coming, old earth,
it is coming tonight;
On the snowflakes which cover thy sod,
The feet of the Christ-Child
fall gently and white,
And the voice of the Christ-Child
tells out with delight
That mankind are the children of God.

On the sad and the lonely,
the wretched and poor,
That voice of the Christ-Child shall fall;
And to every blind wanderer opens the door
Of a hope which he dared
not to dream of before,
With a sunshine of welcome for all.

The feet of the humblest
   may walk in the field
Where the feet of the holiest have trod;
This, this is the marvel
   to mortals revealed,
When the silvery trumpets
   of Christmas have pealed,
That mankind are the children of God.

—Phillips Brooks

Ada's grandchildren, Nellie Beth and Edna Mae Rankin

🌿 O Holy Babe

Through the generations, what depth of passion the birth of Christ has inspired in man. And how beautifully expressed is man's spiritual love in this old hymn, "Love Divine," written by Charles Wesley and John Zundel:

> Love divine, all love excelling,
> Joy of heaven to Earth come down!
> Fix in us Thy humble dwelling;
> All Thy faithful mercies crown.
> Jesus Thou art all compassion,
> Pure unbounded love Thou art;
> Visit us with Thy salvation;
> Enter every trembling heart.

How wonderful is the Christmas spirit that comes to all of us each year and lifts our hearts and calls out kindness, gentleness, and the feeling of goodwill toward others that borders on the divine. Enough so that for a while at least we can dream of peace on earth, harmony akin to the angelic voices of old, greatness of heart that puts Scrooge to shame, and a better world, a better future for our children.

And silently, in the depths of our being, we can cry out for strength to work for as well as dream of that better tomorrow, our legacy to those we love.

ANGEL WINGS

These Christmas cookies are light and sweet. Originally served at Ada's Christmas table, they are a reminder that a messenger from God brought the good tidings of Christ's birth.

4 egg whites, at room temperature	1 cup sugar
¼ teaspoon cream of tartar	1 teaspoon vanilla extract
Dash of salt	⅔ cup shredded coconut

Preheat oven to 275°F. Beat the egg whites with the cream of tartar and salt until they are stiff but not dry. Add the sugar, 1 tablespoonful at a time, beating until stiff after each addition. Fold in the vanilla and coconut. Drop the meringues from a teaspoon or tablespoon onto a cookie sheet which has been covered with heavy ungreased paper, or pipe through a pastry bag onto the paper. Bake until lightly browned, about 40 to 60 minutes. Remove from oven and take the meringues off the paper immediately. Cool before serving.

Makes about a dozen, perhaps slightly more.

GLITTERING STAR CAKE WITH A CLOUD-LIGHT FROSTING

Uncle Bud thought this cake was like "starshine," all white and soft. He wouldn't let the women in his family "mess it up" with chocolate or butterscotch frosting. He thought it should be white "all the way."

2⅔ cups sifted cake flour	⅔ cup vegetable shortening
1 tablespoon baking powder	1 teaspoon vanilla extract
1 teaspoon salt	1 cup milk
5 egg whites, at room temperature	Cloud-Light Frosting (recipe follows)
1¾ cups sugar	

Preheat oven to 350°F. Line the bottoms of two 9-inch round cake pans with waxed paper, then grease the paper.

Sift the flour with the baking powder and salt three times.

In a medium, straight-sided mixing bowl, beat the egg whites until foamy. Gradually add ½ *cup* of the sugar, beating just until meringue forms soft, moist peaks.

In a large bowl, cream together the shortening and vanilla until soft and smooth. Add the *remaining 1¼ cups* sugar, a little at a time, beating for about 1 minute after each addition. Then scrape down bowl and beat about 1 minute longer by hand or with an electric mixer. To the shortening mixture, add about one fourth of the flour, beat for 20 seconds, then add one third of the milk and beat 20 seconds more; continue alternately adding the flour and milk in this way, working quickly until all is used up. Fold in the meringue and mix gently for about 1 minute.

Turn the batter into the prepared pans. Bake until golden brown on top and a toothpick inserted into the center of a layer comes out clean, about 30 minutes.

Remove from oven and let cake cool in the pans about 10 minutes; then loosen sides with a spatula and turn onto a wire rack. Once completely cool, fill and frost lightly with Cloud-Light Frosting.

Makes one 2-layer cake.

Cloud-Light Frosting
To keep the color of this frosting light, we use "winter butter," which is almost pure white, rather than the golden yellow butter of a summer

cow. Store-bought butter is always the color of winter butter, so you can use it in this frosting just fine.

2 tablespoons light-colored butter
2½ cups sifted powdered sugar
1 egg white
About 1 tablespoon heavy cream
¾ teaspoon vanilla extract
⅛ teaspoon salt

Cream together the butter and 1 *cup* sugar. Alternately add the *remaining* 1½ *cups* sugar, then egg white, then cream, until a light spreadable consistency is obtained; beat well after each addition until smooth. Add the vanilla and salt; stir to blend.

Makes enough frosting to lightly frost a 2-layer cake.

DOWNY SOFT CUSTARD
WITH VANILLA-WAFER CRUMBS

When my sister and I were small, times were hard and cookies at our house meant those that Mother made. Then one day Mother bought vanilla wafers at the store to top off this custard, and we were overjoyed because the only time we ever got to eat store-bought cookies was at our auntie's house.

2 cups milk, scalded
¼ cup sugar
½ teaspoon salt
4 egg yolks

2 teaspoons vanilla extract
½ to ⅔ cups finely crushed vanilla
    wafers

Scald the milk in the top of a double boiler. Blend in the sugar and salt. Meanwhile, in a medium-size heatproof bowl lightly beat the egg yolks; then gradually add the hot milk mixture. Strain mixture and return to top of double boiler. Cook over simmering water, stirring constantly and rapidly, until mixture begins to steam and thickens enough to coat a spoon. Immediately remove from heat. Blend in the vanilla. Cool slightly so as not to break the dessert dishes, then pour into 6 glass sherbet dishes. Let cool until lukewarm, then chill in the refrigerator. Sprinkle with vanilla-wafer crumbs just before serving. *Makes 6 servings.*

Aunt Mae's son Jim

LIGHT AND SHADOW

When the scented Yule log burns,
Memories come and go,
Shadowed echoes from the past,
Recollection's afterglow.

Loved ones gone but not forgotten,
Living in ethereal climes
Come again with warm remembrance,
Waking dreams of other times.

When the scented Yule log burns,
Silent voices whisper low,
Reaffirming tender messages,
Spoken softly long ago.

Light and shadow, gently playing,
In the fire's flickering light.
Joy and sorrow stir our heartstrings,
Leaving faded memories bright.

—J.W.H.

A LIGHT IN THE WINDOW

As a child I loved hearing the story of Jim. On Christmas Eve our friend Ada often told us about her Great-aunt Mae, whose only son Jim ran away to sea at age fourteen. Auntie lived in a small cottage tucked away from the howling gales that blew in from the sea. The old woman would never leave home on Christmas because she was afraid that Jim would come sailing in and she wouldn't be there to welcome him. So, Ada, who loved her great-aunt dearly, would plead to go and stay all night with her during the holy hours of Christmas.

They would bake an old-time spice cake and make a few cookies. And Auntie would get out Jim's picture and letters and they would talk about him. And Auntie would read a few lines from Jim's favorite poem:

—From SEA FEVER

I must go down to the seas again, for the call of the running tide
Is a wild call and a clear call that may not be denied . . .

—John Masefield

From *THE SHEPHERDS IN JUDEA*

Oh, the Shepherds in Judea!—
   Do you think the Shepherds know
How the whole round earth is brightened
   In the ruddy Christmas glow?
How the signs are lost in laughter, and the laughter brings the tears,
As the thoughts of men go seeking back across the darkling years
Till they find the wayside stable that the star-led Wise Men found,
With the Shepherds, mute, adoring, and the glory shining round!

                                —Mary Austin

GREAT-AUNT MAE'S CHRISTMAS CAKE

This old-fashioned cake with its currants, citron peel, and strong coffee, has a flavor and texture all its own. Served when Aunt Mae was a girl at home and when scalloped oysters as well as ham, turkey, and pressed chicken graced the Christmas dinner table. This honey-brown fruitcake was eaten last, along with the mints.

    Made just before the holidays and aged only long enough to mellow, thin slices, one after another, fairly melted away amid "wonderful" and "how delicious," and "so good and rich."

2½ cups almonds or pecans
   (preferred) or other nuts,
   thinly sliced
2½ cups plump, dark raisins, finely
   chopped
1 cup dark or light currants
½ cup candied lemon peel

½ cup candied citron peel
4½ cups all-purpose flour
½ cup butter
1 cup, packed, light brown sugar
½ cup light molasses
½ cup strong black coffee

8 eggs, separated and at room
  temperature
1 teaspoon ground cinnamon

½ teaspoon baking soda
½ teaspoon freshly grated nutmeg
¼ teaspoon ground cloves

Preheat oven to 350°F. Generously grease a 10-inch tube pan; line bottom of pan with waxed paper, then grease paper. In a medium-size bowl, combine the almonds, raisins, currants, lemon peel, and citron peel. Dust lightly with ½ cup of the flour; set aside.

In a large bowl, cream the butter with the sugar; mix in the molasses and coffee, then the egg yolks. Sift in the *remaining 4 cups* flour, cinnamon, baking soda, nutmeg, and cloves and beat gently until blended. Fold in the nut-fruit mixture. Beat the egg whites until stiff and lightly fold them into the batter. Turn batter into the prepared pan. (*Note:* I have 2 tube pans, 1 used only for angel and sponge cakes, the other for cakes requiring a *greased* pan.)

Bake until lightly browned and firm to the touch, about 1 hour. Remove from oven and let sit 15 minutes; then loosen cake from the pan with a spatula or knife (run blade between the pan and cake around the sides and around the center cone). Using 2 plates, turn cake out of the pan onto 1 plate, then turn right side up onto the other plate. When cool, cover well with waxed paper or aluminum foil and allow the cake to mellow overnight at cool room temperature (even better, mellow 2 days). Serve thinly sliced with coffee after dinner or along with mints.

Makes 1 tube cake.

GREAT-AUNT MAE'S
SEED CAKE

One of Ada's favorite stories about her great-aunty was about the Christmas Eve they opened her great-great-grandmother's trunk. It was full of wonderful musty things with traces of lavender—no longer very fragrant —strewn about.

There was a pair of yellowed lace gloves with no fingertips made on them, several colorful fans, and a tintype photograph of one of her ancestors—a woman standing behind her seated husband who looked handsome in a Confederate uniform, and behind both of them were aspidistras (plants of the lily family which have dark inconspicuous flowers and large stiff, glossy evergreen leaves), which added elegance to the photograph. There were sets of antimacassars (delicate covers-crocheted, tatted, and embroidered—which were put on the backs and arms of chairs or sofas to prevent soiling), and there was a handwritten recipe book that contained a seed cake recipe.

However, Ada does not believe that this one is the exact-same recipe that her great-aunt had; she remembers that the old one contained rose water and not lemon juice. She believes that through years of being passed from hand to hand through her family the recipe has changed, but it's delicious nevertheless.

3¾ cups sifted all-purpose flour	8 eggs
¼ cup cornstarch	1 cup milk
2 teaspoons baking powder	2 tablespoons strained lemon juice
1 teaspoon salt	1 tablespoon vanilla extract
1 teaspoon freshly grated nutmeg	1 teaspoon finely grated lemon peel
1 pound butter or margarine (don't use light margarine), softened	½ cup candied citron, shaved or finely minced
3 cups sugar	2 teaspoons caraway seed

Preheat oven to 350°F. Grease two 8x4x2-inch loaf pans. Then cut 2 pieces of parchment paper, each about 10x7½ inches; line the pans with the paper so that an inch or more of paper extends above the pan on all sides. (The excess paper makes it easier to remove the cakes from the pans.)

Into a large bowl, sift together the flour, cornstarch, baking powder, salt, and nutmeg; set aside. In a second large bowl, cream the butter thoroughly; gradually add the sugar, beating until light. Add the eggs, 1 at a time, beating well after each addition. To the milk, add the lemon juice, vanilla, and lemon peel. Then alternately add the flour mixture and milk mixture to the buttter mixture; stir only until well blended. Fold in the citron and caraway seed.

Pour the batter into the prepared pans. Bake until loaves are firm to the touch and light brown, about 65 to 70 minutes. (You may also test doneness with a toothpick; if it comes out clean, the cakes are done.) Remove from the oven. Let the loaves sit in the pans for about 10 minutes, then carefully remove from pans and transfer to a wire rack to finish cooling before serving. Serve, thinly sliced, at an afternoon tea or serve as a light dessert.   *Makes 2 loaves of cake.*

HARK! THE
HERALD ANGELS SING

At Christmastime, we would gather at Mother's to sing a few carols and reminisce about holidays past, until memories of childhood and youth overpowered us and familiar old hymns, learned from Mother and the church choir leader, drifted gently to mind. My sister and sometimes one of her girls would begin to sing "'There's a peace in my heart that the world never gave,/A peace it cannot take away;/Tho' the trials of life may surround like a cloud,/I've a peace that has come here to stay!'"

And Mother would lead out with "Amazing Grace" or "Shall We Gather at the River," and during the quiet times when the singing stopped, talk about Grandpa and his sisters and how they sang in the choir and what a lovely tenor voice Grandpa had when he was young and how everyone loved to hear him play the mandolin.

Eventually we would all be singing, "Tell me the story of Jesus,/Write on my heart every word,/Tell me the story most precious,/Sweetest that ever was heard./Tell how the angels, in chorus,/Sang as they welcomed his birth,/'Glory to God in the highest!/Peace and good tidings to earth.' "

And all of us then, caught up in the moment, nostalgic, and filled with memories, listened as Mother told stories about times past, about the Mighty Osage River, the Christmases of her childhood, and tales about loved ones who had gone before.

WHAT THE MISTLETOE DID

A pretty doll in a stocking hung,
While near her a soldier doll bravely swung,
When, lo! the timepiece struck twelve o'clock,
And gave the mistletoe quite a shock.
Then the startled doll heard the soldier say:
"All right, little neighbor!
  It's Christmas Day."

—Joel Stacy

JANE WATSON HOPPING

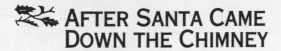 # After Santa Came
Down the Chimney

From *PARENTAL CHRISTMAS PRESENTS*

Parunts don't git toys an' things,
Like you'd think they ruther—
Mighty funny Chris'mus-gif's
Parunts gives each other!—
Pa give Ma a barrel o' flour,
An' Ma she give to Pa
The nicest dinin'-table
She know he ever saw!

—James Whitcomb Riley

Old-fashioned Christmas trees in town homes and in prosperous farm homes were laden with teddy bears and tin soldiers, tiny English tea sets, toy pianos, baby chairs and rocking chairs, rocking horses, doll houses, and tin horns. Then, of course, there were the splendid presents we imagined they gave each other.

Way out on hard-scrabble farms, the fresh-scented Christmas tree was plainer but lovely, all draped in popcorn strands with little cones hung on its branches and with a polished apple hung here and there. The presents were few but brought sheer pleasure to those who received them. Men and boys each got a pair of new overalls (because the old ones "were letting the light in"), and women and girls got shoes for winter and perhaps a piece of dress goods.

Even so, much or little, the joy in each home was about the same because Christmas has always been a matter of the heart.

GREAT-GRANDMA'S "GOLDEN BUCK"

More than a hundred years ago, Great-grandma learned to make this "golden buck" from Dr. Alvin Wood Chase who wrote for farm people of the time, teaching them new ways to use and preserve their home-grown products, how to care for and medicate their animals, how to care for human invalids, and how to cook and serve health-giving dishes.

Through the years the family cooks have made, tasted, and added to the "recipe," and while it may not be quite the same as it was in the mid-1800s, it is still a favorite Christmas breakfast dish.

2 tablespoons butter
½ pound sharp golden cheese, finely grated
1 teaspoon Worcestershire sauce
½ teaspoon salt
½ teaspoon paprika

¼ teaspoon prepared mustard
½ cup ale
1 whole egg, lightly beaten
3 whole eggs, unbeaten
3 thick pieces of toasted bread

Melt the butter in the top of a double boiler. Add the cheese, Worcestershire, salt, paprika, and mustard; cook until cheese is soft (work with a spoon). Stir in the ale, then the beaten egg. Continue cooking until thick. Remove from heat; cover to keep warm while poaching the 3 unbeaten eggs.

To poach the eggs, heat about 1 inch of lightly salted water in a medium-size frying pan just to the boiling point. Meanwhile, break the 3 eggs, 1 at a time, into a bowl without breaking the yolks. Gently slip the eggs into the hot water, then remove pan from heat. Cover and let sit until egg whites are set, leaving the yolks soft; if the yolks aren't completely submerged, spoon the hot water over just long enough to set the whites.

When the eggs are done, spoon the cheese sauce over the toast, spreading the sauce out. Use a skimmer or slotted spoon to gently lift the poached eggs out of the water and onto the "golden buck's" back. Serve while piping hot.   *Makes 3 servings.*

CHRISTMAS TEA RING

This delicious tea ring not only satisfied those family members who wanted something a little sweet to top off breakfast, but it was a ready-made snack for those who were getting too impatient for Christmas dinner.

1 cup milk
1 tablespoon dry or granulated yeast
¼ cup warm water (105°F to 115°F)
½ cup sugar
1 teaspoon salt
About 5 cups all-purpose flour

2 eggs, well beaten
¾ cup butter or margarine, softened
1 teaspoon butter or margarine, melted
Raisin Filling (recipe follows)
Powdered Sugar Frosting (recipe follows)

Scald the milk in a small saucepan; set aside. In a small bowl soften the yeast in the lukewarm water; set aside to proof for 5 to 10 minutes.

Combine the sugar and salt in a large bowl. Add the scalded milk and stir until sugar and salt are dissolved. When mixture is lukewarm, blend in 1 cup of the flour, beating until smooth. Stir in the softened yeast, mixing well. Add 2 cups more flour, beating until very smooth. Beat in the eggs, then vigorously beat in ½ cup of the softened butter, 2 to 3 tablespoons at a time.

Finally beat in just *enough of the remaining flour* to make a soft dough (one that can barely be handled without becoming sticky). Turn dough onto a lightly floured surface; let rest 5 to 10 minutes, then knead adding more flour as necessary if it gets sticky, until it is supple and has a satiny sheen. Form dough into a large ball and place in a deep greased bowl; turn dough to bring greased surface to top. Cover with waxed paper and a clean dish towel and let stand in a warm place until doubled in bulk, about 45 minutes.

Punch the dough down with your fist, then pull the edges of the dough into the center and turn dough completely over in the bowl. Cover and let rise again until nearly doubled in bulk, about 30 minutes.

Punch dough down again and turn onto a lightly floured surface. Divide in half and shape each portion into a ball. Roll each into an 18x9-inch rectangle. Spread each rectangle with 2 *tablespoons* softened butter. Now make the raisin filling and sprinkle half over each rectangle of dough.

Beginning with the longer side, roll dough tightly into a log shape and press edges down to seal. Place each log on a greased baking sheet and pull ends together to form a ring; press ends lightly together to seal.

With scissors, snip at 1-inch intervals through one side of the ring almost to the center; turn each section on its side. Repeat with the second ring. Brush tops lightly with the 1 teaspoon melted butter. Cover and let rise until doubled in bulk, about 45 minutes.

Meanwhile, preheat the oven to 350°F. (Note: Bake the rings at the same time if pans will fit in the oven side by side. If one must wait, set one in a cool place while the first ring bakes.) Bake rings until risen and light brown, about 20 to 25 minutes.

While rings are baking prepare the frosting. Once rings are done, remove from oven and transfer pans to wire racks; cool until lukewarm in pans, then frost. Serve warm or cold. *Makes 2 tea rings.*

Raisin Filling
¾ cup, packed, light brown sugar
½ cup dark raisins

¼ cup butter or margarine,
*   softened*
1½ tablespoons ground cinnamon

Combine all the ingredients in a small bowl; blend well.

Makes enough to fill 2 tea rings.

Powdered Sugar Frosting
½ cup powdered sugar
1 tablespoon milk or light cream
½ teaspoon vanilla extract

In a small bowl, blend all the ingredients together until of a spreadable consistency. *Makes enough to frost 2 tea rings.*

CHRISTMAS AFTERTHOUGHT

After a thoughtful, almost painful pause,
Bub sighed, "I'm sorry fer old Santy Claus:—
They wuz no Santy Claus, ner couldn't be,
When he wuz ist a little boy like me!"

—James Whitcomb Riley

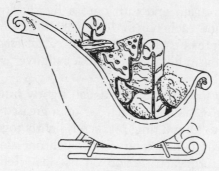

COOKS AND CHRISTMASES

In the old days women on farms across the nation had only three fats to bake with: lard (rendered pork fat), heavy cream (about half butter fat and half milk), and butter, which had to be churned. Aunt Clary grew up using such fats, each for a special purpose. One Christmas Day she laid down her knitting and told sister and me about those days:

"We didn't have no ready-mades like you girls have. In the fall we butchered the hogs and rendered the lard to put away. It would keep all through the winter, sweet and nice and white, if you cooked all the moisture out of it. We used it for frying and for making biscuits—which we done sometimes three times a day. I always rendered the leaf lard (the fat that hangs around the kidneys) for my Christmas pies. It was the nicest lard of all and made a real crisp crust. Generally you didn't use lard for cookies or cakes, though you could if you didn't have nothing else. We made them with butter or with cream to give them a good rich taste. All my little fancy cookies, like snickerdoodles, was made with butter and some of my special cakes was butter cakes. I used cream—'cause it didn't have to be churned—for everyday cakes and for short-cakes. You just use one cup of heavy cream and one half cup milk to make a regular cake that calls for one half cup fat and one cup of milk. It's the same thing whether the fat's in the cream or whether it's churned to hard butter.

"My mother made pork cake for Christmas. She used ground salt pork for it. It made a rich spicy loaf with raisins in it when we could get them. Things like cake and bread wasn't as light then as now, but they had more flavor."

OLD-FASHIONED SALT PORK CAKE

Among the women in our family, this recipe was considered Aunt Mae's heirloom recipe because her mother and aunts made it often in the 1880s and served it hot or cold. We usually cut the cake as soon as it was cool; however it will keep for about two weeks under refrigeration.

¼ pound salt pork, finely ground or finely chopped	¼ teaspoon ground cloves
	1 cup dark raisins
½ cup boiling water	¼ cup candied citron, finely chopped
2 cups all-purpose flour	½ cup or more chopped walnuts,
2 teaspoons ground cinnamon	optional
½ teaspoon baking soda	1 egg
½ teaspoon freshly grated nutmeg	½ cup molasses
¼ teaspoon ground ginger	½ cup, packed, light brown sugar

Preheat oven to 300°F. Line a greased 13x9x2-inch baking pan with waxed paper, then grease the paper. Place the salt pork in a large bowl and pour the boiling water over it; let stand until lukewarm, 10 to 15 minutes.

Into a medium-size bowl, sift together the flour, cinnamon, baking soda, nutmeg, ginger, and cloves. (Note: Due to the salt in the salt pork, none is added here.) Fold in the raisins, citron, and walnuts, if using, until well blended. In a small bowl, beat together the egg, molasses, and sugar and add to the soaking pork. Gradually add the flour mixture, stirring until well blended. Turn batter into the prepared pan. Bake until thoroughly done, 1½ to 1¾ hours. To test doneness, press top of cake gently with your fingertips; if done cake should spring back. (If in doubt, also check doneness by inserting a toothpick into the center; if it comes out clean the cake is done.) Remove from oven and cool completely in the pan before serving.   *Makes about 18 generous dessert servings.*

VEDA'S ORANGE RAISIN MUFFINS

On Christmas day when old-time children peeled and ate their rare treats, oranges, mothers like Veda would gather up all the peelings to candy or would grate and dry the orange part (zest) of the peelings—both to be used for later baking. In this old-fashioned muffin recipe, fresh orange peel and juice are used.

2 cups sifted all-purpose flour	⅔ cup blinky (sour) milk or
⅓ cup sugar	buttermilk
¾ teaspoon baking soda	⅓ cup butter, melted
½ teaspoon salt	⅓ cup orange juice
½ cup raisins	1 teaspoon finely grated orange peel
1 egg, beaten	

Preheat oven to 425°F. Into a large bowl, sift together the flour, sugar, baking soda, and salt. Mix in the raisins. In a small bowl, combine the egg, milk, butter, orange juice, and orange peel. Add the wet ingredients to the dry ingredients, mixing only until the dry ingredients are dampened; don't beat. Fill 12 greased muffin cups two-thirds full. Bake until brown, about 25 minutes. Serve piping hot with fresh butter.

Makes 1 dozen muffins.

A DAY OF FEASTING AND FAMILY

CHRISTMAS GREETING

A word of Godspeed and good cheer
To all on earth, or far or near,
Or friend or foe, or thine or mine—
In echo of the voice divine,
Heard when the Star bloomed forth and lit
The world's face, with God's smile on it.

—James Whitcomb Riley

With tender heart I remember when our daughter Colleen was a little girl, tiny and thin with long arms and legs, looking for all the world like an Indian maiden with long red-brown hair with glints of gold in it.

Long before Christmas morning came she started making gifts for everyone, and in time her pile of presents grew and grew until finally, baby Jesus' birthday arrived and she could put the well-counted hand-made gifts, all decked out in festive ribbons, under the tree.

Small though she was, she was a dynamo of Christmas spirit. She worked tirelessly on crayon-colored cards with loving messages written inside. Everywhere about the house one could see her handiwork: piles of colored paper chain to hang from the ceilings, vases filled with fake holly berries, wreaths made from the boughs of the cedar and fir trees that stood in the front yard.

Now that Colleen is a woman, her list grows longer to include in-laws and friends and their children. Colleen is a giver of thoughtfulness, all year long. As I watch her with a mother's love, I see that she has found the secret for a happy and abundant life.

From "*DAS KRIST KINDEL*"

And in a vision, painted like a picture in the air,
I saw the elfish figure of a man with frosty hair—
A quaint old man that chuckled with a laugh as he appeared,
And with ruddy cheeks like embers in the ashes of his beard.

—James Whitcomb Riley

CHRISTMAS DINNER

When my husband, Raymond, was growing up, Christmas dinner meant a gathering of the family. His Grandma White would come early to spend the evening before the holiday with her daughter, Raymond's mother, and their family, picking pinfeathers out of a farm-grown goose, cracking nuts, making cranberry sauce, and baking pies. Then sometime late, after midnight, the work would be done. There would be quiet woman-talk, and a check of the Christmas tree, under which small gifts for all would be piled high. Memories would rise as conversation drifted back to Christmases in New Castle, California, when all of Grandma White's children were still at home—Ralph, Olive, who would become Raymond's mother, Herbie, and Lois, who was born last. One, and then another would eventually recall other special Christmas dinners.

Everyone's favorite was the Christmas when Great-grandfather White, in Wisconsin, sent a record of Christmas greetings to his son Wilbur, Raymond's Grandpa White. The whole family, all but Grandpa White, knew about the record and that Uncle Ralph, who had come early with Grandma White, had rigged up a special record player that would send a signal to the family radio. Uncle Ralph was ingenious and was especially clever with anything electronic or mechanical. He was always showing up with some amazing contraption or other, which endeared him to the entire family. That night even the smallest child knew what was happening, and that the following day there would be a big surprise for their grandfather.

Eventually even the grown-ups went to bed, to sleep a little before the children woke. The presents wouldn't be opened until all the family —aunts, uncles, and cousins—arrived after church on Christmas Day, at which time every woman and some of the girls would be needed to finish cooking dinner and get the table set. As Raymond's mother began to thicken the gravy, the children and some of the grownups began to take quick peeks out of the windows, knowing that Grandpa White would arrive all spruced up just in time to carve the goose.

Punctual as usual, Grandpa White drove up just as the last preparations were being made. The little children got so excited about his surprise that the adults had to stop what they were doing to calm them down and remind them not to give away the secret. When Grandpa walked into the kitchen, Olive gave her father a small glass of eggnog. The children had already taken his coat and hat and carefully laid them on their mother's bed. Men and older boys had left their conversations to greet him: "Hi, Pa, Merry Christmas" and "Merry Christmas, Grandpa!"

When the amenities were over, everyone settled at the table, the blessing was said, and Grandpa stood to carve the goose, knife in one hand and fork in the other. At that moment everyone heard clearly Great-grandpa White's voice booming over the radio, which sat on top of the piano in the living room; Grandpa could look through the wide arching doorway and easily see it.

"Hello there, Wilbur, this is Mother and Father in Wisconsin." Grandpa whirled and stood frozen, staring at the radio, listening, unable to believe that it was his father's voice speaking to him, a voice he had not heard in many a year. Of course, only a few homes had a telephone at that time, and no one in Raymond's family had one. So as the family began to whisper and the children began to giggle, Grandpa said, "Shut up! Shut up!" and they all saw the strong Victorian man of granite—the husband, father, and grandfather they all loved, respected, and feared just a little bit—crack for a moment before them and show tender feelings for his parents, a side of him they had never seen before.

And Uncle Ralph, whom they already held in high regard, went up another notch.

GREAT-GRANDMA'S CHRISTMAS GOOSE WITH APPLE AND PRUNE DRESSING

My Great-grandma Meekins was particular about the goose she roasted. She thought a goose was of prime quality at about ten months of age. (On farms, geese are born in early spring and kept on feed until Christmas, when they're either eaten or sold.)

Domestic geese have much more fat under the skin of the breast than do wild geese; therefore, some of it must be removed during the cooking process. Mother, who hated grease of any kind, parboiled hers.

1 (10- to 12-pound) goose, all excess fat removed
    For parboiling goose:
      Boiling water
      2 ribs celery
      1 carrot, unpeeled
      1 small onion, peeled
      1 bay leaf
      1 teaspoon salt
      ½ teaspoon black pepper
2 teaspoons salt
½ teaspoon black pepper
1 small orange, unpeeled

1 tart apple (preferably Winesap), unpeeled
1 rib celery, cut into 2 or 3 pieces
1 carrot, cut into 2 or 3 pieces
Half an onion, peeled
4 prunes (with pits or pitted)
1 recipe Honey Butter Glaze (page 57)
Parsley, green, red, and black olives for garnish, optional
3 tablespoons toasted sesame seeds
Apple and Prune Dressing (recipe follows)

To parboil the goose, prick the skin over the breast. Place goose in a large kettle and cover with boiling water. Add the remaining ingredients for parboiling the goose. Return water to a boil over high heat and continue boiling for 25 to 30 minutes.

Meanwhile, preheat oven to 350°F. Once goose has finished parboiling, drain. Lightly season with the salt and pepper inside and out, then stuff the cavity loosely with the orange, apple, celery and carrot pieces, onion, and prunes. Place the goose breast side up on a rack in a large roasting pan. Cover and roast until done, allowing 25 minutes per pound; open the pan now and again and prick the skin on the breast so the fat will continue to render out as the goose cooks.

When the cooking time is about up, start checking for doneness by inserting a meat thermometer into the breast. Once it reads 170°F (don't leave thermometer in the goose while cooking), spoon on a little honey glaze and sprinkle with sesame seeds. Return to oven, uncovered, and brown lightly. Remove from oven and discard fruit and vegetable stuffing. Place goose on a serving platter and garnish as you wish. Serve with Apple and Prune Dressing. *Makes 10 to 12 servings.*

Apple and Prune Dressing

¾ cup prunes (with pits or pitted)
1½ cups boiling water
7 cups small pieces of heavily-
    grained whole-wheat bread
    (leave crusts on)
3 cups unpeeled and finely
    chopped apples
1½ cups chopped celery ribs and
    leaves

¾ cup finely chopped onions
1 cup butter or margarine
¼ cup minced fresh parsley
1½ teaspoons dried oregano leaves,
    pulverized
1 teaspoon salt
½ teaspoon black pepper

Place the prunes in a small bowl, pour the boiling water over them, and let them sit to plump for about 30 minutes. Once plumped, drain, reserving the soaking liquid. Pit the prunes, if needed, then chop and place in a large pan or bowl; add the bread and apples. Set aside.

In a large skillet, cook the celery and onions in the butter until vegetables are clear but not browned. Stir in the parsley, oregano, salt, and pepper, then add 1 cup of the reserved prune soaking liquid. Pour the cooked ingredients over the bread mixture. Fold together, adding a bit of hot water as needed to make a fairly moist dressing (dressing should be neither wet nor dry).

Turn the dressing into a greased 13x9x2-inch baking pan. Bake in the oven with the goose until well risen, browned and firm to the touch, about 40 to 45 minutes. (*Note:* To gauge timing put dressing in the oven when you uncover the goose to brown it.)   *Makes about 10 cups.*

VEDA'S ROASTED PHEASANTS

It was always delightful to have the folks come down out of the hill country and bring wild game or game birds for the Christmas feast. Veda always brought a large covered pan of pheasants.

2 pheasants, each about 3½ to 4
    pounds dressed
Butter or margarine
Salt and black pepper
1 tablespoon dried chervil leaves

½ teaspoon dried sweet marjoram
    leaves
4 to 6 thick slices farm-style bacon
¼ cup water, if needed

Preheat oven to 300°F. Rinse pheasants under cool running water, then wipe them clean with a damp cloth; rub generously inside and out with butter, then season with salt and pepper. Rub the chervil and marjoram between your fingers to pulverize it and sprinkle over the pheasants. Place the birds in a close-fitting pan and cover with bacon. Bake uncovered until a meat thermometer inserted in the breast reads 180°F, about 1 hour. If the pheasants are not yet tender once the thermometer registers 180°, add ¼ cup water, cover, and bake until tender.

Makes 4 servings.

CHICKEN WALDORF SALAD WITH LEMON MAYONNAISE

This delicate salad is perfect for Christmas. We like to arrange beds of red-leaved lettuce in small glass fruit dishes and fill each dish with about half a cup or more of salad topped with slivered almonds. In the old days, women often used tender white cabbage leaves for cups—for garnish only and not to be eaten—because there was no lettuce at Christmastime.

Red-leaved lettuce, washed and
  thoroughly dried
1 cup chopped apples (Golden
  Delicious preferred)
¾ cup boned and cubed cooked
  chicken (breast meat preferred)

⅔ cup thinly sliced celery
½ cup cubed Swiss cheese
¾ cup slivered almonds
Lemon Mayonnaise (recipe follows)

Set out 4 to 6 glass fruit dishes; arrange a bed of lettuce leaves in each. In a medium-size bowl, combine the apples, chicken, celery, cheese, and ½ cup of the almonds. Toss with the mayonnaise and spoon into the prepared dishes. Garnish with the *remaining ¼ cup* almonds.

Makes 4 to 6 individual salads.

Lemon Mayonnaise
Stir 1 *tablespoon strained lemon juice* into ⅓ *cup mayonnaise* (preferably Easy-to-Make Mayonnaise, page 116). Add ⅛ *teaspoon salt* and *a few grains of white pepper* if you have it, otherwise black pepper will do; stir to blend.

Makes about ⅓ cup lemon mayonnaise.

GREAT-AUNT MAE'S
SCALLOPED OYSTERS

Ada recalls that Aunt Mae had a great deal of sentiment for this dish because it was served in her childhood home and was a memory of better days. Auntie would say, "Papa always chose the oysters himself. Nothing was too good for us before the war."

1 pint oysters
1 cup crushed soda crackers
¼ cup butter or margarine
1 cup milk, or ½ cup light cream
   mixed with ½ cup milk, or ½
   cup light cream mixed with ½
   cup oyster liquor

½ teaspoon salt
¼ teaspoon black pepper
Paprika

Preheat oven to 450°F. Grease a 1-quart casserole dish (round preferred). Drain the oysters, reserving the liquor; remove any bits of shell. Wash oysters quickly and lightly under cool running water; set aside in a small bowl. Scatter a thick layer of cracker crumbs over the bottom of the greased dish, then add a layer of oysters over crumbs; sprinkle lightly with some of the salt, pepper, and paprika. Repeat layering the crumbs and oysters alternately until all are used up; end with a layer of crumbs. Slowly pour the milk (or cream-milk mixture or cream-oyster liquor mixture) along the sides until moisture shows at the top of the dish; use all the liquid if it will fit in dish. Dust with paprika. Bake until top is crisp and brown and the center is moist, buttery, and succulent, about 20 minutes. Serve immediately.   *Makes 3 to 4 servings.*

WINTERTIME SALAD BOWL

Effie was a daring cook who never hesitated to combine ingredients if she thought they would blend well together. Therefore some of our favorite Christmas salads were surprises concocted by Effie to add sparkle to the festive holiday dinners.

1¾ cups peeled and diced apples
   (Winesap or Jonathan
   preferred)
¾ cup peeled and shredded sweet
   raw turnips
¾ cup chopped celery
¼ cup minced fresh parsley

¼ cup minced chives
¼ cup Homemade French Dressing
   (recipe follows)
¼ cup mayonnaise (preferably
   Homemade Honey
   Mayonnaise, page 224)

1 small head lettuce, separated   Pitted black olives, for garnish
   into leaves, rinsed and dried

In a large mixing bowl, combine the apples, turnips, celery, parsley, and chives. In a small bowl, mix together the French dressing and mayonnaise (we like just enough dressing to moisten the salad, but make a little more or less if you wish); toss with the apple mixture until all ingredients are lightly coated. Arrange the dressed salad in a serving bowl that's been lined with lettuce leaves. (Old-time cooks lined the bowl with Savoy or red cabbage; in those days lettuce was not in season.) Garnish with black olives. Serve immediately.   *Makes 8 to 10 servings.*

Homemade French Dressing

¾ cup salad oil   Dash of paprika
¼ cup lemon juice or vinegar   ¼ teaspoon sugar
¾ teaspoon salt   1 whole, peeled garlic clove
Dash of pepper

Combine ingredients in a jar and shake until well blended. Store in refrigerator. Shake again before using.   *Makes 1 cup.*

CARROTS GLAZED WITH BUTTER AND HONEY

Uncle Bud loved these carrots—he thought they tasted like a dessert. But then, of course, he loved carrot pie, and carrot bread, carrot pudding, and any other carrot dish if it had butter and honey added.

2 pounds small tender carrots   2 tablespoons light-colored honey
2 tablespoons butter   About ¼ to ½ teaspoon lemon juice
2 tablespoons water   Dash of freshly grated nutmeg

Cook the whole carrots in a very small amount of boiling salted water until just tender. Drain and place in a heavy skillet with the butter. Cook over medium heat until the butter melts. Add the water and honey; continue cooking until the carrots are well coated and have glazed (they will look shiny), stirring constantly. (Note: Take care not to let the carrots scorch; a glaze made of honey scorches easier and more quickly than one made with sugar.) Remove from heat and season to taste with lemon juice and nutmeg. Serve piping hot.

Makes about 8 servings.

LIGHT AND SWEET DINNER ROLLS

Ada called this a sweet-bread recipe because she made it into cinnamon rolls, Christmas wreaths, and filled coffeecakes, all of which were delicious. Effie, who also liked to make this dough, turned it into light, golden dinner rolls.

1 pint heavy cream mixed with
  1 pint milk or 1 quart half
  and half
2 tablespoons dry or granulated
  yeast
½ cup lukewarm water (105°F to
  115°F)

4 eggs, well beaten
½ cup sugar
1 tablespoon salt
8 to 9 cups all-purpose flour
¼ cup butter or margarine, melted

Warm the cream-milk mixture to lukewarm; remove from heat. Meanwhile, in a small bowl, combine the yeast, water, and eggs. Add the sugar and salt to the lukewarm cream-milk mixture, stirring until the sugar dissolves, then add the yeast mixture, stirring well. Stir in just enough flour to make a thin dough (sponge); you will need to use about 4 cups flour for this. Scrape the bowl down, cover with a clean cloth, and let the sponge rise in a warm place until doubled in bulk, about 35 minutes.

Stir down the sponge and add about 6 to 7 cups of flour or enough to make a medium-thick dough. Turn dough onto a generously floured surface and knead enough additional flour into it to make a medium-stiff dough; the dough should be firm enough to knead easily and yet not stick to your hands.

Grease a large (about 17x11-inch) baking sheet. Pinch off egg-sized pieces of dough and form into smooth balls, dusting the dough and your hands lightly with flour as needed; fill the baking sheet with them, fitting dough against the sides of the pan snugly together. Cover lightly with a towel and let rise in a warm place until doubled in bulk, about 35 to 40 minutes.

Bake in a preheated 400°F oven until golden brown, 35 to 40 minutes. Remove from oven and let cool on the baking sheet for about 10 minutes, then lightly butter the tops and serve while still piping hot.

Makes about 2 to 3 dozen rolls.

DADDY'S CREAMED BABY ONIONS

Our father loved this dish and thought it went well with everything, even roasted goose. Mother preferred it with roasted chicken.

1½ pounds baby white onions or
    pearl onions
2 tablespoons butter or margarine
2 tablespoons all-purpose flour

Salt
⅛ teaspoon ground black pepper
1½ cups light cream

Peel and rinse the onions, leaving them whole. Place in a large saucepan and add 3 to 4 inches of salted boiling water (use ½ teaspoon salt to each cup boiling water). Cover and bring to a boil; reduce heat and simmer until tender, about 15 to 20 minutes. Drain.

Melt the butter in a medium-size saucepan over low heat. Stir in the flour, ½ teaspoon of salt, and the pepper. Cook over low heat, stirring constantly, until sauce is smooth and bubbly. Remove from heat and stir in the cream. Return to high heat, bring to a boil, and let sauce boil only 3 minutes. Pour over onions and fold together. Serve piping hot.

Makes 4 to 6 servings.

AUNT MAE'S
MINCEMEAT-CUSTARD PIE

Many old-time recipes combined fruits like pears, peaches, and apples with custard in a pie, as Aunt Mae has done here with mincemeat. This is a wonderfully rich, sweet pie.

Flaky Pastry Dough (page 163)
  2 cups Eva Mae's Favorite
    Mincemeat (page 29)
1½ cups milk

⅔ cup sugar
3 eggs, lightly beaten
1 teaspoon vanilla extract or rum
  flavoring

Prepare the pastry dough; wrap in waxed paper or aluminum foil and chill for at least 15 but not more than 30 minutes before rolling out.

Preheat oven to 450°F. Remove the pastry dough from refrigeration, turn out onto a lightly floured surface, and roll out slightly less than ¼ inch thick. Line a 9-inch pie pan with the dough, letting it overlap rim 1 to 1½ inches; trim off excess. Then tuck overlap under between dough and pan; flute with your fingers or a wide-tined fork. Spread the mincemeat over the bottom of the pie shell.

In a large bowl, combine the milk, sugar, eggs and vanilla; stirring until sugar dissolves. Gently pour the custard over the mincemeat. Bake in the 450° oven for 10 minutes; then reduce oven setting to 350° and continue baking until filling is firm, about 45 minutes longer. Cool to room temperature then serve. Refrigerate leftover pie.

Makes one 9-inch pie.

ONCE IN ROYAL DAVID'S CITY

Aunt Clary, whose singing voice was so lovely that it often brought tears to the eyes of the church folks for whom she most often sang, loved the hymns and carols written by Mrs. Cecil Frances Alexander and usually sang her favorite for the Christmas program: "Once in Royal David's City," accompanied only by the church organist.

Mrs. Alexander, Aunt Clary often told us, was the wife of the primate of Ireland in the 1800s. Many of her most beautiful hymns, such as "There Is a Green Hill Far Away," were written especially for children, to help explain the gospel messages to them. Aunt Clary always said that whether the songs were for children or not, she and other adults, as well as the little ones, were inspired by them.

ONCE IN ROYAL DAVID'S CITY

Once in royal David's city
Stood a lowly cattle-shed,
Where a mother laid her Baby
In a manger for His bed;
Mary was that mother mild,
Jesus Christ her little Child.

He came down to earth from heaven,
Who is God and Lord of all,
And his shelter was a stable
And His cradle was a stall;
With the poor, and mean, and lowly,
Lived on earth our Saviour holy.

And, through all His wondrous childhood,
He would honor, and obey,
Love, and watch the lowly maiden
In whose gentle arms He lay;
Christian children all must be
Mild, obedient, good as He.

For He is our childhood's pattern,
Day by day like us He grew:

He was little, weak, and helpless,
Tears and smiles like us He knew;
And He feeleth for our sadness,
And He shareth in our gladness.

And our eyes at last shall see Him,
Through His own redeeming love;
For that Child so dear and gentle
Is our Lord in heav'n above;
And He leads His children on
To the place where He is gone.

Not in that poor lowly stable,
With the oxen standing by,
We shall see Him, but in heaven,
Set at God's right hand on high;
When like stars His children crowned,
All in white shall wait around.

—Cecil Frances Alexander

PLUM PUDDING WITH HARD SAUCE

Great-aunt Alice, who immigrated from England in 1903, used to tell us
that plum pudding was first made by an English king and his hunting
party. She said they were lost in a blizzard the day before Christmas and
put all their remaining provisions (meat, flour, apples, eggs, brandy and
sugar) in a cloth bag to be cooked; the result was a satisfying, rich
pudding. Royal cooks later refined the pudding, which became a popular

national dish and a Christmas tradition, though why it's called plum pudding I still don't know.

In our family, this lovely old-fashioned pudding has always been eaten late in the day, after our Christmas dinner has had a chance to settle.

⅓ cup butter or margarine,
   softened
1 cup, packed, brown sugar
4 eggs, well beaten
¼ cup sifted all-purpose flour
2 teaspoons baking powder
1 teaspoon salt

1 teaspoon ground cinnamon
½ teaspoon freshly grated nutmeg
1½ cups raisins
½ cup chopped candied orange peel
½ cup chopped nuts
2½ cups dried breadcrumbs

In a large mixing bowl, cream together the butter and sugar until fluffy; add the eggs and stir to blend. Into a medium-size bowl, sift together the flour, baking powder, salt, cinnamon, and nutmeg; add the raisins, orange peel and nuts, stirring to blend. Stir the flour-fruit mixture and breadcrumbs into the creamed butter-sugar mixture, blending thoroughly. Pour into a generously greased plum pudding mold. Cover mold and fasten securely. Steam for 3 to 3½ hours as directed below. Serve warm with hard sauce. *Makes 8 to 10 servings.*

To Steam the Pudding
Many old-time puddings were steamed in a coffee can that had a tight-fitting cover and smooth sides. When no lid was available, the mold was covered with waxed paper fastened securely on top. (The mold was sometimes paper-lined.)

Place the mold in a steamer or deep covered kettle. Add enough boiling water to the steamer to come halfway up the mold. Cover. Cook until done, keeping the water boiling rapidly and adding more water as necessary to keep the correct depth. Remove the pudding from the

324   *JANE WATSON HOPPING*

steamer and take the cover off. If desired, place pudding in a moderate oven (350°F) for about 5 minutes to dry the top a bit.

Hard Sauce

⅓ cup butter or margarine, softened
  at room temperature
1 cup powdered sugar, sifted

A grating of lemon rind (about ⅛
  teaspoon)
½ teaspoon lemon juice, strained

In a pint-size bowl cream butter until very light, then stir in the sugar, grated lemon rind and lemon juice. Blend well together. Cover and set in a cool place until needed. Serve over hot pudding.

Makes 4 to 6 servings.

🎄 THE FADING EMBERS
OF CHRISTMAS

When the day is spent and evening comes at last and the guests have all gone home we stop, share bits of family gossip, and enjoy again the day's memories, especially of the children in the family. We talk about how they have grown and how beautiful they are: Ada's grandchildren and Effie's. We count and recount the progress each one has made in school and praise again those who are musically inclined: Aunt Clary's great-grandchild Billie and several others. And with hearts warming, we talk about the babies that have been born during the year, three of them. And about what good mothers the young women have become. We worry together about loved ones who are getting old, especially Aunt Clary.

Then we nibble a bit, drink a little cold cider, and mix up a small batch of eggnog for those who might not have gotten enough earlier. And we listen to the church bells, ringing their haunting melodies in the distance.

Baby's first Christmas

🌿 SHEILA'S CHRISTMAS BELLS

When Sheila lived in Missouri, women there made pillow tops using coarse cotton fabric for "candlewicking," taking threads from the cut edges of the fabric to work into a pattern of tufts. While traditionally thick cotton fabric and thread are used for candlewicking (called thus because the tufts on old-time handwork somewhat resembled a frayed candlewick), pillow tops may be made of various fabrics and embroidered with floss or light yarn.

The secret for making this lovely handworked pillow is in the choice of fabric and thread. Wool fabric and wool yarn can be used, as can heavy muslin or linen fabric with cotton thread, or even raw silk with silk thread. One must also choose the colors carefully, using thread or yarn that matches or harmonizes with the tones of the fabric.

MATERIALS

Two 24-inch-square pieces of yardage
3 hanks of embroidery floss
132 inches of ungathered lace or 1½ yards
of gathered lace
Pillow stuffing
Fabric Carbon

To enlarge the bell pattern, make a grid of 1-inch squares on paper (24 x 24 inches) and draw the pattern in the squares. Then, using fabric carbon, trace the paper pattern onto the right side (top side) of one of the fabric squares. (*Note:* If you wish you may enlarge pattern on a copy machine.)

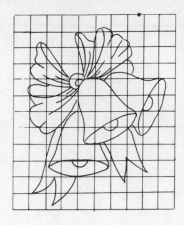

Using embroidery hoops and embroidery floss, outline the bell shapes and ribbon with *chain stitches.*

Work the rest of the design with *French knots:* To make a French knot, bring the thread out at the required position. Hold the thread down with the left thumb and wind the thread twice around the needle. Still holding the thread firmly, twist the needle back to the starting point and insert it close to where the thread first emerged. Pull thread through to the back and secure for a single French knot or pass on to the position of the next stitch.

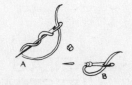

To assemble the pillow, machine-stitch the two pillow squares together with a ⅜-inch seam, leaving a stuffing hole on one of the edges. Stuff the pillow until firm with cotton stuffing. By hand, stitch the stuffing hole closed.

When the pillow is finished, measure around the perimeter, then double the number of inches measured. Make hand-crocheted lace for heavier fabrics—light wool, heavy cotton, or linen. For lighter fabrics you may want to use a lighter-weight store-bought lace.

SNOWFLAKE LACE
WITH
SHELL-AND-PICOT EDGING

This lace is quite lovely. The shell-and-picot top edge forms a small ruffle.

MATERIALS

250 yards of size 20 crochet thread
Size 12 hook

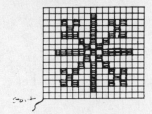

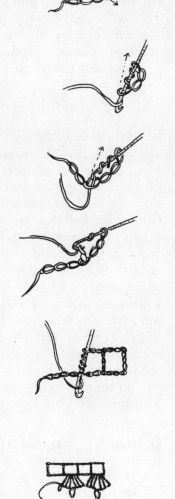

Row 1: For a foundation chain, crochet 51 *chain stitches.* Then *treble crochet* in the 8th stitch from the hook. Chain 2, then skip 2 foundation chain stitches and treble crochet in the next chain stitch, which forms an *open mesh square.* Continue until 15 mesh squares are made. Turn, treble crochet in the first chain stitch. Then crochet 2 chain stitches, skip 2 chain stitches, and treble crochet in the next chain, which forms an open mesh square. Continue to the end of the second row.

Following the visual guide, make open and *filet mesh squares.* (*Note:* A filet mesh square is one that is filled, made by crocheting 4 treble crochet stitches one after the other. See the visual guide.) When the first block of lace is finished, repeat until the lace is twice the length of the perimeter of the pillow.

When the Snowflake Lace is completed, crochet a *shell-and-picot edging* the full length of the lace on both sides (do not crochet edging on ends).

Start the edging in the first open mesh square, double crochet 3 times. Then make 6 chain stitches. Single crochet in the last chain of the 3 treble crochet stitches to form a picot (see visual guide). Next, treble crochet 3 times, skip one space, and repeat all along the lace.

To gather the lace for the pillow, weave ¼-inch ribbon in the top row of open mesh squares. Using a whipstitch, hand work the gathered lace onto the edge of the pillow. (If you wish, very lightly starch the lace before weaving in the ribbon.)

EGGNOG CHRISTMAS PIE WITH GRAHAM CRACKER AND ALMOND PIE CRUST

Aunty loved beautiful things and fancy cooking! This is one of her favorite pies.

1½ cups milk
1 envelope (1 tablespoon) unflavored gelatin
¼ cup cold water
3 eggs, separated (2 tablespoons egg white will be reserved for the pie shell)
½ cup plus 2 tablespoons sugar

⅛ teaspoon salt
Graham Cracker and Almond Pie Crust (recipe follows)
½ cup heavy cream
1 tablespoon brandy or 1 teaspoon brandy flavoring
¼ teaspoon freshly grated nutmeg
Finely shaved almonds

Scald the milk in the top of a double boiler. In a small bowl sprinkle the gelatin over the cold water; let soften about 5 minutes. In a medium-size bowl, lightly beat together 1 egg white with ¼ cup of the sugar and the salt; mix in the 3 egg yolks. Pour the scalded milk slowly over the egg-sugar mixture; stir to blend. Return the mixture to the top of the boiler. Cook over hot (not boiling) water, stirring constantly, until custard begins to steam and thickens enough to coat a spoon. Stir up the gelatin and add to the custard, stirring until dissolved. Cool at room temperature until thick enough to mound when dropped from a spoon. Beat 2 egg whites until frothy; reserve 2 tablespoons for the crust. Slowly add ¼ cup sugar and continue beating until stiff. Gently fold into the custard mixture. Pour the filling into the baked pie crust and chill until set. Meanwhile, combine the cream, brandy (or brandy flavoring), and the remaining 2 *tablespoons* sugar and beat until soft peaks form; refrigerate until ready to use.

Just before serving, top the pie with the whipped cream, and garnish with almonds.   *Makes one 9-inch pie.*

Graham Cracker and Almond Pie Crust

¾ cups graham crackers, crushed into fine crumbs with a rolling pin
¼ cup finely ground almonds
¼ cup sugar

⅛ teaspoon freshly grated nutmeg
⅛ teaspoon salt
4 tablespoons butter, softened
2 tablespoons reserved egg white, beaten to a froth

Preheat oven to 350°F. Generously grease a 9-inch pie pan. Combine the cracker crumbs with the almonds, sugar, nutmeg, and salt. Work the butter into the crumb mixture with the back of a spoon until well blended. Stir in the egg whites. When the mixture is cohesive, press it with the back of a spoon into the bottom and onto the sides of the pie plate; do not spread up onto the rim. Bake in the center of the oven until done, only 5 minutes. Cool on a wire rack before filling.

Makes one 9-inch pie crust.

AFTERGLOW

After the angel voices
Died from the solemn night,
Some of the echoes lingered,
Left by the wondrous flight.

After the shepherds came
Back to their waiting flocks,
Some of the glory tarried
There on the hillside rocks.

After the questing Magi
Journeyed from Bethlehem,
Much of the night's elation
Never departed from them.

After the star had faded
Some of its radiance stayed,
Thrilling their hearts forever,
Well were their gifts repaid!

This is the joy we capture
Brought by the Child Divine,
Lighting the world at Christmas . . .
May it be yours and mine!

—Mary B. Wall

AFTERGLOW

The in-between days, those during which we take the tree down and decide what to do with all the leftovers, are warm restful days. None of us can quite forget the second-grade choir at the Eltonville Elementary School that so touched our hearts as their baby voices sang "O Holy Night." Or the special Christmas Eve service we went to at Ida Marie's country church, which is a lovely, simple church graced with only one stained-glass window, a few hard wooden benches, and a giant, black woodstove that gives off puffs of smoke now and then. The organ is missing one key and yet the congregation sang with a purity that spoke of a depth of spirituality that most never reach.

AFTER THE STAR HAS FADED

Sister Mary Elizabeth O'Brien expresses more eloquently than any of us her emotional legacy from the Christmas season:

"The whole wonderful season leaves me with such an afterglow. Each year as the season of Christ's birth approaches, I can feel my heart melting at the sight of even the hardest-hearted sinner coming out of

himself enough to wish another soul a Merry Christmas. It fills me with love to watch neighbors put away their fighting and scrapping long enough to shake hands and wish each other well.

"For me, the celebration of the birth of the wee baby Jesus is a very holy day, a very spiritual day. But that does not lessen the thrill I feel when other Christians and non-Christians alike take pleasure in the chiming bells, the glitter and pomp, the gift-giving, and the children waiting for Santa Claus. All about me I can hear and feel the hope and joy. And I thank God that, for a while at least, we are reminded of 'how it could be' and of God's greatest gift to mankind, His own Son."

EFFIE'S HONEY-BAKED APPLES

After all the Christmas feasting, our mother thought we should "eat light," so she would set out for each of us bits of leftover meat, a little bread, a glass of icy-cold milk, and one of Effie's delicious honey-baked apples with a little cold sweet cream to spoon over it. My father thought Effie's baked apples were "something special."

6 firm baking apples (Cortland,
   Stayman, or Winesap preferred)
1 cup water

¾ cup honey, at room temperature
1 tablespoon butter
Cold sweet cream, optional

Preheat oven to 350°F. Lightly grease an 11x7x1½-inch baking pan. Wash and core the apples. Peel them about one third of the way down from the stem end so they won't burst while baking. Arrange in the prepared pan, pared side up.

In a small saucepan, boil together the water, honey, and butter for 10 minutes, then pour mixture over the apples. Bake until the apples are tender and lightly colored and the syrup is thick, about 45 minutes, spooning the syrup over the apples several times while the apples bake. Remove from oven and dish up with or without cold sweet cream.

Makes 6 servings.

DELICIOUS OLD-FASHIONED GOLD CAKE WITH APRICOT SAUCE

Apricots have always been a treat in our family. Each apricot season we buy a few for eating out of hand and we use some for canning, particularly for making apricot sauce to serve at Christmas or New Year's.

¾ cup butter or margarine
1½ cups sugar
1 teaspoon lemon extract
8 egg yolks, well beaten
3 cups sifted cake flour

1 tablespoon baking powder
½ teaspoon salt
1 cup milk
Apricot Sauce (recipe follows)

Preheat oven to 375°F. In a large bowl cream the butter until smooth; gradually add the sugar, beating well. Add the lemon extract and stir to blend, then add the egg yolks and beat well. Into a medium-size bowl, sift together the flour, baking powder, and salt. Alternately add the flour mixture and milk to the butter-sugar mixture, beating well after each addition. Turn into a greased 13x9x2-inch baking pan. Bake until the cake is golden brown, pulls away from the pan when tipped, and springs back when lightly pressed, about 30 to 35 minutes. Remove from the oven, let cake cool in the pan for about 10 to 15 minutes, then serve immediately with sauce over it. *Makes about 12 servings.*

Apricot Sauce
2 cups canned apricots, drained,
   pitted, and pureed (use home-

   canned or store-bought)
¼ cup cornstarch

⅓ cup water
1 tablespoon butter

Sugar, to taste
Dusting of freshly grated nutmeg

Bring the pureed apricots to a boil in a heavy saucepan. Meanwhile, dissolve the cornstarch in the water. Once the puree boils, stir in the cornstarch to thicken. Cook and stir until clear, then stir in the butter, sugar, and nutmeg and remove from heat. Let the sauce stand until warm before serving.

Makes about 2 cups.

SONG OF THE NEW YEAR

I heard the bells at midnight
  Ring in the dawning year;
And above the clanging chorus
  Of the song, I seemed to hear
A choir of mystic voices
  Flinging echoes, ringing clear,
From a band of angels winging
  Through the haunted atmosphere:
    "Ring out the shame and sorrow,
      And the misery and sin,
    That the dawning of the morrow
      May in peace be ushered in."

And I thought of all the trials
  The departed years had cost,
And the blooming hopes and pleasures
  That are withered now and lost;
And with joy I drank the music
  Stealing o'er the feeling there
As the spirit song came pealing
  On the silence everywhere:
    "Ring out the shame and sorrow,
      And the misery and sin,
    That the dawning of the morrow
      May in peace be ushered in."

—James Whitcomb Riley

JANE WATSON HOPPING

🌿 RING IN THE DAWNING YEAR

Invigorated, somewhat relieved to see old things pass away, reaching out, hoping the New Year would bring with it a new start—new dreams —we used to celebrate by breaking bread with friends.

Born on the farm, and still milking cows and feeding chickens, Ada and Aunt Mae were always up and about doing chores at dawn and were the first to arrive with treats for the midmorning festivities. Soon everyone had come—even the men, who came late after feeding cattle and horses, sometimes pigs and other livestock, and getting themselves all spruced up.

In no time the kitchen table was covered with mouth-watering dishes and the dining table was crowded with familiar faces, those who shared with us the joys of everyday living. Usually, the meal began with Jake,

Ada's husband, a tall quiet man whose face seemed unwrinkled by time and who spoke in a soft, confident way, asking God to bless and guide each one of us through the new year.

ADA'S
OVEN-COOKED CANADIAN BACON
WITH ORANGE MARMALADE GLAZE

This is an absolutely delightful dish to serve on New Year's Eve or when celebrating the newly arrived year at breakfast with friends. It may be eaten hot or cold, and either way the meat slices to good advantage.

3 pounds or more of Canadian
   bacon
1 cup orange marmalade

1 teaspoon natural stone-ground
   mustard

Preheat oven to 350°F. Lay the bacon out on a rack in a shallow roasting pan. Bake uncovered until a meat thermometer reads 150°F, about 30 minutes, then combine the marmalade and mustard in a small bowl, blending well and spread this glaze evenly over the top of the bacon. Continue baking uncovered, watching carefully and frequently, until the internal temperature of the bacon rises to between 165° and 170°, or less if the glaze is getting too brown. This will take 15 to 20 minutes. (*Note:* Don't overcook; if cooked beyond a temperature of 170° the meat will be dry.) Remove from oven; let set out about 5 minutes if you plan to serve this hot; or let cool, then refrigerate if you wish to serve cold.

Makes about 10 to 12 servings.

AUNT MAE'S PRESSED CHICKEN

Aunt Mae thought this was an elegant dish for a Christmas Eve or New Year's Eve supper or for a New Year's Day breakfast with friends. Most old-time cooks made this loaf the day before it was needed, then unmolded it shortly before it was time to serve.

1 (4-pound) chicken
4 cups hot water
1½ teaspoons salt
1 small rib celery
1 small carrot, peeled and sliced
1 small onion, peeled and chopped
1 small bay leaf

2 envelopes (2 tablespoons)
   unflavored gelatin
½ cup cold water
3 tablespoons minced fresh parsley
Garnishes:
   Delicious Stuffed Eggs
   (page 213)

Pitted black olives
Sprigs of parsley

Wash the chicken including the neck, gizzard, and heart (discard liver or save it to cook for another time. Place the chicken, neck, gizzard, and heart in a large saucepan or kettle. Add the hot water, salt, celery, carrot, onion, and bay leaf. Cover closely and simmer until the meat falls away from the bones, about 1 to 1½ hours.

With a slotted spoon, remove the chicken meat and bones from the broth. While the meat is still warm, remove and discard all the skin and bones; separate light and dark meat. Set the broth aside to cool so the fat will rise to the surface. (Note: If you wish, drop several ice cubes into the broth; stir them about as the fat collects on them, then remove before they melt.)

Now measure the broth; there should be about 3 cups. If less, add water to make 3 cups. Sprinkle the gelatin over the cold water and let soften about 5 minutes; stir, and add to the hot broth, sprinkle minced parsley over the broth, and continue to stir until the gelatin dissolves (reheat broth if necessary). Pour enough of the broth into a 10x5x3-inch loaf pan to come up the sides about ¼ inch. Arrange the light and dark meat in alternate layers on top. Then slowly pour more of the broth over the chicken to cover it completely. Chill until set, at least 6 hours, preferably overnight. Just before serving, unmold onto a serving platter; garnish with Delicious Stuffed Eggs, olives, and parsley sprigs. (Note: Stuffed eggs made with bantam chicken eggs are quite small and look particularly festive as a garnish for this dish. If you don't have them use store-bought small eggs.)   Makes 6 servings.

FANCY CANDIED YAMS

This puddinglike dish goes very well alongside turkey, goose, ham, or pork, especially leftovers! Also serve a Young Cook's Cabbage and Carrot Salad with Homemade Honey Mayonnaise (page 224) for a flavor and texture contrast.

6 medium-size yams, peeled and
   quartered (about 2 pounds)
Boiling salted water, to cover
  potatoes
2 tablespoons butter
½ cup strained orange juice
½ cup roasted pecans, chopped

⅓ cup, packed, brown sugar
1 teaspoon ground cinnamon
½ teaspoon freshly grated nutmeg
½ teaspoon salt
6 large or 12 small marshmallows
  (cut large ones in half)

Grease a 1½-quart broilerproof dish. Place the potatoes in a saucepan, add boiling salt water to cover, and cook until tender (test by piercing with a fork), about 20 minutes. Meanwhile, set temperature control of range to broil. Drain the cooked potatoes and dry by shaking pan over heat. Next, warm a potato masher and mixing bowl with boiling water, then mash the potatoes and whip until fluffy. Stir in the butter, orange juice, pecans, sugar, cinnamon, nutmeg, and salt. Spoon into the prepared broilerproof dish; top with marshmallows. Place dish under the broiler, 4 inches from the heat source, and broil until marshmallows are delicately browned and slightly melted. Serve immediately.

Makes about 8 servings.

OLD-FASHIONED SPANISH CREAM

As this cream cools it separates, leaving a light frothy top over the custard base.

1 envelope (1 tablespoon)
    unflavored gelatin
⅛ teaspoon salt
½ cup sugar
2 eggs, separated and at room
    temperature

2 cups milk
½ teaspoon vanilla extract or brandy
Orange marmalade, for garnish,
    optional

In a large saucepan, combine the gelatin, salt, and ¼ *cup* of the sugar. Blend the egg yolks with *1 cup* of the milk, then pour over the gelatin mixture and stir to blend. Place over low heat and cook for about 5 minutes or until the gelatin has dissolved, stirring constantly. Remove from heat. Add the *remaining 1 cup* milk and the vanilla or brandy. Chill the cooked mixture until slightly firm.

Beat the egg whites until they stand in soft peaks; as you beat, add the *remaining ¼ cup* sugar to them, 1 tablespoon at a time. Fold the egg whites into the chilled custard, then pour into a serving bowl or into 4 individual serving dishes. Garnish with a dot of orange marmalade if you wish.

Makes 4 dessert servings.

A Day of New Beginnings

Each year Aunt Clary's favorite holiday was New Year's Day. She told anyone who would listen that it made her feel lighthearted and "eager to go" again. Her laughter enlivened the gatherings, and everywhere she told stories about the old days in the Ozark Highlands of Missouri, where she was raised, and "clogged" a bit for the children. Clogging is a noisy, jumping shuffle-step done in heavy shoes or boots that pounds out a rhythm, rather like a heavier form of tap dancing. My grandfather clogged when he went around corners in a square dance, and we children learned to do it, too.

Sometimes in a wavering voice Aunt Clary sang old Irish songs for us, those she said had been kept alive in the hills. She ate heartily, taking more than one serving of Uncle Bud's fresh roast pork ham, and if any one dared to scold her for the onslaught on her ancient digestive system, she would hoot and tell them she had grown up on "side pork" (fresh bacon) and good old-fashioned cured hams.

Watching on the sidelines, nieces and great-nieces always worried that Aunt Clary was overtaxing herself. But when asked softly if she would like to sit down a bit, she would laugh and tell the worriers that she was eighty years young, not eighty years old.

UNCLE BUD'S FRESH PORK HAM

Uncle Bud raised Hampshires, black hogs with a white band around the front part of their bodies. Such pigs were not large—full grown boars weighed only 800 pounds—but they produced many young, were "easy keepers," and were well known for the quality of the hams.

By late December the fall litters were nearly ready for market and were eating Uncle Bud out of house and home, so he would invite the whole family over—thirty or forty strong—for New Year's dinner and he would provide the roasted young pork hams. A fresh ham yields a high percentage of lean meat to bone, making it an excellent choice for serving a large number of people.

1 leg of fresh pork (about 8 to 10 pounds)	1 clove peeled garlic
Salt and black pepper	2 teaspoons pulverized dried sweet marjoram leaves

Preheat oven to 325°F. Remove the hock (ankle) and rind from the leg of pork and trim away all but about ¼ inch fat. Set out a 15x10x2-inch flat roasting pan fitted with a rack. Sprinkle the leg of pork on all sides with salt and pepper. Rub the surface with a cut clove of garlic and sprinkle the marjoram over the top. Place fat side up in the roast pan. Insert a meat thermometer through the fat side of the leg of pork so that the tip rests in the thickest and leanest part of the meat. (*Note:* For an accurate reading, the tip should not be embedded in fat, nor should it touch gristle or bone.)

Roast, without adding water or basting, until the thermometer reads 185°F, or bake 40 to 45 minutes per pound. When done, remove from oven and place on a heated serving platter. Keep warm until ready to serve. *Makes about 3 servings per pound of uncooked leg of pork.*

JANE WATSON HOPPING

AUNT CLARY'S
TART YELLOW AND GREEN STRING BEANS
WITH BACON

In the old days, vegetables in winter were stored from one season to the next by either drying them or home-canning them. For this bean dish, Aunt Clary canned yellow and green string beans in the same jar for color.

6 or 8 slices farm-style bacon, cut
   crosswise into ½ inch pieces
⅔ cup finely chopped onions
¼ cup sugar
¼ cup vinegar
¼ cup water
½ teaspoon salt

⅛ teaspoon black pepper
1 quart home-canned yellow and
   green string beans (or use about
   1½ pounds fresh cooked beans
   or 2 cans store-bought beans;
   see Note)

Note: Home-canned beans are always opened and boiled about 10 to 15 minutes before tasting or serving.

Place the bacon in a large cold skillet. Cook slowly until pieces are browned and crispy, stirring frequently; once all pieces are done, pour off any remaining fat from skillet. (Note: The fat may be reserved for making cornbread or biscuits, or for frying or seasoning.) Remove pieces from skillet as done and drain on paper towels.

Return all bacon to the skillet; add the onions, sugar, vinegar, water, salt, and pepper, stirring well. Drain the beans and add to the skillet; toss to mix. Heat to serving temperature.   *Makes about 8 servings.*

ADA'S RIBBON POTATOES

These golden deep-fried ribbons were one of Ada's favorite garnishes for a beef roast.

4 to 6 large potatoes
Vegetable oil, for deep-frying
Salt and pepper, as desired

Wash and peel the potatoes, removing blemishes and eyes; peel with a sharp knife around and around into thin ribbons. Fry in hot oil (375°F.) until light brown, 5 to 6 minutes. Drain on absorbent paper towels or a folded brown bag. Sprinkle with salt and pepper. Serve hot or cold. If serving hot, arrange on a platter alone or around a roast; if serving cold, place in a bread basket lined with a folded napkin.

Makes 8 to 12 servings.

AUNTY'S NEWFANGLED
CHOCOLATE BAVARIAN CREAM

As the Great Depression began to ease, the women in our family began to splurge "just a little," especially our aunts who had no children to support. Christmas, New Year's Eve, New Year's Day, and birthdays saw a proliferation of fancy desserts.

Often on New Year's Eve we serve this dessert with hot coffee just before the midnight bells toll. When I was a child, the New Year was ushered in with whoops and yells and shotgun blasts.

2 cups milk
6 ounces semisweet chocolate, cut
   into small pieces
2 envelopes unflavored gelatin
½ cup cold water
4 eggs, separated
¼ cup granulated sugar

Pinch of salt
2 cups heavy cream
3 tablespoons powdered sugar
Honey and Spice Whipped Cream
   (page 163), nuts, or chocolate curls
   (for garnish)

In a medium-size saucepan, heat the milk and chocolate together, stirring constantly, until chocolate is melted. Remove from heat; set aside. In a small bowl, sprinkle the gelatin over the cold water; let stand until softened, about 5 minutes.

In a large bowl, beat together the egg yolks, granulated sugar, and salt until mixture is thick and lemon-colored; then gradually stir in the milk-chocolate mixture, blending well. Place in the top of a double boiler; adjust heat so the water under mixture simmers (not boils). Add the gelatin and cook and stir until gelatin dissolves, about 5 minutes. Remove from heat and place the top of the double boiler in a large bowl of ice cubes; stir until mixture has the consistency of thick cream.

In a large bowl, whip the cream and powdered sugar into soft peaks (don't beat too long or cream will begin to turn to butter). Gently fold the gelatin mixture into the whipped cream. Pour mixture into a 2-quart mold or into 10 to 12 individual glass dessert dishes. Refrigerate to chill for 5 to 6 hours. To serve, garnish with Honey and Spice Whipped Cream, nuts, or chocolate curls. *Makes 10 to12 servings.*

Howard Chandler Christy · 1902

THE GOOD
OLD-FASHIONED PEOPLE

The Hale,
Hard-working People
The Kindly Country People
'At Uncle Used to Know!

With Christmas still lingering in their minds and hearts, old-time country folks knew they had to get back to work. There were harnesses to mend, storerooms to put in order, equipment to repair, daily chores to do. And men who worked hard through all of the seasons took advantage of cold wintery January to fix up something for the woman of the house, maybe build a new cupboard or repair the old ones.

The new year was at hand—everyone felt it in their bones. Even children sensed that it was a time of fresh starts, a chance to make changes. And it was a time to sit gathered about the fire while grandparents, uncles and aunts, and parents and we children listened to the rain on the roof and lost ourselves in stories of the past.

THE GOOD, OLD-FASHIONED PEOPLE

When we hear Uncle Sidney tell
   About the long-ago
An' old, old friends he loved so well
   When he was young—My-oh!—
Us childern all wish we'd 'a' bin
   A-livin' then with Uncle,—so
We could a-kind o' happened in
   On them old friends he used to know!—
      The good, old-fashioned people—
      The hale, hard-working people—
      The kindly country people
         'At Uncle used to know!

They was God's people, Uncle says,
   An' gloried in His name,
An' worked, without no selfishness,
   An' loved their neighbers same
As they was kin: An' when they biled
   Their tree-molasses, in the Spring,
Er butchered in the Fall, they smiled
   An' sheered with all jist ever'thing!—
      The good, old-fashioned people—
      The hale, hard-working people—
      The kindly country people
         'At Uncle used to know!

He tells about 'em, lots o' times,
   Till we'd all ruther hear
About 'em than the Nurs'ry Rhymes
   Er Fairies—mighty near!—
Only, sometimes, he stops so long
   An' then talks on so low an' slow,
It's purt' nigh sad as any song
   To listen to him talkin' so
      Of the good, old-fashioned people—
      The hale, hard-working people—
      The kindly country people
         'At Uncle used to know!

        —James Whitcomb Riley

INDEX

breads (cont'd)
glazed cinnamon buns, 138–39
graham muffins, 209
Great-Grandma Meekins's dunkin'
doughnuts, 286–87
Johanna's Christmas stollen (fruit loaf), 155–
56
light and sweet dinner rolls, 319
molasses oatmeal, with easy-to-make lemon
glaze, 69–70
Mother's dunkin' doughnuts, 251–52
Norwegian Christmas (Julekake), 187–89
pumpkin raisin, with nutmeg glaze, 121–22
quick buttermilk buns, 117–18
roly-poly snowmen with lemon icing, 227–28
Schnecken (caramel buns), 21
Sheila's southern corn muffins, 95
soda biscuits: an old-time basic recipe, 138
sweet Swedish rye, 214–15
Veda's orange raisin muffins, 308–9
whole-wheat yeast muffins, 288–89
breakfast:
Aunt Clary's "Handy Andy," 142
easy-to-make golden fritters, 234
Great-Grandma's "golden buck," 303–4
oats, 70
"Bring a Torch, Jeanette, Isabella" (Nunn), 265
Brine, Mary Dow, 136–37
Brooks, Phillips, 217, 289–90
butter:
carrots glazed with honey and, 318–19
honey glaze, Aunt Mable's imitation boar's
head pork roast with, 56–57
lemon glaze, Aunt Mae's Christmas cream
cake with, 238–39
lemon glaze, old-fashioned spice cake with,
42–43
rum frosting, Aunt Clary's old-fashioned
raisin buns with, 237–38
buttermilk:
buns, quick, 117–18
molasses drops with raisins, Effie's soft, 140

cabbage:
and carrot salad with homemade honey
mayonnaise, a young cook's, 224
and fruit salad with orange cream dressing,
150–51
sweet and sour red, with apples, 161
Cady, Daniel, 26
cakes:
angel, 34–35
Aunt Clary's bramble, 245–46
Aunt Clary's old-fashioned fruited
gingerbread, 233
Aunt Ida Louise's chocolaty wacky, with
dusted powdered-sugar lace, 27–28
Aunt Irene's angel torte with light cream-
cheese frosting, 219–20
Aunt Mable's peppermint-stick-candy sheet,
with seven-minute frosting, 263
Aunt Mae's burnt sugar, with burnt sugar
frosting, 172–73
Aunt Mae's Christmas cream, with lemon
butter glaze, 238–39
Aunt Peg's silver, with snowy lemon frosting,
111
best-ever, with whipped snow frosting, 106–7
Christmas pound, studded with candied
cherries, 124–25
delicious light fruitcake, 46–47
delicious old-fashioned gold, with spiced
apricot sauce, 335
Dutch apple, 137–38

easy-to-make coconut snowballs, 34
easy-to-make orange, with orange filling and
creamy orange frosting, 122–23
Effie's chocolate Yule log filled with
sweetened whipped cream, 59–60
glittering star, with a cloud-light frosting, 292
Great-Aunt Mae's Christmas, 296–97
Great-Aunt Mae's seed, 298–99
Great-Grandma Meekins's dunkin'
doughnuts, 286–87
Irish potato, with chocolate glaze, 71–72
lady golden, 267–68
light-as-a-snowflake gingerbread, 274–75
lovely chocolate leaves for, 184–85
Martin's peanut butter, 174
Mother's dunkin' doughnuts, 251–52
Mrs. D's applesauce, 43–44
old-fashioned applesauce fruitcakes, 183
old-fashioned dried-apple fruitcake with
George's favorite cider glaze, 281–82
old-fashioned mincemeat, with fudge frosting,
60–61
old-fashioned salt pork, 307–8
old-fashioned spice, with lemon butter glaze,
42–43
our family's eggnog sponge, 256–57
pumpkin and walnut, with caramel frosting,
203
simple fruitcake, 274
"sugar and spice and everything nice" with
oatmeal crisp topping, 277–78
swansdown loaf with orange mist frosting,
244–45
Will's favorite applesauce fruitcake, 33–34
Yuletide carrot, 118–19
Canadian bacon, Ada's oven-cooked, with
orange marmalade, 338
candy:
Ada's dipped chocolates with simple-to-make
fondant centers, 76–77
Aunt Mae's saltwater taffy, 100–101
Betty's chocolate mounds, 229
brown sugar caramels, 99
the children's almond brittle, 48
the children's favorite caramel corn, 277
Colleen Jane's pecan date seafoam, 66
easy-to-make chocolate fudge with roasted
pecans and candied cherries, 98–99
Effie's stained-glass Christmas, 97–98
Esther's after-dinner peppermint wafers, 80–
81
golden apricot nuggets, 248
Grandma Hopping's Turkish delight, 218–19
lovely chocolate leaves, 184–85
old-fashioned "apricotlets," 134–35
old-fashioned date and nut smash, 179
old-fashioned sugarplums, 64–65
Raymond's favorite graham cracker fudge, 41–
42
rubies in the snow, 268
Sheila's cherry bliss, 65–66
Sytha Jane's sugared walnut meats, 179–80
caramel:
buns (Schnecken), 21
corn, the children's favorite, 277
frosting, pumpkin and walnut cake with,
203–4
caramels, brown sugar, 99
carrot(s):
and apple salad, easy-to-make, 262–63
Aunt Mable's roast chicken with potatoes
and, 130–31
and cabbage salad with homemade honey
mayonnaise, a young cook's, 224

dressing, salad:
  boiled, 149–50
  golden sour cream, 117
  homemade French, 318
  orange cream, 151
Dwight, John S., xxvii

eggnog:
  Auntie's, for growing children, 250
  Christmas pie with graham cracker and
    almond pie crust, 330
  filling, 257
  sponge cake, our family's, 256–57
eggs, delicious stuffed, 212–13
elderberry wine, Grandpa's, 204
Emerson, Ralph Waldo, 190
"Exceeding All" (Riley), 225

"Feel in the Chris'mas Air, A" (Riley), 53–
  55
Field, Eugene, 104–5
figs:
  old-fashioned sugarplums, 64–65
  preserved green, 36
flaskkarre (roast loin of pork with prunes and
  apples), 212
"Folks at Lonesomeville" (Riley), 96
Freeman, Delphia Cline, 269
fritters, easy-to-make golden, 234
"From First-Name Friends" (Guest), 197
"From the Old Home Folks" (Riley), 110
"From the Snowstorm" (Emerson), 190
frosting:
  burnt sugar, 173
  caramel, 203–4
  cloud-light, 292–93
  creamy orange, 123
  fudge, 61
  lemon, 228
  light cream-cheese, 220
  orange mist, 245
  powdered sugar, 306
  rum butter, 238
  seven-minute, 246, 263–64
  simple powdered sugar, 24
  snowy lemon, 111
  thin powdered sugar, 35
  whipped snow, 107
  see also glaze
fruit:
  and cabbage salad with orange cream dressing,
    150–51
  chocolate drops, Aunt Clary's, 257–58
  filled cookies, 10
  see also specific kinds of fruit
fruitcakes:
  delicious light, 46–47
  Great-Aunt Mae's Christmas, 296–97
  old-fashioned applesauce, 183
  old-fashioned dried-apple, with George's
    favorite cider glaze, 281–82
  simple, 274
  Will's favorite applesauce, 33–34
fruited gingerbread, Aunt Clary's old-fashioned,
  233
fruit loaf (Johanna's Christmas Stollen), 155–
  56
fudge:
  balls, Ma's Christmas, 151
  easy-to-make chocolate, with roasted pecans
    and candied cherries, 98–99
  frosting, old-fashioned mincemeat cake with,
    60–61
"Funny Little Fellow, The" (Riley), 20

ginger nuts, old English, 252–53
gingerbread:
  Aunt Clary's old-fashioned fruited, 233
  boys, little, 50
  Gretchen's honey Lebkuchen with a simple
    powdered sugar frosting, 23–24
  light-as-a-snowflake, 274–75
glaze:
  chocolate, 72
  cocoa, 45
  easy powdered sugar, 156
  easy-to-make lemon, 70
  George's favorite cider, 281–82
  honey butter, 57
  lemon butter, easy to make, 70
  nutmeg, 122
  simple powdered sugar, 187
glögg, the Swede's, 215–16
"God Bless Us Every One" (Riley), 216–17
"God Rest You Merry, Gentlemen" (Rimbault),
  253–54
"golden buck," Great-Grandma's, 303–4
"Good, Old-Fashioned People, The" (Riley),
  348
goose, Great-Grandma's Christmas, with apple
  and prune dressing, 314–15
graham cracker:
  and almond pie crust, eggnog Christmas pie
    with, 330–31
  fudge, Raymond's favorite, 41–42
gravy:
  caramel-colored, 200
  cream, Maryland fried chicken with, 91–92
  pan-dripping or stock, 223
Guest, Edgar A., 68, 83–84, 129, 197
gumdrop cookies, Helen and Esther's, 80
gumdrop jumbles, Archie's Christmas, 227

ham, old-fashioned, with raisin sauce, 260–61
ham, Uncle Bud's fresh pork, 342
"Handy Andy," Aunt Clary's, 142
Harding, John P., 31
Harries, Margaret, 235
Harrington, Karl P., 254–55
"Heap O' Livin', A" ("Home") (Guest), 129
"His Christmas Sled" (Guest), 83–84
Holland, Josiah Gilbert, 254–55
honey:
  allspice tea with, 175–76
  apple-butter sauce, Ada's baked sweet
    potatoes with, 261–62
  baked apples, Effie's, 334–35
  butter glaze, Aunt Mable's imitation boar's
    head pork roast with, 56–57
  carrots glazed with butter and, 318–19
  Lebkuchen, Gretchen's, with a simple
    powdered sugar frosting, 23–24
  mayonnaise, homemade, a young cook's
    cabbage and carrot salad with, 224
  oat crunch, our family's favorite, 222
  and spice whipped cream, Uncle Bud's creamy
    pumpkin pie with, 162–63
  whole-wheat rolls "plus," Effie's, 174–75

"If" (Kipling), 89–91
Irish potato cake with chocolate glaze, 71–72
"It Is Coming Tonight" (Brooks), 289–90

jellied tomato salad, Ada's, with homemade
  lemon mayonnaise, 58
jelly:
  Effie's grandmother's wine, 256
  Effie's rose-petal, with graham muffins, 208–9
  jeweled cranberry apple, salad, 266–67

About the Author

JANE WATSON HOPPING grew up in a large old-fashioned extended family that added depth and richness to her childhood. She now lives and works on an old farmstead in Southern Oregon.

Jane Hopping's first book, *The Pioneer Lady's Country Kitchen,* was published in 1988. She is now at work, standing at her stove and seated at her kitchen table (which doubles as a desk), on her third book.